Moving

---

a Mary Daisy memoir

Artistic Director/Founder Actors Workout, Inc., a 501©(3) Arizona theater corporation

PublishAmerica

Baltimore

First printing

Persons, places, and activities below [renowned included) in "Moving" are part of Mary Daisy's personal experience unless otherwise noted.

ISBN: 1-4137-5911-4
PUBLISHED BY PUBLISHAMERICA, LLLP
www.publishamerica.com
Baltimore

Printed in the United States of America

Moving *is dedicated to*
All That &
All Who
Have loved me.
All That &
All Whom
I love.

Preface

When visiting the ball gown and wedding dress collection of a major museum I asked, "Why are there no *everyday* clothes?" I was informed that if such items were ever found they would be worth a great deal, since people customarily wore them out or discarded them.

Perhaps the following will someday be worth a great deal. It is *three-quarters of a century* in the life of an "ordinary" American female, born just 30 days before the stock market crash of October 24, 1929, living in freedom at or below the poverty level the first seven and all of the adult years of her life, yet with many out-of-the-ordinary moments.

*"During its moment all that is remembered joins and lives, the old
and the young, the past and the present, the living and the dead."*
Eudora Welty

Contents

Part One: *Pre-dawn*
1929-1950 – The Great Depression, WWII, Creative Beginnings
…11

Part Two: *Sunrise*
1950-1963 – The Baby Boom, Korean War, Family
Beginnings
…45

Part Three: *Morning*
1963-1975 – Assassinations, Vietnam War, Back To My Roots
…87

Part Four: *Noon*
1976-1986 – Phoenix Car-Bombing, Iran-Contra, Creative Growth
…133

Part Five: *Afternoon*
1986-2001 – Whittier(L.A.) Earthquake, Persian-Gulf War, New Start
…167

Part Six: *Sunset*
2001-2004 – 9-11, Afghanistan War, Actors Workout,Inc.
…199

Part Seven: *Evening*
2001-2004 – 9-11, Iraq War & After, Family, USA, God, *Moving*
…231

Part One
Pre-dawn

1929-1950 – The Great Depression, WWII, Creative Beginnings

Moving on a Giant Spaceship

I am aware the earth is *moving*, not just because I've read about it in books. I'm aware of it for two reasons. First, because my kitty, Halloween, who lived with me on the upper level of my office studio, got to be carried downstairs to the swimming pool between 4 and 5a.m. in the summer so she could eat grass. I'd look up at the stars and moon. If Halloween and I stayed there for an hour the stars and moon would appear to *move* (I know, of course, it is the giant space ship I ride on that *moved*, spiraling completely on itself every day). Then the horizon would faintly glow. As the mornings became cold, the spot on the spaceship I occupy had *moved* away from the hot sun. Second, because I watched the light of the summer solstice creep down then up an opposite side wall of the acre of top floor of the Burton Barr Phoenix Public Library, June 21, 2003. My spaceship earth had *moved* closer to the sun! Since I live on a giant spaceship called Earth, which turns on itself every day between sunrise and sunset, I have *moved* 27,375 times riding on Earth, plus almost 75 times on Earth around the sun, Earth's star!

Moving Being Born

September 24, 1929. I must have *moved* through the tunnel of the birth canal. I'm here! My mother, at the height of F. Scott and Zelda Fitzgerald's flapper age, even though living in Nebraska (an uncle had allowed her to usher in his store-front silent movie house in Elwood, Nebraska, when she was a child), must have been pretty sexy, because she told me the intern attending my birth (in Lincoln, Nebraska) was a former medical student she had been engaged to before she eloped with my dad! She'd even worn his ring for awhile! Imagine her surprise while her tummy was *moving* like crazy to push me out seeing her former fiancé! Imagine looking up to see who was checking you with your legs in the air! *What an entrance for me! What drama!*

I'm part of Einstein's curved space-time, his general theory of relativity and the paradoxical predictions of quantum mechanics, Stephen Hawking's theory of time, Julian Barbour's "The End Of Time," Jesus' "many mansions," the Seth books, Edgar Cayce's seaside resort in Nebraska, and the Vishnu Schist(oldest geological formation on the face of the earth at the bottom of the Grand Canyon). I am ubiquitous *moving* and before I know it I will be gone, but not gone, either. Like the tiniest grain of sand in the Grand Canyon at sunrise, little pieces of me will hang around to *move* things.

"We are made of elements forged in the stars and scattered through space. We are recycled stardust with the gift of consciousness," says John Noble Wilford, (New York Times, February 13, 2000).

Moving from Body to Energy.

Halloween(my kitty) was very sick for two weeks. She had stopped eating and drinking.

She pooped only twice during that entire time. I gave her fur ball medication I got at PetsMart. I syringed purified water, tuna juice(her favorite treat), prune juice into her mouth and forced suppositories up her little behind. She was thirteen years old. I was devastated watching her suffer, but I couldn't afford expensive vet bills. I decided if she wasn't better by the upcoming Saturday she would have to *move* from her black kitty cat body and the Humane Society would do it for $25. Holding her I cried in my office/studio and I cried a lot when the Humane Society put her in a plastic cage and carried her away. Not just because I would miss her so much but because I hated to think she was in such pain and she must have died terrified with me saying goodbye to her there in the cage, not holding her for whatever comfort that would give. Twenty-five dollars was all I could afford.

Moving Through an Explosion.

Author Joseph Campbell's (*The Power of Myth*)wife Jean said of me ,"You write like James Joyce." That's the way my mind travels.

The sun gets very hot in Arizona in the summer. Hot enough to fry an egg on the pavement they say, though I've never tried it. That's because our small part of the Earth in Arizona is tilted more toward the sun and closer to the sun in its orbit on the days of 115 degrees. It was on a frying- egg-on-the-pavement day that a bomb exploded under a car, killing Phoenix, Arizona investigative reporter Don Bolles who'd been reporting on the mob, shattering his body so badly he died in days. I was at Surgi Center undergoing a diagnostic and therapeudic D&C for a troublesome fibroid tumor and as I was coming into consciousness from the anesthesia I heard an announcer on the radio say, "Investigative reporter…has been rushed to the hospital in a critical condition after a bomb exploded under his car!"

"I know him!" I cried out. Like a circle of psychic energy I not only knew him, but was *moved*, after the fact, into the vortex of one of the darkest dramas that ever occurred in Phoenix.

There was a Big Bang 13 million years ago, when all matter burst into superclusters of galaxies and billions of stars!

Moving into My Life.

I was born a year and a half after my big brother Bob and exactly 30 days before the "crash" on September 24, 1929. My maternal grandpa's, William Reynolds, parents, seeking opportunity, rode a covered wagon along the Platte River (snakes crawled through the roofs of the mud huts Grandpa slept in on the trip) to settle first in Elwood, then Omaha, Nebraska. I proudly learned very early in life I am the sixth cousin of Abraham Lincoln on my maternal grandmother's, Daisy Johnson Reynolds, side, via the Mudd family of Springfield, Illinois. I watched Grandma Daisy work all day to prepare a farm legacy dinner-size meal at lunch and again at dinner; scrub clothes on a washboard, hand wring them, then hang them to dry on the line outdoors in summer, or in the cellar in winter. I watched her live an unceasing life of labor, the only relief being church on Sunday or a quilting bee in her parlor (I hid under the frame as the ladies gathered around). It was at Grandma Daisy's house, after the ice man delivered a big block of ice for the bottom of the "ice box," that I got ice chips to suck on, picked out tunes on the piano, began acting and directing in her back yard, had a buddy in my Aunt Gladys (whose waist length red hair I brushed before bedtime), fell from the porch to have three stitches on my forehead, and endured castor oil. When Christmas came, it was to my maternal and paternal grandparents' homes we drove over bleak Nebraska winter roads from Lincoln to Omaha (counting Christmas lights in farm house windows along the way). We never had our own Christmas tree in those Depression years, so I never believed in Santa Claus.

The Great Depression began on October 24, 1929. My dad must have been under enormous pressure to earn though he didn't lose his job. It was the era of the WPA Writers Project in Nebraska and the American Guide Series: Nebraska, The Cornhusker State. My dad was the son of a printer, Fred Oliver, with presses near the stockyards (I have a vivid memory of the horrific odor near my grandfather's shop). Dad's mother, Elizabeth Rhodes Oliver, was a prudish English teacher with a Master's degree in English from Blair, Nebraska, who had married and become pregnant late in her life only to have a "blue" baby. Protective of my dad, my grandmother taught him at home through the third grade.

As a teenager, Dad learned the advertising business by offering to work for nothing for Mr. Bozell and Mr. Jacobs (founders of the worldwide Bozell & Jacobs advertising agency, begun in Omaha, Nebraska). He worked free at Bozell & Jacobs on Boys Town (made famous by Spencer Tracy as Father Flannigan in the film when it was just a store front) and Nebraska Public Service Company between 9a.m. to 5 p.m., then he went to work in a gas station from 5 p.m. to midnight to earn some money!

Though he drove one of the first cars in the area and took my mother to see the first cross-country airmail flight landing, my dad never graduated from high school because he and my mother eloped. The newlyweds moved into the home of my paternal grandparents, a reciprocal housing debt my mother would pay through ten of my growing-up years and twenty into my adulthood. My dad must have been very good and very creative at Bozell and Jacobs, because he soon was hired by Nebraska Public Service Company as their advertising director. I can remember Sunday trips in Lincoln, Nebraska, when my mother would buy three chickens for a dollar, which would become the "big" family Sunday dinner that had to stretch into several more dinners over the week. We were completely unaware that Hitler was about to embark on WWII, that would lead to the Holocaust.

Even in our modest circumstances (my brother Bob, a year and a half older than me, my brother Dick, a year and a half younger, and I slept in one bedroom in our small house in Lincoln, Nebraska), Dad loved to entertain his business associates at home. His signature entertainment was the outdoor steak fry (Nebraska being beef and potatoes country) and at every house in which we thenceforth lived he gathered stones and built an outdoor fireplace. Dad would keep his dinner guests plied with martinis until 9:30 or 10 p.m., while they inhaled the aroma of steaks cooking over the open fire so praise would be lavished on the chef! I came to hate steak fries because I couldn't stand blood oozing from the charcoal-broiled meat (I'm a decades long vegetarian today). Just at the right moment, when everyone was feeling mellow, Dad would sing the University of Nebraska fight song with such gusto one would believe him to be a distinguished grad:

"There is no place like Nebraska
Dear Old Nebraska U
Where the girls are the fairest
The boys are the squarest
Of any old school that I knew!
There is no place like Nebraska
Where everyone's true blue
We'll all stick together
In all kinds of weather
For dear old Nebraska U!"

Dad attended to business away from home a lot and on the day of my sibling Dick's two-year-old birthday, Dad was gone. Dick had no party and no gifts as Mother awaited Dad's return home. I can still see Mother and my brother Bob in a doctor's office that day as Dick played with his only toy—an empty oatmeal box! I felt very sorry for adorable little Dick!

However, we (as part of America's industrial age) were upwardly mobile because my dad was an avid reader and self-educated scholar and was supported enthusiastically by my mother. Due to both of my parents' incredible industry, entrepreneurism, and risk-taking, I eventually had the advantage of good homes—homes near fine schools (my mother made eighteen homes across America following my dad's career)—so I gained armor to face "hardships, incredible sorrow and obstacles…"even though, as an "artist"in performing arts I've lived at or below the poverty level all of my adult life!

We girls are *so* lucky to have been born in America, this iddy-biddy span of homo sapiens on earth, this mini-fraction since Jesus, this infinitesimal-micro-mini-fraction of time in eternity. Why was *I* so lucky? Why has so much blood been shed, so many minds been fired up, so much "sweat and tears," so much Passion been expended on *me?*

Why wasn't I born in the Middle East, where women hide behind veils and are the property of men with no rights at all?

Why wasn't I born in Africa, where young girls, if they have not been starved to death before they are five years old, are circumcised without anesthesia?

Why wasn't I born in China, where they abort most baby girls or kill them at birth?

Why wasn't I born a slave somewhere?

Why wasn't I born Anne Frank, whose brilliance was snuffed out in her second decade, the victim of the unimaginable evil of the Holocaust?

Why wasn't I born to become a waitress, engulfed in flames and rubble in the fall of the World Trade Center?

Why wasn't I a baby killed by Saddam's biological weapons of mass destruction or a baby killed by American bombs in Iraq?

Moving through Dreams

I was still living in Nebraska (before age seven) when I moved into a recurring nightmare. I once heard that maybe the *I* in all the bodies we inhabit from babyhood to old age is the *real I we visit in dreams.* I dreamed my mother made me wear red slippers to go down to the cellar (common in the Midwest due to tornadoes) to get a jar of jelly. In tears I would plead with her *"Please don't make me do it, Mommy!"* But she prevailed. In the dream I moved down several steps and was engulfed in flames and oil and woke up screaming. I couldn't seem to stop the dream. Are we humans still hating, warring and torturing, going after sweet jelly to be consumed in flames?

Much later in my life there was a dream about my baby (the one who died of neuroblastoma cancer). I was standing at the bottom of a roller coaster and I could see my baby ravished by the cancer, looking like a little yellow skeleton from a Nazi concentration camp, strapped to the first hill on one of the rails. I tried and tried to climb the rail, but I couldn't do it. I kept sliding backward, trying and trying to get to his little shackled body, crying out in despair. Eventually, my cries and moans woke me up. My baby son had been dead for a month.

Today I feel warm sun on my face, my eyes closed but seeing red. I feel luscious water on my skin swimming or under the shower. I feel a soft breeze riding my bike, eat warm oatbran, smell the delicious aroma of coffee perking and bread baking, see leaves back lit by the sun, or rich magenta bougainvillea and a field of African daisies blowing in the wind. I mentally envision my beloved Impressionists—Monet, Van Gogh, Matisse, Cezanne, Renoir—and I wonder anew why my beautiful, happy baby son's life stopped after only a year and a half.

In another dream, coming out of dental anesthesia, I re-lived the creation of the universes! Stars exploded and in the midst of the huge explosion was a nimbus of molten love.

Moving in Awake Dreams – Acting and Directing

Acting is not just getting a new life. It's getting a *new self.* My Great-aunt Lois may have been my motivation when she held me on her lap in the rocking chair saying "There was a little girl who had a little curl right in the middle of her forehead. When she was good she was very, very *good.* But, when she was bad she was horrid!" Already I had two selves! Acting for me began in my Grandmother Daisy's backyard in Omaha. I was allowed to wear her wedding dress and create "shows" using her sheets drying on the back clothes line as curtains. I had all the open space of her back yard to play my drama! Directing began in the same backyard when I plucked the blossom off a hollyhock, pealed the green cap away from the stem to expose the holes, plucked a hollyhock bud with a bit of stem and inserted it in the hole making a lovely lady with a long colorful skirt! With several of these homemade hollyhock dolls moved about, I created stories. As I grew older I also created hours' long dramas with paper dolls. My Aunt Gladys (mother's older sister, a poet who was published in the *Ladies Home Journal*) told me one day I'd written a poem when I declared in Grandma Daisy's backyard: *"The sky has taken off its old grey dress and put on its beautiful blue one!"*

As a child (never reinforced by professional theater, great literature, fine art or performers), I found myself in a space, using its possibilities, using the objects lying about, playing games of design, body and voice, light and colors, emotional triggers with the five senses, movement and stillness, adapting to the place, time and people of *"imagination"* (think Kris Kringle in *Miracle On 34th Street*). Sticks became a boat, (in the infrequent rain of Lincoln, Nebraska) and I sailed joyously in my stick boats in the gutter in front of our house. Trees become another town or city, fort or castle. A swathe of cloth became a queen's gown (unless I luxuriated in my grandmother's wedding dress). Rose blossoms crushed became "perfume." Shirley Temple was all the rage and I had a "Scoodles" doll with a wooden head. My doll had to go to the doll hospital when I cracked her head in many places, a tragedy on the level of the Trojan Wars of Greece!

I did have the opportunity to take dance because my mom's cousin had a small studio, so my brother and I could take lessons free. At age five or so, with my brother I did an acrobatic show (in our "show" my brother wanted a sucker stuck in my sock and every time he made a dance move toward it I did a cartwheel or sommersault). The dance show must have been funny or charming because my mom's cousin made arrangements with all the local hotels in Lincoln so my brother and I got to perform it about five times for large audiences. I frequently got "stage fright," leg aches cured by my mom, who gave me an aspirin. My brother and I got no pay for these performances. However, we were given hotel dinners which seemed very grown up and I was given a complimentary shampoo and hairdo at the hotel beauty shop. It was during these performances *I discovered the joy of audience ovations*!

After working for money as the ad director of Nebraska Public Service Company, my dad got a job offer to work in the advertising department of Westinghouse in Mansfield, Ohio. My brother Bob (a year and a half older than me, was always bright, because when my Grandpa Oliver offered a handful of coins, Bob picked the dime even though the nickel was bigger) and my brother Dick (today a multi-millionaire, who has the first nickel he ever received, according to my brother Bob) and I created comic book stories on the long car trip by drawing on sheets of toilet paper, a project that happily covered many hours and miles! We stopped at a Chicago hotel with small soaps wrapped in paper (a never-before-seen miracle) on the way. My mom put the three of us—Bob, Dick and me—at the bottom of the escalator in Marshall Fields and urged us to ride up and down. (Which was marvelous free child sitting for her, as we kept it up for an entire morning!)

Moving Accidently to See my First Live Show—a Strip Tease!

During the period of my life when I lived in Ohio, between age seven and eleven, I saw my first live stage show at the movies. It was the period in American exhibitor history when live touring shows came to movie houses and were performed along with a film. My whole family went one night to see *Andy Hardy*, starring Mickey Rooney and Judy Garland. The stage show began when the film ended. The curtains opened to reveal a beautiful, nubile girl with long black hair, wearing blue chiffon, flanked by cages of white pigeons. Music began and the girl danced from one side of the stage to the other opening the cages. The pigeons flew out and one by one plucked blue chiffon handkerchiefs from the lovely girl's body until finally she was naked! My brothers and I sat open mouthed in awe at this wondrous sight, while our parents, conditioned by their Victorian–Puritan upbringing, sat like stone monuments. As we walked to Isley's, the ice cream parlor we always frequented as a treat after the show, I kept expecting my parents would say something about the naked girl with the pigeons but they did not. However, the experience made such an impression on me I did strip teases for the kids in the neighborhood for the next two weeks! Much later in New York I saw Mickey Rooney in (a déjà vu moment) *Suger Babies*. I delighted in the fan dance number, reliving white pigeons swooping down to help dancers strip tease!

Moving to See my First Great Film in Philadelphia

My paternal great-great grandfather had been sent by Queen Victoria to be Methodist–Episcopal Bishop of Philadelphia, so it was revisiting family ancestral history when my dad was hired by a top Philadelphia advertising agency! Thus began the only decade-long period in my life when I've lived above the poverty level, though my dad's salary had to cover many people, college educations, homes beyond our means. There was never money for new clothes, travel or culture. Our family of five drove through the tunnels of the Pennsylvaina turnpike to the Main Line of Philadelphia (made famous by the film *Kitty Foyle* and so named because there is a commuter railroad that runs through all the old money towns). While my parents hunted for a house to rent on the Main Line we stayed in a downtown hotel. One day our exhausted-from-house-hunting mother gave my brothers and me some money to go to a downtown movie palace to see Charlie Chaplin in *The Great Dictator*. (This is prior to Adolph Elizabeth Hitler in the smash Mel Brooks' Broadway hit musical *The Producers*, with"Don't Be Stupid/Be A Smarty/

Come And Join The Nazi Party").Hitler was satirized brilliantly by Chaplin. We country bumpkin kids lined up at the ticket window to learn mother hadn't given us enough money to get in! Ashamed and scared by the cross cashier, standing in the middle of a big unfamiliar city, I began to cry. The manager was summoned and somehow, via my emotional outburst and my brothers' hard luck story about just arriving from Ohio, he decided to let us in to stand in the rear without paying—probably to get rid of the noise in front of a theater playing the biggest hit of the year!

Chaplin's genius vied with reality for the most indelible memory of the day! Back in Ohio, Mother had deposited the three of us at Mansfield's movie theater with a dime each and we saw two feature films, three serials, a news reel, and several cartoons over a span of five hours!

American History *Moves*!

It changes me.
It changes my family.
Incredible difficulties and tragedies—wars, diseases, deficit finances, failed projects and dreams, divorces and deaths—we've overcome with heroic struggles! But, up to now, we've never lost our *optimism,* the typically American belief we will win!

Moving to Pearl Harbor, America vs. Japan and Hitler – Mom's New Baby

On Pearl Harbor Day, December 7, 1941 (a day of "infamy"), I can vividly remember sitting around the family's big radio hearing the news of the Japanese attack. Roosevelt had sealed a deal with Churchill to "lease" needed armaments to Britain in an attempt to keep America out of WWII but, that day the President of the United States declared "America is at war with Japan and Germany."

Almost to the day, nine months before the Japanese bombed Pearl Harbor, my brother Tom was born on March 8, 1941. I vividly remember that night too. A blinding blizzard enveloped Merion, Pennsylvania, a suburb of Philadelphia where my parents had rented a house. We lived on Philadelphia's old money

Main Line. Our home was a "test house" for electrical appliances due to my dad's job. Therefore, ours was the only house in the neighborhood *without* a maid, *but we had a dishwasher*! Mother had hired an African American maid, Connie (who made mouth-watering apple pies), solely to help at the time of my mom's labor and post partum however. Dad was away at a meeting the night my mother went into labor. Connie and I watched from a second story window as my mother struggled between labor pains shoveling snow along with my big brother Bob, gradually pushing through foot-high snow drifts. They finally got our car moving. It went only as far as the middle of the street where it remained all night. Dad ultimately—more than an hour after mother and Bob had begun their heroic snow shoveling—returned in a taxi to take Mother to the hospital! The car remained "snowed in" in the middle of the street all night long.

When mother returned home I was entranced with baby Tom! He was a gorgeous, picture–perfect baby frequently photographed. Though I was only ten years old I happily "baby sat" my brother Tom around twenty hours a week. It was risky for my mother to allow this. My mea culpa was walking down the cellar steps carrying baby Tom one day and tripping at the bottom over a step which was higher than the rest. I dropped baby Tom on his head on cement! He turned blue but didn't cry. Surprisingly, mother did not go into hysterics or verbally abuse me, which I undoubtedly deserved. Mother instead was amazingly calm and forgiving. Tom amazingly survived my immaturity.

My dad talked about enlisting when America entered the war but, with a very large family to support, including a wife, four children and his parents who had come to live with us, he had to focus on getting a better job. He went to work as Vice President of Proctor Electric, earning citations making munitions parts.

> "The most important things in this war are machines. The United States has proven that it can turn out from 8,000 to 10,000 airplanes per month. Russia can only turn out, at most, 3,000 airplanes a month. England turns out 3,000 to 3,500, which are principally heavy bombers. The United States, therefore, is a country of machines. Without the use of those machines, through Lend Lease, we would lose this war." (Stalin speaking in *Franklin and Winston* by Jon Meacham)

Mother started a huge vegetable garden in the vacant lot next to the house my parents had purchased (with my grandparents' financial help) on Howe

Road in Wynnewood. The stress during these difficult times must have been enormous. I remember one bitter fight my parents had when I came downstairs to find a huge spot on the wall where dad had thrown an ink bottle while drunk. The stress was caused both by the enormous responsibilities of my dad's job and my mother's household burden with three pubescent children, a baby and her in-laws to care for. It was not enough to be the only person on the block to have a *dishwasher*.

While my future husband marched across France and Germany among the GIs to liberate Buchenwald as part of Patton's Third Army, I, ten years younger than he, was shielded from WWII's direst truths. *Still the war pervaded everything.* Servicemen were everywhere. I, meanwhile, attended a superb American public school, Bala Cynwyd Junior High School, where an oil painting of my brother Dick as "The Ideal Junior High School Boy" still hangs in the cafeteria. Bala Cynwyd was only a brief walk or bike ride from our house. My brother Bob was a year ahead of me and won elections as president of his class. Therefore, it was easy for me to became vice president of the school (name recognition on the bulletin board posters!).

My boyfriend, Phil Hungerford (later a Princeton grad, president of a South Carolina bank and a veteran of urban renewal in Pakistan), was president of the school. I was a member of the Student Council and a cheerleader. I rediscovered the joys of acting when I was cast as the Virgin Mary, taking center stage in a spotlight, wearing a lovely pale blue chiffon costume and head shawl, feeling very beautiful and "chosen." I also won a poetry contest, and most significantly, won the public speaking contest, competing against James Billington, now America's Librarian of Congress and author of many historical books on Russia. Jim was so brilliant that, even in junior high school he was studying Russian on his own. However, I "held the audience in the palm of my hand," causing mothers of servicemen overseas to cry with my winning speech, "Half the War Is Over." I was so amazed to beat the brilliant Jim Billington, I shyly focused on the red ducks on my white pique dress, burying my head when it was announced I was the winner(so my mother told me)!

Just before entering high school I lost all my popularity and subsequently all elections. While riding my bicycle down a steep hill the steering gear went bad. I dragged my feet to stop sliding into the V of my girl's bike. My mouth hurtled down, glancing the middle screw of the steering wheel. My bike zig zagged to finally crash when it hit a fence post. My front tooth broke as it went through my lower lip! The tooth could not be capped until my braces came off at the end of twelfth grade! While my brother Bob was editor of the yearbook and my brother Dick was a scrappy back on the football field (who ruined his knee in his sophomore year), I never smiled for three years!

Without smiling I made over my one formal dress ten times for school dances and co-edited my school paper, *The Merionite*. The faculty advisor of the Merionite took me and the truly gifted editor of our school paper to New York City for a high school journalism conference where the glamorous couple Jinx Falkenberg and Tex McCreary were highlighted speakers! Inspired by their talks I tackled my first big interview. I rode the Main Line railroad along the Schuylkill River into Philly's downtown. (Famous as a George Washington Revolutionary War site—one could see the statue of William Penn with his hand blessing the city, which when backlit in the sun, making him appear to be in tumescence!) An African American called Father Divine claimed to be God (he'd just had a picture spread in *Life* magazine). As I arrived at his headquarters I saw blocks of his believers of all races waiting to see him. Though just a frightened kid in high school, I had made an appointment to meet the famed God-man, but was not allowed into his presence until I had been interrogated by his Caucasian wife.

I asked Mrs. Divine how her husband got any rest with the hundreds of cold, hungry, homeless, badly clothed people standing in line day and night, waiting to offer him all their worldly goods. She responded "God never rests!" Her statement became the headline of my story positioned on the front page of my school paper! My story told of Mrs. Divine and her husband being transported every day in a Cadillac sedan to their luxurious home (where I presume they slept and ate wonderful meals). When I finally was shown in to see the great Father Divine, I found a short, rotund little man, wearing a suit jacket covered with medals, looking, sounding and perspiring very much like an arrogant human being!

I regained some popularity by winning the lead (the mother Penny) in the venerable, thought-provoking *You Can't Take It With You*, which was our class senior play. Penny has all the wonderful funny punch lines, so I was a big hit with the audience. I loved creating the laughter as I did double takes and pauses and delivered the punch lines. My drama teacher and director, Mr. Hand, figured I had a great career ahead of me. My dad also thought I was destined for a Broadway career. He got me a pass to see Mae West in *Diamond Lil* at a theater in downtown Philly. It was my first professional show. Ms. West was grossly over made up at sixty years old and I thought her "Come up and see me sometime" line *disgusting*. (How could Mae West have sex at sixty years old? How naive I was! Today I realize what a great performer, an unforgettable icon, she was to continue to fill seats with only illusion!)

Moving to College

In 1947, I graduated from Lower Merion Senior High School as a member of the National Honor Society. My yearbook picture had the epitaph *"Happiness is a rare cosmetic."* I was accepted at Goucher College, in Baltimore, Maryland, the college of my journalism teacher, Mrs. Hay, who must have been instrumental in my being accepted. Now that my braces were off and my front tooth capped, I could smile again! Most importantly, amidst brilliant minds and culture my soul could grow.

Goucher was the first accredited school below the Mason–Dixon Line in America. In the throes of expansion from a many decades downtown campus, Goucher was in the process of moving to many beautiful acres in Towson, on the outskirts of Baltimore. Its faculty boasted brilliant scholars from Wellesley, Vassar, Harvard, etc. I was academically challenged by third and fourth year Latin, physiology taught by an MD from Johns Hopkins University (during which I had to dissect a rat while keeping the heart beating), philosophy, South American history, history of fine art, the Bible as history, but I did well only in the history courses and was lucky to pass my sophomore exams with average grades.

What I learned there came not only from difficult classes, however. My stretching came from living in Baltimore at the historic Goucher House, former home of college founder Dr. Goucher and his wife (who would figure in my first summer college job) and rooming with the very-mature-for-her-age Margie Gerke who introduced me to Gibran's *The Prophet*. While at Goucher House I also made friends with the daughter of an USA ambassador, Aida "Curly" Schoenfeld, who had studied ballet in Europe. Curly (Aida, who has been a life-long friend) introduced me to classical music at concerts and urged me to listen with her to Stravinsky, Mozart, Bach and Beethoven recordings.

One night I was given the option to take off from my spending-money-waitress-duties at the dorm to dine with poet-laurate Archibald MacLeash (later an American Librarian of Congress)! I took the exciting opportunity to dine with the famous literary figure who became Librarian of Congress. I have now dined with two Librarians of Congress, having, in recent years, re-united with my public speaking competitor James Billington, for lunch, on the Library of Congress deck overlooking the Capitol of United States!

Additionally, my art class professor and Director of the Corcoran and Phillips galleries took we students monthly to his gallery in Washington, D.C., where we sat "up close and personal" with Renoir's *Boating Party*, Cezannes, Monets, Manets, Van Goghs, and Braques! Inch by inch, my Goucher art professor explained to we young ladies what artists do with brushes, pallet knife and paints. He taught me to *see*, how to look at art! Our trips to D.C. usually culminated also with a visit to the National Gallery, where he inspired me how to seek out great museums and galleries (which I would later do in New York City, London, and Los Angeles)! As a part of Goucher's Glee Club during the pre-Christmas season, I sang alto in a *Messiah* concert with paid soloists at famed Annapolis Chapel. After the broadcast event I danced with a Midshipman to traditional "Sleepy Time Gal" at midnight.

Big Wheel On Campus, Nancy Clark (daughter of United States Senator Clark, who later became special assistant to Governor of California-then-President Reagan) was all the rage at school. Probably because my friend and sophomore roommate Alice "Bubbles" Falvey, herself a fine athlete, recommended me, I became Secretary to the Athletic Association. I was therefore pictured on the front cover of a Goucher brochure with the already "hot" Nancy Clark!

Six-foot-six-inch, Greek-god-looking Villanova basketball player Fred Raker came as my date to a Goucher dance. I also took train weekend passes to the University of Pennsylvania, Amherst, Princeton (as the date of my junior high school beau, Phil Hungerford), and Dartmouth. Though at a women's college I had plenty of male company! I had quite a crush on a located-in-Baltimore tall, lanky Johns Hopkins University boy, from Warren, PA. My brother Bob (at Dartmouth) invited me to attend his Dartmouth Winter Carnival (famous for its ice sculptures) so, "in love" at the time, I invited my Johns Hopkins beau as my date. My beau's father was a Warren corporate executive who frequented New York City, so he and his wife invited us to stop in the Big Apple as their guests for dinner and hit Broadway show *Brigadoon*. With utmost tact and kindness, my beau's father taught me to eat my first blue point oysters on the half shell which I first attempted to cut with a knife and fork! The Bobby Lewis-directed *Brigadoon*—company, set, dance and music—blew me away! (Years later I would meet Bobby Lewis in Hollywood when he accepted me as an actress to his matchless acting class.) The choreography was by Agnes DeMille. Ms. DeMille, who had made story-telling choreography history in musical theater when she did the musical *Rodeo*, was magic. (I would meet Ms. DeMille in Arizona when I did a magazine story on her.) Later she made story-telling and dance history when she did the American Ballet Theatre's Lizzie Borden ballet.

The impact of "Brigadoon" cannot be overemphasized regarding my soon-to-be-made decision to leave college.

Goucher also gave me a lifetime way to exercise with joy. I took crash courses in swimming! Having begun life in the dull autumn green, and flat brown summer landscape around Lincoln and Omaha, Nebraska, where there was no water—no ocean, no lake, no stream, no swimming pools, where even rain was an event causing me to dance around the front yard dressed only in panties reveling in the scent of rain on the wind—I was actually afraid of water when my Grandfather Oliver took me and my two brothers on the Tunnel of Love boat ride at an amusement park (water depth was probably only one foot).

At Goucher, however, I took crash courses and earned Red Cross Life Saver and Instructor certificates. My friend "Bubbles" Falvey (she lived next to the Kennedys in Hyannis Port summers) recommended me for a summer job teaching swimming to very young children at Camp Cloudmarch, in Damarscotta Mills, Maine. The camp was owned and managed by the widowed wife of Goucher's first president. Swimming in spring-fed pools at Camp Cloudmarch, then later to the center of a lake at night, floating on my back miles from shore, gazing at universes of stars in New England, I discovered a life long serenity and passion that has also helped keep me fit. Later I taught my own four children how to swim before they could walk.

While at Camp Cloudmarch, the counselors organized a field trip to Boothbay Harbor where counselors and children camped in the open overnight. At 5 a.m. we climbed Camden Mountain, which borders the Atlantic ocean. I was transported into ecstasy watching gold, rose, purple, blue and pink mists part to reveal a single white sailboat bounce on the surf far below!

Swimming brings to mind one of my favorite stories about the actress Katharine Hepburn and Irene Selznick (Broadway producer and daughter of L. B. Mayer). Apparently the two great friends decided they would swim across Los Angeles! They entered strange backyards and swam laps, then went on to another pool ending in Malibu and the Pacific ocean! One outraged homeowner came home just as they were climbing out of the owner's pool! Kate merely pushed by the complete stranger, declaring, "We were just swimming a few laps. What's all the fuss about?" Then the intrepid actress and producer sped off in their car! I kinda did the same thing when I was attempting to move my career from Phoenix to Los Angeles. I would work all day in Phoenix, drive all night, then go to auditions in Los Angeles all day. I'd stop along the way between the two cities and pop into the pool of a strange motel, do a few laps to regain my energy and move on!

I love to see the peaceful green-blue environment *under* water. One of the most magnificent experiences I've had seeing underwater was at Arizona's Lake Powell, the man-made reservoir behind the Eisenhower Dam in northern Arizona. Lake Powell has a coast line longer than America's Pacific coast! The water is so blue-green-clear you can see fifty yards ahead of you underwater! I've swum in the ocean from beaches on the East and West coasts plus in Mexico. I've swum in the Gulf of Mexico. For several years I leased a guest studio under the Mummy Mountain house of Jack Stewart, founder of Camelback Inn. The studio I lived in was glassed in on one side, overlooking 350 miles of metropolitan Phoenix surrounded by its small mountain ranges. I had the opportunity to swim in an outdoor heated pool year round! Access to swimming has always been a priority to me when seeking housing.

My sophomore and final year at Goucher was highlighted by two adventures. Classmate Jane "Honey" Harmeling invited four of us Goucher classmates to spend spring break at her home in Clearwater, Florida. At the time, the New York Yankees were in training in Clearwater and one day we five girls went to the Yankee practice as only a group of very young college girls can do, and brashly pushed our way into the dugout, where we took snapshots of Joe DiMaggio! Yankee first baseman "Mapes" encircled all five of us in his long arms for a photo!

My college chums and I also took an overnight at the home of Goucher gym teacher "Punky" Stokes in Glencoe, Maryland, a home hidden away in a dense thicket of trees and brush. It was a mysterious structure with secret stairways, doors and passageways, adjacent to an innocent appearing private girls preparatory school! We learned the house was used by the OSS (Office of Stragtegic Services, the forerunner to the CIA) during WWII, so our imaginations ran rampant!

Moving Closer to Who I Am

Sophomore year exam–cramming loomed and I realized intuitively I was on the wrong path. At the time there were many summer stock theaters in the East, but only one was considered the best—the Bucks County Playhouse in New Hope, Pennsylvania, north of Philadelphia. The producer of the Bucks County Playhouse, Theron Bamberger, was located in New York City. I wrote him a passionate letter telling him I believed my destiny was to work in the theater and asked for an appointment. Several weeks later I was invited to meet him at his office in New York. I took the train from Baltimore and found myself climbing the rickety stairs of an old brownstone building with theater posters on the walls picturing theater greats, i.e. Helen Hayes, Katherine Cornell,etc. Unbelievably, Mr. Bamberger invited me to be one of only two apprentices! He would have one girl and one boy! I went back to Goucher in ecstasy. My future was sealed!

I passed my sophomore exams at Goucher and went home to wait for the day I would leave for Bucks County Playhouse. I needed money from my parents only for food. Five days before I was to leave my father announced he would not give me the money needed for food because he believed if I went to Bucks County my morals would be ruined by "theater" people. (My morals were ruined anyway!) He threatened to expel me from the family if I left for the Bucks County Playhouse. I realize now my father must have been crushed that I had decided not to take my college degree. A college degree had eluded him and he felt his career had been hurt by that. He wanted all his children to have a college degree. I was not "tough" enough at that time of my life to give up my family (I have never been tough enough to give up my family). However, I was brokenhearted to lose what clearly would have been the opportunity of a lifetime—the opportunity to learn my craft from the greatest American stars.

Moving to New York

It was 1949. My father probably felt guilt about stopping me in my first "big break." He allowed me to audition for the American Academy of Dramatic Art in New York City(alma mater of Spencer Tracy), which was, at the time, the most prestigious theater school in America. It was located in Carnegie Hall.

I passed the audition and was admitted (for a huge tuition which I believe was a waste of money, though at the end of my first year there, one of the auditors wrote "She has gift") and it was arranged I would live at the expensive Three Arts Club for women, near Riverside Drive in New York City's Westside 90s blocks. The faculty at the American Academy could not measure up to the brilliance of my Goucher college professors and I found myself searching elsewhere for a top teacher. However, New York City itself was an astonishing teacher and constant joy!

"Here Is New York" was published in the late '40s and became a kind of handbook to me. Near the end of the short book is this paragraph:

> This race—this race between the destroying planes and the struggling Parliament of Man [the United Nations]—it sticks in all our heads. The city [New York) at last perfectly illustrates both the universal dilemma and the general solution, this riddle in steel and stone is at once the perfect target [foreseeing 9-11] and the perfect demonstration of nonviolence, of racial brotherhood, this lofty target scraping the skies and meeting the destroying planes halfway, home of all people and all nations, capital of everything, housing the deliberations by which the planes are to be stayed and their errand forestalled.

I loved to walk to school through Central Park, put nickels in the Automat, crawl into the unlocked door at the top of Carnegie Hall to watch *Toscanini* rehearse! What a breathtaking, soaring, astonishing experience I *stole* doing that! From New York City I would go by train to my parents' home in Connecticut, carrying two large empty suitcases. I would fill them with my mother's produce and canned goods, then back at the Three Arts Club I would make cabbage sandwiches to survive while I used all the money I had to buy standing room only at shows! Broadway musicals were in their Golden Age. Great dramatists like Tennessee Williams and Arthur Miller had long runs. Stars like Sir Alec Guiness, Sir Lawrence Olivier, Vivian Leigh, Marlon Brando, Julie Harris, Ethel Waters, Audrey Hepburn, Jessica Tandy, Mary Martin and Judy Garland were to be seen. It was also the tail end of radio drama produced in Broadway houses with name stars "holding book" (to which I, as a student, received free tickets). Some nights I would go Big Apple crawling with my best friend Betty Leigh Herbert (a chum at the American Academy of Dramatic Art, later a fine art painter with a show in the United States Capitol rotunda and with a painting destined for the Louvre) to explore Chinatown, Little Italy and the Bowery. Occasionally my father would come to town and invite me out to dinner. In one evening the check for dinner would exceed what I would spend in two months at the Automat!

Moving from Philadelphia to a "Farm" in Connecticut

While still living on the Main Line of Philadelphia, my father had an affair with an editor of the *Ladies Home Journal*. He courted her in New York City. It was a terrible time for my family. I can still remember watching from the stairs as my mom groveled on the floor in front of an open fire, begging my dad not to divorce her. Dad even brought his lover home one weekend and I had to give up my room and bath to her. I can remember seeing her in the bathtub and how hard she tried to ingratiate herself to me. Eventually my mom went to New York (she told me this story very late in her life) to the hotel where my dad was staying with his mistress. She told him he could either give up his lover or get a divorce. *If he chose divorce he would have to take the kids and his parents too*! She made it as far as the elevator before he came rushing after her, promising to break off his affair. Dad did give up his lover (who may have been the love of his life). He also must have made a great effort to patch things up with my mom because he impregnated her with my brother Ron (ten years younger than my brother Tom). Ron was a beautiful child, but sadly in poor health from the beginning. He died tragically and mysteriously in his early twenties.

Meanwhile, part of my parents' clean break was for my dad to take a job as Vice President of Universal Small Appliance Division, in Berlin, Connecticut. Dad was always getting offers but, up to that time, to maintain we three older children in the same excellent high school (a choice of courage on my dad's part), we remained on the Main Line of Philadelphia. In Harwinton, near Berlin, my parents purchased from a millionaire "Highfields," a 350-acre Connecticut property, with a house built in 1812 (the kitchen portion was built in 1749), five fireplaces, and polished wide floorboards with hand wrought nails. Surrounded by New England stone fences, the property had a wonderful old barn, a multi-car garage with a guest house above, acres of vegetable gardens, an acre of strawberries (when the berries came in, Mom put us older kids to work as stoop labor picking the fruit which Mom put in fifteen-cent baskets and sold by the road for only twenty-five cents a basket!), twenty kinds of fruit, active bee hives, a hundred chickens, a couple of turkeys and a lamb. There were also collie dogs. It was a glorious R&R place for me to come from New York!

My brothers or my dad would take me out in the Jeep (named after the General Purpose vehicle of WWII) over the expansive property. There was a hill opposite the house at Highfields, a hill I would climb to gain a view of the Litchfield Hills fifty miles distant, which was a breathtaking sight during the fall at sunrise and sunset. In summer the flowers were like a Monet painting. I would clamber out to the blueberry bushes and pick my breakfast. I would watch the bee keeper gather the luscious nectar for my mom's homemade biscuits. I would hike the paths into the fragrant evergreens and be blissfully enveloped in earth's moss and music. At Christmas time, I would tramp the woods with my dad looking for small evergreens to chop so every member of the family would have their own little tree with presents on separate tables! In addition we chopped a huge, beautifully proportioned tree for in the living room. My mother began decorating for Christmas the day after Thanksgiving.

My brother Dick, who was studying at Brown University, spent every available hour he could at Highfields. I have a clear picture of him sitting on a tractor mowing acres of lawn. It was there, I believe, that he discovered his life's work because he received the gift of a "shopsmith" from my parents. He decided to cut a birch tree into sections about two inches tall, then drilled a hole large enough for a big red candle in the middle of each cutting, placed decorative ropes on the sides of each piece and thus created his first gift items! He had a problem, however—that of finding a market for them after they were handcrafted! Fortunately, my mother empathized with his problem! Christmas was approaching so she bought the entire lot for Christmas gifts. Dick's advertising and distribution problems were solved! Another of his building schemes involved a fresh water spring on the property. Dick decided to create a fresh water swimming pool at the site, which I thought a wonderful idea since I'd swum in a fresh water pool when I taught swimming in Maine. All summer long Dick hauled in sand, cement, pipes and other supplies, but at the end of the day the pool would not hold but a puddle of water! On one of my dad's showing-visitors-around tours he approached the project, saw a snake swimming in the middle and exclaimed "Quite a lot of money and labor to create a swimming pool for a snake!"

Dick eventually bought his own custom shutter manufacturing company in Santa Fe Springs, California, Steiner & Mateer, one of southern California's largest shutter manufacturering companies. His "shop smiths" (manufacturing machines) are as big as a house on several acres! He's added a retail company and an industrial paint company called Aqua Coatings on his own property, so today he is a multi-millionaire from his one-time hobby!

Mother's responsibilities? She had two college age sons and their friends, me and my friends from New York City, a ten-year-old boy (brother Tom), a baby and my aging paternal grandparents to care for. Into this mix my father, so proud of his gentleman's "farm," brought business associates for bucolic weekends. They could eat my mom's incredible fried chicken, vegetables and fruits picked fresh on the property, and excellent current pies. Dad, of course, would charcoal broil steaks and sing "There Is No Place Like Nebraska!"

But, I can remember cradling my exhausted mother moaning with servile grief in my arms, as if *I were her mom*. My mother had only one employee, Surdan, who came for half days. Surdan forced me one day to watch while he wrung the necks of chickens for my mom's fried chicken. The "farm"work family members did was a drop in the bucket compared to the eighteen hour days of my mother. I helped all I could, especially with the ever present child care, and on the business weekends with food preparation and flower arrangements.

I watched mom's misery and vowed *to somehow escape my mother's fate!*

I must find a way to become an actress in New York City. Inspired by words in Maxwell Anderson's essay:"…Thespis never knew what became of his decision to become an actor…[Thespis stepped out of the Chorus to speak alone and thus became the first actor and the first playwright] …theatre at its best is a religious affirmation, an age-old rite restating and reassuring man's belief in his own destiny and his ultimate hope. The theater is much older than the doctrine of evolution, but its one faith… is a faith in evolution, in the reaching and the climb of men toward distant goals…"

I was determined to follow my intuition, to become whom *I knew I am.*

The summer after the Bucks County Playhouse disappointment, before attending the American Academy of Dramatic Art in New York City, I got a job in Connecticut summer stock as a prop mistress. All summer long, while carefully handing hand props to Actors Equity Association[the actors union) actors on cue, I was keenly aware of the fact that I could, instead, have been doing walk-ons and small roles *learning from and watching great actors* like Helen Hayes. I did get to perform in one show that summer. I performed the can-can in the melodrama *Streets of New York*.

Moving Toward Understanding My Mother

Understandably, from backbreaking work, my mom's appearance became that of an overweight peasant (she had been a beautiful little blonde haired girl with hair tied up in a big hair bow and a lovely, sexy, desirable young woman!) by the time of the Connecticut years. Mom never had time or money for grooming and wardrobe. A local artist saw her and wanted to paint her in her garden with her chickens. I'm sure the painter perceived, with a fine artist's inner eye, great beauty in my mother's heroic industry. The artist probably looked at her and saw a Vermeer, but my father would not allow her to be painted. He was ashamed of her appearance and did not want it memorialized. Sadly, my father took no conscious responsibility for the effect his infidelity had on mother's self-esteem or for the toll her inhuman work load (including frequent business guests for the weekend) took upon her. A renowned mural painter (father of the fine artist who wanted to paint my mother) invited me to be the model for a twenty foot mural he did of the Angel of Annunciation in a Connecticut small church. I accepted, so I assume I still stand there twenty feet tall!

I am ashamed to say I, too, was ashamed of mother's appearance, though I understood all too well what motivated it. Mother and I argued because I could not condone her allowing herself to become a victim. But, I felt helpless. I do not believe she realized what a sexist, chauvinist family ours was. Mother was very defensive about my dad. Already I had come to believe *every* person's health—physical, emotional and mental—in a family should be revered. Mom never had *time* even to be affectionate (though she may well have had these feelings). It wasn't until the very end of her life, after my youngest brother, my paternal grandparents, and my dad had died, that my mother and I could become friends and have "fun." How sad that we missed so many years and so much we could have shared! In my view, my mother was the tragic victim of her era—the industrial age. (Today my neice Cheryl declares my mom was definitely smart enough to have had a career!) My dad most certainly was the love and lover of her life but, upwardly mobile and focused on his demanding career as he was, *my dad betrayed my mother's love*. She became an uncherished slave to a huge household on a fabulous but demanding property.

Though never on anyone's payroll, Mother did triumph in several ways. Her pro bono career was to remodel and landscape all the homes my dad's career took her to. Each time they moved my parents made a profit on real estate. One time Mom's persuasiveness with bankers produced loans which allowed my parents to buy investment lots, which were later sold at a profit, stanching a hemorrhaging family financial wound. My dad had lost one million dollars in the stock market on one airplane flight!

Moving Toward Understanding Myself

At that time in New York City, my good friend at the Three Arts Club and fellow student at the American Academy of Dramatic Art, Betty Lee Herbert and I decided to take our acting training into our own hands. Stanislavski in America leaders, the founders of famed Group Theatre, had created the Actors Studio which was spearheaded by Elia Kazan, director of Tennessee Williams' *Streetcar Named Desire*. Kazan became too busy commercially to continue leading the Actors Studio so Lee Strasberg assumed leadership (this was the status of the Actors Studio when Vanessa Redgrave attended sessions). Stella Adler, breaking with Strasberg over method, because she had actually traveled to Moscow to study under Stanislavski, became one of the greatest coaches in America, with many successful students, including Marlon Brando.

Knowing the Adler family history (starting with the great Jewish actor Jacob Adler) I was excited to learn Stella's sister Frances gave private coaching lessons. Betty Lee Herbert and I decided to buy private coaching lessons from Ms. Frances Adler, quite apart from the work we were doing at the American Academy. The night of our first session we were admitted by a grotesque (though probably at one time striking) woman wearing a see-through blouse with no bra which exposed ample breasts—Ms. Frances Adler herself. It was like sitting in a room with a naked stranger!

Betty Lee and I were acutely uncomfortable and embarrassed by this nudity which fazed Ms. Adler not at all. She proceeded to *read to us* for an hour, then requested our money. Finally her partner, a mannish-coifed, heavy set woman made an appearance, called one of us "Little Puppy" and the other "Little Kitten" and we hastily left. Betty Lee and I were shocked by our first overt encounter with lesbianism, though we probably could have grown accustomed to that had Ms. Adler's coaching been exciting. We decided after two sessions not to continue because all we did was listen to Ms. Frances Adler read from Shakespeare, Shaw, Chekhov and O'Neill! We had simply become her audience and we could do that for less money at the theater!

Moving Up

It was 1950. Trying to think through what to do next, since I did not want to return to the American Academy of Dramatic Art, I became a "church tramp." I went to hear sermons of great theologians—Norman Vincent Peale, Ralph Sockman, Harry Emerson Fosdick, the bishops at St. Patrick's Cathedral and Riverside Church. Some nights I would ascend to the top of the Empire State Building (memorialized in the Cary Grant film *An Affair To Remember* and in the more recent *Sleepless In Seattle*). Stunned by the effervesence, glint, sparkle, glitter and glisten of *millions* of lights meeting the millions of stars in the universe, I felt close to God. I asked to be given answers.

Many years later I retraced my Empire State Building ascent and walked slowly around the entire observation deck looking at my life in my former hometown below. There was Times Square and Broadway, site of hundreds of hours "making the rounds" as a poor actress and hundreds of hours attending performances of the best and the greatest performers in the English speaking world. Below was the Hudson River, with ocean liners close to the harbor and uptown, Riverside Drive close to Grant's Tomb, the route of the double decker bus I loved to ride, and the Three Arts Club, my first home in New York. Clearly sighted down there was Central Park, site of my early hiking to and from the American Academy of Dramatic Arts at Carnegie Hall. Soon I saw CBS and Madison Avenue, site of my early work in network television drama's "Studio One." Moving around I saw the East side, where I shared an apartment with two actresses, not too far from the UN building, close to my brother Tom's apartment (after he'd been a VP of American Airlines Tom was a VP of Great Britain's Thomas Cook with residences in NYC and the U). On the East River stood the New York Hospital where my first baby James was born. Near Washington Square in Greenwich Village was the Evangeline, a women's hotel catering to young women starting their careers, where I got a room and two meals a day, plus an Olympic-size swimming pool privileges, roof deck, music room and laundry privileges for only $13 per week! The Evangeline was owned and managed by the Salvation Army and one night, urged by the Army officers, I went to the Bowery Mission for a service attended by homeless drunks of lower Manhatten. Nearby was Wall Street—close to the site of 9-11—where I worked part-time as a hat check girl,till I was given a $100 tip at Christmas, which I wasn't allowed to keep due to restaurant policy that employees must pool all tips! And finally, in New York Harbor were the Staten Island Ferry and the Statue of Liberty (which I would memorialize in the book I wrote for Al Campanis/VP of the Los Angeles Dodgers who, having crossed the Atlantic for many days to escape Mussolini's Italy, upon seeing Lady Liberty, tugged at his mother's skirts and said, "Mama, mama, who is that lady with the fire in her hand?")

Given the power to *see* by my art professor at Goucher, I also sought answers at a world retrospective of Van Gogh's work at the Metropolitan Museum. My D.C. experiences did not prepare me to encounter a life's work of Van Gogh's paintings! The show, which began with his early work—dark browns, blacks and umbras—clearly demonstrated his ability to paint reality. But, as I moved into the cinema verite of his most famous canvases, I entered into thick palet-knife styled peacock blues, lemon yellows, kelly greens, magenta, hot purples and oranges, thick globs of paint that made the world explode! I am fully convinced that Van Gogh in his madness perceived and predicted the atomic age. He must have realized quintessence passes through the earth itself! He must have realized in the simplest sunflower is the energy of the farthest star! The show so viscerally affected me I could not stay! I had to leave after a half hour then pay to come again and again! Colors! How they impacted my psyche! How amazing that in his lifetime, Van Gogh sold nothing and today his canvases sell for millions of dollars. The world catches up slowly! Van Gogh's colors dominate print advertising, the internet, and fashion today! When my husband and I built our home in Arizona (with the help of a generalist Frank Lloyd Wright builder), I opted to decorate with Van Gogh's palette.

One weekend I went by train from Grand Central Station to tony Westport, Connecticut, to see a play at the Westport Country Playhouse (recently graced by Joanne Woodward's artistic director leadership and her husband actor Paul Newman's talent playing the stage manager in venerable *Our Town*). I walked into the lobby amid a leviathan of incoming theatergoers who suddenly parted as if they were the Red Sea! Two ladies passed through the opening and it was whispered one of the ladies was none other than Helen Keller (made famous on Broadway and in film via *The Miracle Worker*, starring Anne Bancroft and Patty Duke)! It astonished me that a blind/deaf person would come to a play! It was spoken among the patrons nearby that Helen could see the play by feeling vibrations and hear the dialogue as her teacher signed in her hand. *I would later make the connection* (just as Helen did when she felt water splashing on her hand, prompting her to say "Waaa Waaa"{water}as her teacher signed the word water in her hand), *between an actor's emotional trigger*(based on the playwright/screenplay writer's script)*and his expressed action.* One follows the other! First there must be an *experience.* Only then may the actor *move and speak*!

In my searching I experienced a conjoining with God when I went to the Civic Center Theatre to see Gershwin's masterpiece, the opera *Porgy 'n' Bess.* New York's Civic Center Theatre was, at that time, a venue of short runs and I worried for the black company that they'd soon again be out of a job. I needn't have worried! The *Porgy 'n' Bess* company I saw toured Russia, Europe and South America for the next four years!

A study of good and evil, poverty and power, Dubose Heyward's 1925 "Porgy" first appeared in the Charleston News Courier. It is the story of Samuel Smalles, a crippled beggar who tried to shoot his lover's pimp. In the show Samuel (Porgy), who can't walk, befriends a prostitute (Bess), taking her into his small shack to live with him. Porgy falls in love with Bess ("Bess, You Is My Woman Now"). On the day of the town's island picnic, Bess' former pimp, Sportin' Boy, a mulatto purveyor of "happy dust,"sex, violence, religion and love, played by Cab Calloway in the production I saw, arrives and rapes Bess, then forces her to accompany him back up North. At the end of the show, Porgy decides to travel all the way from the Deep South to New York City to rescue the love of his life traveling on a small goat pulled cart!

The set for *Porgy 'n' Bess* had fifty doors and windows that opened and shut, plus the company had lead black actors with opera trained voices, a hundred singers and dancers (including an unknown Maya Angelou) moving around the set every moment, yet at any given moment, if you were to stop the action, there was a perfect design of blues, yellows, greens, reds, and purples, as if the precenium held an Impressionist painting lovingly swept along by Mr. Gershwin's glorious music! I wept. I angered. I feared. I was ashamed. I was aroused sexually. I was physically abused during the rape scene. And I was eventually in a cathedral of worship at the show's denouement. The show conveyed a message of erotic and agape love, forgiveness, redemption and triumph. I was in *church!* The show changed my life because it defined what great theater *is. Great theater, the weaving together of optical, aural and emotional threads, is joined at the hip to spirituality!*

I knew after I saw *Porgy 'n' Bess* I had to strike out on my own! I had to find a teacher for this kind of theater! With my limited experience, contacts, theater background, and money, how would I do this? Where could I start?

Moving Toward Financial Independence

First I had to find a place to live cheaply and safely with maximum benefit. That's when I heard about the Evangeline and moved to Greenwich Village for only $13 a week! That's also when I began a series of part-time jobs, including one as a hat check girl near Wall Street. I got a few acting jobs. In Connecticut non-union summer stock I got a job playing Laura in Tennessee Williams' *Glass Menagerie* and Alice in *You Can't Take It With You*. Off Broadway I did a new play called *Noah's Ark* at the YMHA Playhouse, and for the Jackson Heights Players (first home for actor Richard Widmark) the title role of Elizabeth in the comedy *Ring Around Elizabeth*.

Constant auditioning got scary at times. One night, after a late rehearsal, I found myself on an express subway that took me all the way to Harlem! I had stepped onto the wrong train! It was 2 a.m. when I moved off the subway into a dark, deserted station and made my way up to the street. Lost I saw nothing but a bar lit up not too far away. I walked into the bar which was full of African American faces and asked the first person I saw if he would direct me back to the entrance of the subway (which I fully expected he would do because I have always sensed a kind of "bubble" around me, an Angel protecting me). When we got to the entrance of the subway a mounted policeman stood guard and made sure I got on the subway train headed back home safely. Another time, after "doing the rounds" (actor jargon for calling on casting directors and agents), I found I didn't have bus fare home. I walked up to a police officer and asked him for the money which he gave me along with his address so I could mail it back (which I did!). Manhattan, despite its reputation, is a city of millions people offering kindnesses toward strangers and the crime rate per capita is very low. New York City, an island of only four miles by thirteen miles, embraces nine million residents and at least double that number of commuters and visitors daily. The real miracle of New York City is that all these people live, work, play and evolve together, largely without violence, enjoying each other's many differences. Another miracle is that all the toilets flush!

Big Apple actors (including Dustin Hoffman at one time) get jobs in Macy's toy department following the Macy Thanksgiving Day parade (made famous by *Miracle On 34th Street* starring child actor Natalie Wood) and I was no exception. The toy department in Macy's at Christmas was located *with* Santa and his jillion pint-size solicitors. It is an experience in survival! Lines for clerk service were almost longer than the lines for Santa Claus! One day, exhausted after working eight hours and expecting to be paid because I was broke, I was told I had to work another four hours into the evening. I did not realize Macy had a policy of giving employees a free dinner when such a request was made so I worked on without anything to eat. Aching with fatigue and hunger when 9PM came, I learned it would be a week before I could collect my paycheck! I had no money to get from Macy's down to Greenwich Village, thirty-five blocks away! Macy's entire city block display window had animated toy figures, a family going to Grandma's house in the snow, moving to "Sleigh Bells." The window with its gay Christmas music became my mental focus (a technique used by Viktor Frankyl in his practice of psychiatry) as block after block my feet grew wet, slogging through slush and new snow. That was *acting!*

Finally I got a first small union acting job on live television drama's *Studio One*! In those experimental days of television, famed *Studio One*, *Playhouse 90*, etc. were dramas shot "live" with three cameras, recorded on kinescope at the time of the broadcast. It was like doing a Broadway opening night each broadcast! The three huge, cumbersome cameras moved about the set as actors made costume changes behind set pieces. Timing was critical and sometimes, if the drama itself ran overtime, the drama was cut to allow time for the commercial! Betty Furness, week after week, opened Westinghouse refrigerators! I persuaded the CBS casting director to allow me into the control room to watch the director (famed Worthington Minor, who had directed the American's leading acting couple, Alfred Lunt and Lynn Fontanne, in Robert E. Sherwood's *Reunion In Vienna*) choose his shots moment by moment from a bay of monitors. There was only one "take" to get it right! There were no multiple lense takes of the same scene or post-production editing (as in film where only two to three minutes of usable film per day result. When the British produce their dramas the BBC goes on location and shoots with eight cameras, realizing fifteen minutes of usable tape per day). The three camera shoot including a live audience to assure spontaneity is the way sitcoms are produced today.

In addition to making contact with great writing on *Studio One*, i.e. Paddy Cheyevsky (*Americanization of Emily*, *Network*, and the Emmy- and Oscar-winning *Marty*), I finally got to watch and work with great actors: Beatrice

Straight(who won the Oscar for *Network*), John Forsythe (later the star of *Dynasty*, with Joan Collins and Linda Evans), Maria Riva (Marlene Dietrich's daughter), Felicia Montelegra, (wife of Leonard Bernstein, *who visited the set*), and Leslie Nielsen, who stars regularly in television and film to this day!

Once I had set up these ways to survive and grow I could continue my search for training. I auditioned for Margaret Webster and was accepted to the Old Vic School in Great Britain but, received a follow-up letter saying inadequate funding forced the Brits to cancel classes the year I was accepted! I was thrilled to be accepted and keep Ms. Webster's letter to this day. I do not know where I would have found the money to travel to and study in England but, I know had that materialized I would have grown as an actress. At any rate, it was not to be.

Suddenly, it came to me—Ms.Mildred Dunnock, star as Willy's wife of Arthur Miller's *Death of a Salesman*, was currently playing on Broadway! Ms. Dunnock had graduated from Goucher prior to gaining her master's degree from Columbia, then joining Lee Strasberg's Actors Studio! As an ex-Goucher student, I decided to try writing Ms. Dunnock a letter. "Millie" amazingly answered my letter, invited me to see a performance of *Death of a Salesman*, and on another day invited me to be her guest at lunch at the Yale Club! As we talked I realized she understood the intellectual challenges I had left when I left Goucher and the disappointment in the faculty of the time I'd had at the American Academy of Dramatic Art. That lunch meeting resulted in my being *sponsored (based entirely on Millie's referral!)for acceptance in famed coach Sanford Meisner's "professional" class* (for union working actors on Broadway and off Broadway, in film or live television drama). Fortunately, by that time I was eligible for this special group, because I was a member of TVA, Television Artists of America (forerunner of AFTRA, the American Federation of Radio and Television Artists) due to jobs on *Studio One*.

"Sandy" (whose students included Montgomery Clift and later Marlo Thomas) had directed *Men In White*, the first play ever produced by the Group Theatre. The Group Theatre emerged after Russia's Moscow Art Theatre stunned New York critics with reality-based performances. It included, in addition to Sandy, Lee Strasberg (at the helm of the Actors Studio, taking over when Kazan became too busy), Elia Kazan (director of *A Streetcar Named Desire*), Stella Adler (actress and coach), Harold Clurman (director), Clifford Odets (playwright of *The Country Girl, Waiting For Lefty*) and Hollywood actress Frances Farmer (whose tragic lobotomy story is told in the film

Frances for which Jessica Lange won an Academy Award). Millie also mentored me for Joseph Anthony's professional class. Joe directed *Rainmaker* for the Broadway stage and later would direct *Rainmaker* as a film. At last I had found my teachers! Both of these superb, brilliant theater professionals taught scene work via improvisation based on the scenes' characters "through line of action." *Not until an improvisation had connected the actor to a personal "memory of emotion" was the actor allowed to speak the words of the playwright* or screenplay writer, a far cry from saying lines on cue! Actors were mandated to chose real prop objects to work with, i.e. if an actor's character drank something, the actor must bring the vessel to drink from and something to drink. On my own knowing I needed movement as an actress, I began classes with Martha Graham and Merce Cunningham.

*I was truly delighted with every class, without knowing I was at the core of what would **move** entertainment and all forms of drama—theatre, film, television, cable, cassettes, CDs around the world*!

After I had married and moved to Arizona I visited Joe Anthony (who by that time had directed Broadway's *Mary, Mary*, starring Barbara Bel Geddes of later *Dallas* fame) at his farm in New Jersey. His wife served homemade mustard, the gift of a neighbor, *the* Madame Boleslavsky, *widow of Richard Boleslavsky*, author of the famed, beloved short text for actors, *Acting – The First Six Lessons*. Boleslavsky had appeared with the Moscow Art Theatre in New York then stayed to make a career in Hollywood director. Because it was raining when I left, Joe gave me an umbrella which became a cherished "thing" kept for a decade.

After she left *Death Of A Salesman*, Millie Dunnock rehearsed *Peer Gynt* with John Garfield at the ANTA (American National Theatre and Academy) Playhouse. I received an invitation to the rehearsal, so was privileged one day to be only three feet away from the famed-in-the-McCarthy-era and unfairly black listed John Garfield. I was too young and inexperienced to realize the agony of members of the Actors Studio! They had to make the choice of *not being able to work at the only work they knew,* or *snitch on their friends and families, declaring them Communists*! John Garfield was a brilliant artist with integrity. He refused to "name the names" of his colleagues and family, though he was not a communist himself. His heroic act would destroy his career and undoubtedly caused his premature death. The day I watched his *Peer Gynt* rehearsal I was simply aware of the fact that I was *in the presence of a great actor.*

I dated a featured player, Larry Gates, in Rex Harrison and Lili Palmer's *Bell, Book & Candle* (the film version starred Kim Novak instead of Ms. Palmer). It may have been an accident that went so well the first time it happened, the stars decided to keep the accident as part of the show but, the night I saw *Bell, Book & Candle*, about a sexy witch on the prowl, an amazing thing happened! Rex and Lili—married in real life at the time—"flew up,"or forgot, their lines! They stood staring at each other for several moments. Silence. It seemed an eternity! Finally with great grace they took hands and asked each other "Can you remember your line now?" "Are you ready?" Then Rex and Lili walked to the footlights, took a deep bow and while the audience thundered its applause, stepped back into character and picked up the play! I learned from that experience even great artists make mistakes! When they do, they handle them with dignity and professionalism! The audience loves their vulnerability! They get ovations! (Or perhaps it was great showmanship!)

I would finally realize my inheritance and renew my gratitude to my mentor (the generous Mildred Dunnock), when, after two decades in Arizona, I moved to Hollywood, to pick up the threads of my career. There I discovered my resume (with such credits as Sanford Meisner, Joseph Anthony, Martha Graham, and Merce Cunningham) would *always* be "hot"! Most of America's top actor-director talent owe a debt to Stanislavski, the Moscow Art Theatre, the Group Theatre, and the Actors Studio! See today's *Inside The Actors Studio* on BRAVO.

The dance world, meanwhile, reveres Ms. Graham and Merce Cunningham as still presenting innovative, remarkable concerts in New York City!

Part Two
Sunrise

1950-1963 – The Baby Boom, Korean War, Family Beginnings

Moving into an Apartment with Two Actresses

I had been in the Evangeline's remarkably cost-efficient housing for over a year. I decided it was time I gave another girl its advantages! I felt "cocky" about my earning power (ah youth!) so I became roommates with two other actresses on the east side of Manhattan in the '50s! But, I was smart enough to realize some stable income would be required so I took a part-time job at McGraw Hill Publishing company's *Business Week* magazine and *Chemical Week* magazine. My job was to work in a typing pool and fill in for secretaries on vacation. McGraw Hill actually allowed me to clock in by the hour when I wasn't on auditions, in workshops or taking acting jobs! It was at the big blue high-rise off Broadway that I would see the ticker tape parade for returning General Douglas MacArthur and would meet my husband-to-be, Art Director of *Chemical Week* magazine, close friend of *Business Week's* Sales Manager and veteran of the atomic-bomb-making Manhatten Project.

Moving Into a Life–Changing Relationship

The first time my husband-to-be, Woodfin Grady Mizell,Jr. (named after the famous American Civil War reconstruction journalist, Henry Woodfin Grady [the school of journalism at the University of Georgia is named for Henry Woodfin Grady])stopped by my desk at McGraw-Hill Publishing Company, he said in a friendly, kind of fellowship-buddies-at-work way "Let's go to lunch." Thinking he meant "dutch treat," I said "No" because, in-between jobs as an actress, carrying no money except bus fare home, I'd brought my own sandwich and an apple! It was the *way* Woody said it that made me refuse! I was not privy to the rules of conduct at the McGraw-Hill workplace. Certainly I was up for a *free* lunch! Though he was ten years older than me.

What I did not know was that Woody, small town Southern boy pre-WWII, was remarkably "green" and uptight around girls! Infatuated with many of the handsome men I encountered regularly in show business, Woodfin Grady Mizell, Jr., though tall and lean, athletic and obviously very talented as a designer, was not my idea of matinee idol handsome! Also, his *name* completely alienated me! *Woodfin!* Egad!

I underestimated the *persistence* of my new friend however! He continued to stop by my desk and say "Let's go to lunch." Finally, one day (because peanut butter sandwiches in the ladies room were growing old, plus I had *some* money in my purse, enough to pay for a small salad anyway) I decided to take my chances with Mr. Woodfin Grady Mizell Jr. I said "O.K." Outrageously, I asked almost immediately if I could call him "Bill," even though he was affectionately called "Woody"by everyone at work. More outrageously, he agreed! Woody or "Bill"*reached for our check* at the end of his two martinis and my small glass of wine lunch. After that I said "Yes" to his invitation for lunch at least three times a week! *He* was picking up the check!

I never saw him on weekends because Woody, having learned to ski in Europe after WWII, went skiing to famous ski resorts with his work buddies on weekends. Though he may not have been aware of it, this was the smartest thing he could have done to intrigue me! That he would appear disinterested and unavailable on weekends was a very strong attraction to me! I went away, too, i.e. on a date one weekend to hear Serge Koussevitzky, renowned Russian conductor of the Boston Symphony and Director of the Berkshire Symphonic Festival, conduct at Tanglewood. Koussevitsky was champion of modern music, commissioning and performing new works by Copland, Barber, and William Schumann. I heard Koussevitsky conduct Beethovan sitting on the spacious green lawn of Tanglewood's natural amphitheatre in Massachusetts, with its glorious green hills, music enveloping me in a *Midsummer Night's Dream* kind of magic.

However, in Manhattan, during our McGraw-Hill lunches, my "buddy"Woody's WWII stories began to intrigue me. A favorite of his stories was the story of waiting in Britain for the Allied Invasion D-Day. He was encamped with a million GIs in England and every day while eating Army rations for breakfast Brits would pass by on the road gawking at the Yanks. One day one of them asked Woody what he was drinking. He replied *"Cocoa."*

"Cocoa! " the man said astonished. *"Why even the bloody Queen don' have cocoa!"*Like Tom Hanks' platoon in *Saving Private Ryan*, Woody

walked hundreds of miles across Germany! He went into France over Omaha Beach just after the invasion as part of Patton's Third Army. He learned French and German by talking to the children "Kids use simple words, easy to pick up!" he said. Awesome General Patton passed by Woody's group of men one day and asked Woody how he was. Woody knew enough about General Patton to reply, "Fine, sir"!

Woody came to the end of his trek on VE Day when *his was the first group of American GIs to liberate Buchenwald!* It was a day he never could speak much about, even during the twenty-one years of our marriage (Americans saw no documentaries during the war of the Nazi concentration camps, so we were not exposed to the haunting images which are now familiar to us, nor were the camps in newsreels at the time I first dated Woody). Since Woody was stationed in Europe for more than a year following V-E Day he made maximum use of his leaves to encounter the great art of the Bauhaus, an institute founded in Germany in 1919 in Weimar, for the study of art, design, and architecture, noted for its development of a style of functional architecture and its experimental use of building materials. This experience that would influence Woody's choice of a terminal Bachelor of Fine Arts degree at the University of Georgia on the G. I. Bill when he returned to the states. It would also guide his life's work in graphic design.

Woody's sister Anne, following her service in the WAAC's during the war, moved to New York City. Anne encouraged her brother to do the same. "Get out of the limiting environment of Ozark, Alabama," she urged. Ozark, in Southern Alabama not more than fifty miles from the Georgia border, was the home of Woody's parents. It is a tiny, Deep Southern town. Woody's dad owned the local drugstore. My McGraw-Hill art director friend had, at one time, "jerked" sodas and scooped ice cream. That Woody applied and got a job as an art director at McGraw-Hill Publishing company in New York City was not only a sign of the post-WWII attitude toward veterans but is proof of his gift as a designer.

Meanwhile, abandoning shared space with two actresses in the 50s in Manhattan, I took an apartment by myself in Jackson Heights on Long Island, because new apartment complexes built post-war (following the trend to build Levittowns [low cost single family homes for ownership) all over America) offered much more space for the same amount of money. Woody, who had been leasing an apartment in the 50s too, soon followed my decision by leasing an apartment close by but *several blocks closer to the subway exit*! On freezing cold nights, after "making the rounds" as an actress and working a few hours at McGraw-Hill, I would slip into the Oyster Bar at Grand Central Station for a large bowl of steaming oyster stew and oyster crackers to get my courage up for the walk home after I got off the subway. In those days actresses wore high heels, nylons and skirts and the cross winds from the Atlantic ocean, plus the Hudson and East Rivers, cut with incisive pain into frostbitten toes. On one occasion I was invited to see off a friend in a docked ocean liner completely encased in ice! I got into the habit (which Woody encouraged) of stopping by Woody's apartment on the way home. It was a shorter walk than the walk to my apartment—or so I told myself! Woody was an excellent cook and he enjoyed making dinner for me, culminating with his favorite dessert, stewed apricots and sour cream. It was after one of these dinners, watching the still blizzard conditions raging outdoors, that I finally lost my virginity at age twenty-one and, according to my husband's testimony, he lost his.

Moving Brother Tom's Dreams Into Space

After I moved to the Jackson Heights apartment I invited my young brother Tom, then ten years old, for an overnight in the Big City. I took him on the subway for a visit to the Planitarium in Central Park. He was delightful with his curious and eager mind, plainly entranced with space! Soon afterward I learned Tom had begun what became a beloved hobby, the making of model airplanes.

Continuing to make honor grades wherever he went to school, by the time Tom was in high school in Scottsdale, Arizona, he had written a paper on the operation of the airlines. Submitted to his English teacher (who boarded him his final year in high school because my dad had taken yet another better job back East) the paper earned Tom a deserved A+ but, his English teacher couldn't understand the essay so he submitted it to a friend who was a professor at Arizona State University. The professor couldn't understand it either so dad, in-the-corporate-loop, wrote a cover letter and submitted the essay to the president of American Airlines. Immediately a letter came back from American's President saying Tom had an *"unusual grasp of the operation of a major airline for one so young."* He suggested that Tom take entry level summer jobs with American while at the prestigious Wharton School of Business of the University of Pennsylvania (where Tom had won a place in the honors program). Upon graduation Tom would be guaranteed a position!

Tom took the amazing offer. It would have been a challenge had he been alone, but Tom had already married his high school sweetheart, a brilliant girl named Toni Merrill, and the very young couple had had a little girl, Wendy Beth. Tom was a freshman at the University of Pennsylvania!

When Tom graduated with honors from Wharton, American's president secured Tom a place in American's Executive Training program. Sadly, bi-coastal separations (Toni had elected to get her undergraduate degree from Arizona State University) were too heavy a burden on Tom's marriage, which ended in divorce. Wendy Beth grew up living in many places, sharing time with her mother, her dad and my mother. She, like her parents, is brilliant!

Tom, meanwhile, emerged from American's executive training first as advertising director of American! That job was followed by being named vice president of American Airlines Hotels at only twenty-nine years old, the youngest vice president American Airlines ever had! He married again, this time to his life-mate Jane, who was a supervisor of American Airlines stewardesses. Jane became a homemaker extraordinaire, creating beautiful environments wherever they lived and entering into the adventure of travel accompanying her husband whenever possible. Two sons, Ryan and Brett, were born. Tom's time at American Airlines was followed by a similar position with Thomas Cook based in London (travel expeditor of Great Britain), then Senior Vice President of Federal Express (a company which he helped build in its early stages), and most recently CEO emeritus of Holiday Inns Worldwide/Six Continent Hotels based in London! Tom admitted recently his fascination with space may have started with the visit we shared to the Planitarium when he was a pubescent boy!

Moving so He'd Pop the Question

In Jackson Heights, Woody's skiing weekends became fewer and my dinners on the way home from the subway became more frequent. *Belonging to the era when possible pregnancy* (I was not pregnant at the time, though not protected with birth control and neither was Woody) *meant disgrace or marriage* (which must be why I forsook my beloved acting), I decided to go "home." "Home," at that time in my dad's career (he had become VP of the Westinghouse Corporation) was Mansfield, Ohio. Mother had finally been relieved of the workload of Highfields, though leaving that magnificent property was sad for everyone in the family. I figured correctly that Woody would either make up his mind to propose after I left New York or the relationship would terminate. Many long distance phone calls and passionate letters later, Woody flew out to Mansfield (he had already visited my family when they lived at Highfields)for a weekend with a small ring belonging to his mother which he gave me as an engagement ring. I had been carefully taking my temperature and knew it had only been five days since the cessation of my period so I believed sex would be "safe." We had sex on the floor of my dad's study one evening after announcement of our engagement to my parents (who approved the marriage excitedly). Of course, I immediately became pregnant with my first son, James!

Amid my nausea and general malaise, Mother and I traveled to Cleveland and in a round of many stores bought the most expensive wedding dress we saw, an ivory tone satin gown with a Juliet Cap, seeded with pearls trailing a lovely veil. On that wedding dress shopping trip, I told my mother I was certain I was pregnant. She insisted we proceed with wedding plans as if nothing had transpired. A few weeks later we traveled by car back to Manhattan, where my dad, a member of the Canadian Club at the Waldorf Astoria Hotel, had arranged an engagement party for me culminating in a family dinner at the popular Starlight Roof (in a photo taken at the time I look radiant and my parents look happy and proud).

My wedding was a candlelight wedding in the First Congregational Church of Mansfield. Groomsmen and bridesmaids came from far distances, so Woody and I spent most of the day before the wedding and the day of our wedding going back and forth between the airport and the train station to pick people up, including his parents from Alabama and his sister from New York City. Woody and I spoke our own vows which we had memorized at the service. The reception was at my parents' home, where Mother had prepared a feast but, Woody and I, en route eventually to the elegant Homestead resort in Virginia, left before eating anything. We took only the top of our wedding cake and a bottle of champagne from Mother's feast. The small motel we went to on the outskirts of Mansfield prior to boarding a train for Virginia in the morning had no restaurant! Starving, we spent our wedding night with the top of wedding cake and champagne in our tummies. The owner of the motel saw the story of our wedding in the paper on Sunday and kindly knocked on our door in the morning with a tray of juice, eggs, toast and coffee. Our joy runneth over! Below is an excerpt from the account the Mansfield News Herald had about our wedding:

October 12, 1952
Mary Lynne Oliver Wed At Candlelight church Service
Miss Mary Lynne Oliver, daughter of Mr. and Mrs. Robert Marion Oliver, 583 Russell Rd., became the bride of Woodfin Grady Mizell Jr., Jackson heights, Long Island, N.Y., last night during a candlelight service performed in the First Congregational church.

The Rev. Matthew Madden officiated at the ceremony which was climaxed by the communion service for the couple. Miss Iris Turner,New York City, soloist and Mrs. Rhea Twitchell organist, presented a half-hour prelude of the nuptial music preceding the ceremony. the bride was given in marriage by her father. She carried a white Bible topped with a white orchid. Her attendants were Miss Alice Joan Falvey, Glencoe, MD., maid of honor, Mrs. Andrew Joseph Banks, Akron, matron of honor, and Miss Anne Mizell, New York City, sister of the bridegroom, bridesmaid. They carried deep red Happiness roses with their floor length fur-trimmed gowns. ....Woodfin Grady Mizell Sr., Clearwater,Fla., served his son as best man. Usher duties were performed by Densil R. Adams Jr., New York City, Richard K. Oliver and Thomas R. Oliver brothers of the bride.

The new Mrs. Mizell, a member of the American National National Theatre and Academy, attended Goucher College, the American Academy of Dramatic Arts and the Martha Graham school. She studied with Sanford Meisner of the Neighborhood Playhouse and Joseph Anthony, member of Actors Studio.

The bridegroom attended the University of Alabama. He received his Batchelor of Fine Arts degree from the University of Georgia where he was affiliated with Sigma Alpha Epison fraternity. Mr. Mizell is currently employed as art director and production manager of Chemical Week magazine in New York City.

Moving Into the Dance of Marriage

My new husband was a great dancer and at the elegant Homestead in Virginia that was one thing we actually did of all the activity opportunities during our three days there! Every evening, while dining on entrees that ran the gamut from filet mignon to quail in wine sauce, plus a complete array of hors d'oeuvres, soups, salads, dressings, breads, vegetables and desserts, we danced to a full orchestra in evening clothes!

"You were meant for me.
I was meant for you.
Nature fashioned you and when she was done
You were all the sweet things rolled into one.
You're like a plaintive melody
That never sets me free.
I'm content.
The angels must have sent you
And they meant you just for me."

We also used the swimming pool *once*. Oddly, we were glad to board the train for New York City to get back to the business of setting up a home together in Woody's one-bedroom Jackson Heights apartment and to prepare for parenthood. This meant my abandoning all thought of "making the rounds" as an actress since the only beginning-to-show wardrobe we could afford for me was Woody's army pants left open at the fly with suspenders and one of his shirts! I did buy one good maternity navy blue suit. The navy blue suit took me to Manhattan for appointments with our Blue Cross–Blue Shield obstetrician, who insisted I gain no more than one pound per month. Working hard at learning nutrition, I faithfully ate liver once a week! When I emerged from the doctor's office having gained only one pound per month I celebrated by buying a giant Hersey bar! Then I met Woody near the big blue McGraw-Hill high-rise and we celebrated by going out to dinner!

The *whole adventure of marriage and expectant parenthood was full of drama* because I had elected to be in the first wave of women at New York Hospital on the East River to have "natural" childbirth (birth with little or no painkilling drugs – HBO's *In the Womb* reveals the drama). In the Lamaze method, prospective parents are taught physical and mental techniques for reducing pain and discomfort and participating more fully in the birth process. This meant both Woody and I took a series of classes. Mine were concentrated on exercises for actual labor with stress on breathing techniques. His involved mingling with every race and socioeconomic level of Manhattan's one-world demographic population of expectant fathers to learn to support the mother in labor techniques. Ah-h-h the "old wives tales" stories he came home with! One story he told me was related by the intern instructor to the group in his class. Apparently, the intern, a Caucasian, was called to Harlem to deliver a baby.

In home births in Harlem at the time, all the relatives gathered to watch the birth of the baby! When the expectant mother gave her last big push the infant emerged so suddenly the intern let the baby fall to the floor! The young doctor looked up into a sea of angry black faces and thought quickly. "Sometimes I have to let them drop more than once to make them cry," he exclaimed cheerfully, which probably saved his life!

Thanksgiving was approaching and Woody and I elected to have our first dinner party, following going by subway to watch the wonderful Macy Thanksgiving Day parade. I baked my first turkey (Mom wrote careful instructions for this feat). The dinner had to be carefully planned around our tight budget. We planned to go from the parade to the home of Woody's groomsman, Jack Adams ("Densil R. Adams" in the wedding press announcement) who had invited the group for cocktails (which would be double old fashioneds). *Woody and I had our first major argument over a bottle of wine purchased for this party.* Woody insisted wine must be served with dinner (certainly appropriate for Manhattan dinner parties but, with an eye to our tiny budget for the feast, I asserted Jack's cocktails would be sufficient alcohol for the party). Woody bought the wine and only he elected to have it during dinner. He, in fact, drank the entire bottle (probably to prove a point). By the time dessert was served (my first baked pumpkin pie!) *Woody had passed out* on our bed. I was ignorant of the early symptoms of alcoholism, so this obvious danger signal didn't register on me. In my mind, nothing mattered except our happiness! I was centered on the *adventure* of being married and expecting my first baby!

Only one thing disturbed us emotionally at this time. Woody's parents, reared in the Deep South, upon learning I would be expecting my first baby in six—not nine—months, choose to stop communicating with us! This communication "black out" endured during my entire first pregnancy, including my baby James' birth and my stay in the hospital! In fact, Woody's parents did not re-enter into correspondence with their son and his family until James was three months old! Heartbreaking as it was for Woody and shaming as it was to me (these attitudes are tragically portrayed in an exceptional 2003 Irish film, *The Magdalene Sisters*), the biggest losers were the senior Mizells, because it alienated Woody from his parents for the rest of his life. During years in Europe during and following WWII, plus years in New York City, Woody's mind had matured away from the narrow values of the Deep South.

Moving Into Parenthood

Christmas was coming and to save money for the arrival of our first child, I elected to decorate our tree entirely with hand cut and individually decorated cookies on strings, a project that required two weeks to complete. Woody, meanwhile, utilizing his inventive design ideas, materials and building skills, created a "mobile bedroom" for our baby! Woody probably could have attained a patent on his invention because it was perfect for new parents living in the city in a small apartment! An eye-appealing piece of furniture, our baby's mobile bedroom was a designed-in-width-to-just-fit-through-a-bedroom-door. The wooden boat-shaped bed with foam mattress mounted on wheels had tall sides, with a shelf below for baby clothes, diapers, and supplies! This meant during the day our one bedroom would become the baby's room and at night, wheeled through the door, the living room would become the baby's room! Perfect for city dwelling expectant parents!

A new snow fell that 1953 New Years's Eve. It was a magic, street lights and neon signs making the snow glisten, silent and wonderous night! We newlyweds and expectant parents were full of joy and very much in love! Woody and I elected to make angels in the snow on a walk to see Garbo in *Ninotchka.*

If you take the ferry boat ride around Manhattan island, you will see on the East River two imposing structures, the New York Hospital and the United Nations, almost side by side at river's edge. The famous New York Hospital, Woody's and my first choice of hospital, due to its top reputation and its experiment in"natural" childbirth, was a great choice for my first labor and birth, though my first try at "natural" childbirth turned out to be a disappointment. Many hours before delivery, my water broke just as I got to the hospital. In the labor room my husband held my hand for hours (he said he could not believe the grip I had during contractions!),rubbed my back, and counted the seconds of my deep breathing hour after hour. I was dilated completely (cervix opening to ten centimeters proceeds birth) but my about-to-be-born baby son's head was turned to the side instead of down, as it needed to be. In spite of 30 seconds apart contractions for over an hour, the baby could not move through the cervix. My obstetrician asked if he could clamp ether on my face (I finally gave permission). I was out in seconds. With forceps, Dr. Finn deftly rescued James. I, however, awoke feeling very sick and experiencing deep grief that I had not seen my baby born! Then, when I saw my child all injured, his little head shaped like a teepee, his face bruised and scarred, I was bereft! However, within three days my baby's head was round, his face rosy and clear!

Meanwhile, New York Hospital treated me exactly as if I *had* seen my baby born. As a part of the hospital's experiment with "natural" childbirth, four new mothers shared a huge solarium filled with potted trees, plants and visitor bouquets of flowers! Such a sun-filled, happy place! Even the nurses commented "OB-GYN in this room is the happiest part of the hospital!" It was like being in a garden! The huge room was glassed in on one side so we could see boats moving up the East River! At night we had the illusion we four mothers were on a cruise! Four privileged new dads, draped in white from head to toe, wearing face masks (looking just like doctors prepared for the operating room) were allowed to visit whenever they wished, not just during visiting hours! Four babies were in cribs on wheels beside the beds, not in the nursery. At least four nurses per hour hovered over us at all times. They helped us bathe and nurse our babies, and urged us to use the rocking chairs provided to cuddle and sing to our babies. All this they did plus cared for us, at no extra cost to we patients!

One of the new moms in the solarium was a professional singer in Broadway's *Kiss Me, Kate*.Her husband was a dancer in the same show (one of Broadway's big hits which I had seen), so we formed a wonderful "colleagues in show business" bond that endured beyond the hospital. Due to all the posterior battering I'd endured at the end of labor, none of my plumbing worked. I had to stay in the hospital eight days (unheard of today)!

At last we three could go home. Woody had taken a week off to help me. My mother came from Ohio with my youngest brother Ronnie to see the baby. Her visit of only one day lifted my spirits. She and Dad had made "Jamie" (our name for James until he became an adult) the gift of his first complete layette. Attempting to breastfeed my baby I developed breast mastitis, so most nights during that first week Woody heroically was up walking our baby son! Woody then had to sleep during the day! In the middle of the night one night, Woody had to canvass the streets for a pharmacy to buy formula and prepare it for bottles (pediatrician's order). When the week was up Jamie was a bottle fed baby and I think Woody was extremely happy to return to the office!

Jamie seemed to thrive on formula. My doctor said an extremely wise thing to me in those first weeks as a new parent:"Babies are tougher than we give them credit for! It's the parents who need care!" He advised Woody and me to take a break from the baby at least once a week, go for a walk, go to a movie! We took Jamie for baptism when he was six weeks old. It was Mother's Day and Jamie was as plump as a baby of that age should be! Baptism day was rainy and overcast. We had traveled to the church using an umbrella. Jamie cried quite loudly in the vestibule of the church waiting for his baptism, which was scheduled for the end of a regular church service! In fact, in spite of efforts to quiet him, he was still crying as we walked up the aisle to the alter! We stood beneath the minister just below a stained glass window. Suddenly the sun broke through the window casting a rainbow beam of light directly on Jamie's face! The minister placed drops of water on Jamie's head. Suddenly, our infant stopped crying and smiled! The minister spoke. "James Robert Mizell, I baptize you in the name of the Father, and the Son, and the Holy Ghost," and Jamie was radiant! I have always thought this spiritual moment to be a momentous sign about James' destiny.

Moving Across America to Arizona

The temperature on the 4 of July, 1953, in New York City (before widespread air-conditioning) was 95 degrees, coupled with 90 percent humidity! Woody and I had invested in a large window fan positioned to draw the hot air out the window. But, the hot air would not go! We knew we would be crowded like sardines in a can in traffic on the way to the cool breezes of NYC's favored getaway-Jones Beach. Instead, we chose to celebrate at home with a show biz couple who also had a new baby! What a clever idea! How proud I was of myself for thinking of it! Our friends lived on the first floor of our apartment building, so the travel would be nil! We would outsmart everyone on the highway by having a pot luck picnic with red and white checked tablecloth, potato salad, deviled eggs, sliced ham, and watermelon on our own apartment floor! Long before getting to the watermelon, however, the heat and humidity overpowered us! We could scarcely breathe let alone speak to each other! The heat made the babies miserable, so eventually we elected to take them up to the hot roof where at least a small breeze was blowing. The event was a giant failure!

Knowing we'd need a room for our son soon, we investigated housing we could afford in Connecticut and New Jersey. We learned it would mean a minimum two-hour daily commute for Woody (the Pocono foreclosure housing scandal of 2004 demonstrates this problem still exists for low and middle income families working in New York City) would leave hardly any quality time for our new family. While focusing on the housing problem we witnessed up close and personal the lifestyle of Woody's editor-in-chief. He had at least a decade of seniority in the top position on Woody's magazine, and thus made many times the salary of my husband. We newlyweds/new parents were invited to dinner at the editor's high-rent-district apartment on Park Avenue, near Washington Square in Greenwich Village. How honored we were! But, when we got there we were appalled to learn the editor and his wife had three children in an apartment with only one bedroom, a living room, kitchen and bath!

Though his children and wife were frequently pictured in Vogue magazine enjoying tony, historical Washington Square, the walls of the editor's apartment were completely covered with child grafetti. Two of the children and a mountain of toys occupied the bedroom, but the youngest child, a toddler, slept in an alcove in the hallway (a la *Harry Potter*) and the parents slept on a roll-away in the living room. The evening began with candlelight and martinis, which somewhat obscured the mess, walls, and noise. However, it was ten o'clock after the children had quieted down before we finally ate a very ordinary dinner prepared from cans. Though the editor-in-chief's wife was thrilled with the publicity and extra money her children received as models in Vogue, my husband and I realized Woody's editor spent *all* his salary on inadequate space for his family, private schools for two of his children, "sitters" hired to escort the children to and from school, and booze to obliterate it all night after night! I realized that night I didn't want to rear our son in a brownstone with no grass facing that kind of a future.

It was after those two fiascos that my dad came to dinner one night. Hearing our stories, his response was "Why don't you pick a place in the USA you'd most like to live and go there?"

My dad had been such a successful entrepreneur, starting from nothing, that this logic coming from him made sense! We began sending away to Chambers of Commerce all over America requesting brochures and, in the process, received our first ever copies of *Arizona Highways* magazine! O! The incredible photography depicting awe-inspiring beauty in endless space! Arizona was indeed a strange *open* land, full of promise, albeit thousands of miles west of New York City. Woody and I were on a journey of discovery! Our naiveté and enthusiasm was boundless! We had found the secret to a true *life*—and living at the poverty level was about to begin again!

Dad offered to connect us to his good friend Julia Kiene, head home economist of Westinghouse, author with Betty Furness of Westinghouse's recently published cookbook. Julia, in addition, was a friend to me in my childhood; we shared the same birthday and she always remembered me with a small gift; additionally, as each of my children was born she gave as a baby gift a hand-knitted Christmas stocking with the child's name and the year of his birth, a gift my youngest son Gary has to this day!

Julia's colleague, Mary Marks, had recently married a stock broker by the name of Eric Marks. Eric was active on Wall Street but he also had bought an Inn in Show Low, Arizona. Woody and I went to breakfast with Eric and learned Mary Marks was the chef extraordinaire at Eric's Show Low, Arizona Paint Pony Inn, which was a resort for *invited guests only*—politicians, show business celebrities, and wealthy executives! Eric described this wonderful place and promised to host us at his inn if we moved to Arizona! Before we'd finished breakfast, Eric had also referred us to Fred Eldean, brilliant owner of the largest, most successful public relations firm in America, with General Motors as his principal account. Mr. Eldean's office was in Rockefeller Center, so it was there that we breakfasted with him at a small table close to the skating rink not in use during the summer. Fred told us he had recently built a home in Scottsdale, Arizona, designed by Frank Lloyd Wright architect Blaine Drake. Mr. Eldean expected to move his family to Scottsdale as soon as possible, because his son had health problems. Arizona's climate would be a boon to his son. Of course the Frank Lloyd Wright lure was a magnet to my husband, who had been attracted to the work of the Bauhaus in Germany after WWII.

That breakfast became a turning point in our lives, because though Woody also arranged via a referral a meeting with the advertising director of American Airlines (a man based in Dallas, Texas, who told us "Dallas is the place to move because Dallas has money!"), the lure of breathtaking scenery as pictured in *Arizona Highways*, Frank Lloyd Wright's Taliesin, and the potential friendship of men like genius Fred Eldean and stock-broker-turned-inn-keeper Eric Marks was irresistible! We decided Woody would leave his secure top designer/art director/New York City publishing corporation job and I would leave my opportunity to develop a professional acting career in the major theater market in America, to travel two thousand miles and there begin a remarkable life, contributing to one another, our family and our community life. We were confident these opportunities had been given to us by God, that we were directed to ***move***! Woody gave his notice at McGraw-Hill.

The actual process began as we sold one by one the things in our apartment, keeping only baby equipment and a very expensive bar and stools we had foolishly purchased(the moving costs for the bar and stools was $1200, which would have bought us a house full of used furniture in Arizona). We bought a recent year used Jeep station wagon. Nine-month-old Jamie's new crib would travel with us in the station wagon. When we left our Jackson Heights apartment we left stacks of valuable LP records and storage units in the hall, items that had not yet sold but which we could not carry. We would travel to Mansfield, Ohio, to share our second Thanksgiving with my parents at the site of our wedding. In an old photograph we are pictured beside our jeep station wagon with a snow-covered landscape in the background, about to embark to an unknown future, without jobs, in a journey across America!

The actual trip across America became a second honeymoon! We, in our first fully paid for car, traveled from state to state as I had as a child, when my dad kept getting jobs farther and farther East, only in the opposite direction! We stopped at a motel by 4 p.m. each day. We put our baby Jamie to bed in the motel *bathtub!* It's hard for me to believe today but, once Jamie was asleep in his temporary crib, we stole out of the room for a quick half hour meal in each motel café! Unbelievable! Irresponsible! (Though we felt confident once Jamie was down for the night he would sleep for at least five hours! God must have been watching over us because there were no motel fires or other emergencies.) The only time we ran into trouble using the bathtub for a crib was the morning we woke to find the foam cushions, which lined the bathtub, were all wet because the faucet had a small drip! Amazingly, Jamie was still sunny and agreeable, though soaking wet!

Finally we came to New Mexico, where the earth seemed to open up, and we could see distances of two hundred miles! Sighting the *openness* of the West was love at first sight for both Woody and me. It was our plan to stop in Albuquerque for two nights because Woody had Albuquerque advertising agency job leads he wanted to check on during one full day. He saw a couple of potential employers and came away feeling encouraged he had a job offer. However, we had decided to push on to Arizona because Arizona was our first choice goal of where we wanted to live. That night, in a burst of optimism, I foolishly did not use my birth control diaphragm. The next morning I awoke and *knew* I was pregnant again! When I made that announcement to my unemployed husband, he did not question how I *knew*. He instead shouted at me, "How could you do that? I don't even have a job! I'll leave you in

Albuquerque!"

"If you do," I shouted back,"you'll have to leave Jamie too!"

In spite of our argument we found ourselves simmering down in our jeep traveling into a blizzard toward Arizona. As we approached the Continental Divide, suddenly the keeper came off the accelerator of the jeep so the gas pedal wouldn't work properly! Barely able to see more than two car lengths ahead, Woody courageously kept the car going by turning the key on and off 'til we came to a tiny hamlet called Pietown (featured in Depression–era photos by Russell Lee [*The New York Times*, 5-09-04)). Woody pulled the car into an open mechanic's garage there. A rotund, red-faced-with-cold jolly man, all wrapped up in heavy jacket, pants, tall boots, scarf and knitted cap came out to us and asked what he could do for us. Woody described the trouble and the man suggested Jamie and I go into a nearby café where it was warm while he looked under the hood.

About a half hour later, Woody and the man came smiling into the café to say the trouble had been fixed! Apparently the man had welded a metal *hairpin* bent in just the right way to fix the problem! Expecting to be charged the moon, Woody asked how much we owed. "That'll be fifty cents!" the man said. "And good luck to you!" We could scarcely believe our good fortune!

Having lost many hours with our car trouble, we stopped at the state line of Arizona amid foot-high snow drifts to change Jamie's diaper and to figure the miles yet to go to Eric Marks' Paint Pony Inn in Show Low. We were expected there for dinner. We would be late but, we had no choice but to push on (there were no cell phones then to announce the reason for our delay). With a vast universe of stars now visible in a clear sky, at about eight-thirty or nine o'clock, we drove up to a setting not unlike that in the Bing Crosby movie *Holiday Inn*. Paint Pony Inn was enveloped in evergreens, new snow and festooned in Christmas lights. Eric Marks, in formal attire looking every bit the New Yorker, welcomed us. We must have looked bedraggled in our grubby travel clothes carrying a baby!

Eric ushered us into a large room of never before seen Native American paintings, sculpture, woven blankets and rugs, manos and metates, Kachina dolls, and sand paintings! Native American servants moved about in their colorful native dress wearing silver and turquoise jewelry. A group of Anglos in evening clothes were at the dinner table midway into a wine with dinner meal prepared by gourmet hostess Mary Marks. Eric took us upstairs to a room and (though he'd never before allowed children at his Inn) allowed us to put Jamie to bed in the bathtub! We hurriedly cleaned up as best we could, changed into clothes a bit more appropriate for a formal sit-down dinner, and went down to meet Eric's guests, all well known, established in Arizona and elsewhere VIPs! Eric proudly pointed out his collection of former guests' hats on pegs and mentioned the owner of each hat— Bing Crosby's bill-shaped golf cap, Barry Goldwater's western hat, and others.

Woody and I could not believe the contrast between being stranded in little Pietown and dining on exotic foods in the elegance of Paint Pony Inn with such high powered, yet warm and eager to help, formally dressed people! The next morning, Eric and several of the guests gave us job possibilities' names and phone numbers and pointed us toward the Salt River Canyon that would lead us to Phoenix! We were full to the brim with the kindness of strangers, our own hope and already fulfilled dreams. How amazing it was to travel from snow-covered evergreens, through red rock hanging on the side of a cliff, down to scrub brush and eventually to saguaro and other cacti as we approached Phoenix! It was December 8 1953, just twelve years and a day since the Japanese attacked Pearl Harbor, and what a journey my life had already taken!

Moving Via Woody's Mentor

Just as Mildred Dunnock of Broadway's *Death of a Salesman* had mentored me in New York City, Fred Eldean mentored Woody from the first day we arrived in Phoenix! We checked into a a motel on Van Buren Street and having just a day before come from a blizzard, we went swimming! Such was the wonder of our *adventure*! Fred referred Woody to Arizona Messenger Printing Company about a job as art director. It was bare survival money, $90 a week—what a shock after Woody's salary in New York City!—but Woody accepted the job.

Fred invited us to his Blaine Drake (a former Frank Lloyd Wright architect) designed home on Scottsdale Road. The house was surrounded by desert flora and fauna and a moat, or stream filled with tropical fish. There was a swimming pool also on five acres. We were intrigued with the light decks, angled walls, clerestory windows, built in furniture, and the Native American fine art that decorated the house (all hallmarks of famed architect Frank Lloyd Wright).

Fred's wife, Margie, a down-to-earth and gracious hostess, was a nutrition expert specializing in vitamin C with calcium healings. Margie's nutrition research and experimentation would later impact my family. Fred loved to tell us the story about his visiting dignitaries from around the country who came to see him in Scottsdale. During the serving of cocktails, when guests inquired about a powder room they were referred to one close by. Fred's sons [adventuresome snake catchers) had captured a many feet long *bull snake* which they put in the designated powder room shower. When guests had used the toilet and were washing up they'd hear a noise, peer into the shower stall to satisfy their curiosity, and scream! Such was the sense of humor of our host!

Fred had legitimate *clout!* He was already demonstrating his genius real estate deals by using his policy of marketing with no overhead. As a brilliant researcher, he studied the United States government's releasing of "script"(vast sections of land owned by the government, soon to be made available to private purchasers). In the weeks prior to the day of the Feds' release of the "script" for private ownership, Fred sat in his kitchen, called his friends, clients and associates from across the USA asking them to send him checks for $25,000, $50,000, etc., until he'd accumulated a *million dollars! All this money was collected without contracts of any kind*! With the money, Fred bought "sections" of land on the day "script" was released by the U S government. In one year, Fred turned over a 100% profit to his "investors"who had trusted him so completely, not even a handshake was necessary to complete the deal! In this way Fred launched nonexistent communities—Care Free, Fountain Hills and Laughlin (Fred bought Laughlin for 25 cents an acre!). Fred also purchased all of Arizona's real estate records stored in the basement of landmark structure Luhrs Tower on Jefferson Street in Phoenix. After purchase he trucked the hard cover records to a "barn"(an outbuilding from his house) on Scottsdale Road and transferred them to microfilm, a project that employed his sons and others. Eventually Fred not only knew about every real estate transaction that had ever taken place in the state of Arizona, he became chairman of the board of Arizona's largest land company, the John Page Land Company. (The current President/CEO of Page Land and Cattle Company is Stephen Brophy, whose family founded the Catholic Brophy Preparatory school on Central Avenue in Phoenix.)

Almost immediately after arriving in Phoenix, Woody and I found a small rental house with a bit of a yard on 29th Avenue north of Camelback Road. A photo of Jamie at the time shows a baby touching with complete awe (as he'd never seen it before) brown backyard Bermuda grass! The house had a basement (the builder of these small rentals came from the Midwest and feared tornadoes). We created an art studio in our basement. To earn extra money, we began what continued as a tradition—the making of serigraphs (silk screened) Christmas cards, wall hangings, place mats, etc., for sale and to give as gifts. Following in the footsteps of my brother Dick, with his handcrafted candle holders in Connecticut, family and friends became our first markets for silk-screened products. Sales helped with ever mounting expenses and with Christmas gifts.

It was in the basement, which had a window at the ground level above the bottom step down, that I first encountered scorpions! I'd been warned to watch for their curved, pointed, poisoned tails, so I went down to the art studio equipped with a can of insect killer! I found if I looked out for the scorpions in advance I could deadeye them before they struck! I wasn't bit by a scorpion until years later, in our Scottsdale house.

One of our first Sunday afternoon outings was to drive to Frank Lloyd Wright's Taliesin. When I first sighted it I had the same visceral reaction I'd had at the Metropolitan Museum of Art in New York City's retrospective of Van Gogh! Here was a creator who predicted the atomic age! The architecture seemed to *explode* into its universe.

Moving into the Promise of Arizona

To celebrate Christmas we went shopping on Scottsdale's Brown Avenue, which claimed to be "the West's Most Western Town." There we bought baby Jamie Levi jeans, a western shirt and western boots! At nine months old, he could just pull up on the couch at our little rented house and looked cute as the dickens as a little cowboy! It was a very happy Christmas because we'd decided to take Fred Eldean up on an extraordinary offer! We would purchase from him an acre and an eighth of land on Jack Rabbit Lane, east of Scottsdale Road in Scottsdale (the lot would later become part of Paradise Valley). The land had a stable on it. To buy the land we each had to generate $1000 from each of our parents but, after that, Fred agreed to co-sign a construction loan with the Arizona Bank and to refer his generalist builder, T.P. Furrow, who had worked for Frank Lloyd Wright, to work with us. Thus we could renovate the barn into a Woody Mizell designed house! The property had a clear view to the snow-capped McDowell Mountains seventy-five miles away. Across the street was a thoroughbred horse ranch of twenty acres and we could see jackrabbits leaping in from the nearby desert. Families of quail, the babies trailing after the mother bird, crossed the property as did roadrunners (a famed

Arizona area bird with a long tail that points when it comes to a standstill). Toads and lizards were also in abundance.

The deal was cut and thus began a three year odyssey to gain an FHA mortgage (Woody, post–WWII, qualified). I could not know then that the three years soon to follow would take me from ecstasy to the pits of hell. I would "grow up" during the three years just ahead in ways I could not at the time imagine. One thing I did know at the time the deal was cut! I *was* pregnant again.

Our *Moving* to Arizona Attracts My Family

My older brother Bob, the Dartmouth graduate and Naval officer, who had been in combat zones and hurricanes during the Korean war, decided to quit the Navy when his tour was up. He mustered out in San Diego and elected to drive east with his wife, Beverly, and baby son, Chris. Their destination was Quincy, Massachusetts,(John Adams memorial home) the residence of his wife's family. 1954 was the height of the American polio epidemic. When Bob and his family arrived in Qunicy, Beverly's brother Dudley had already been diagnosed with paralytic polio! The Thomas family was devastated, so no one paid attention to Bob though he knew he was very ill. Finally Bob's temperature reached 105 degrees and he was forced to consult a doctor! It was learned he had *bulbar polio*, the polio that attacks the nervous system and the brain.

Fortunately Bob did not die, but the disease devasted his body. During a year of recovery he, his almost newlywed wife and son had to live with my parents at their Mansfield, Ohio, home. During that time, Bob (always the bright scholar) applied for the GI Bill, electing to attend Thunderbird:The American Graduate School of International Management in west Phoenix. He was accepted and thus moved his family West not long after we made our deal with Fred Eldean. Bob's second child, a daughter, Cheryl, was born in Phoenix. At the Mizell rented house on 29th Avenue in Phoenix, a backyard photo shows baby Cheryl in a carriage covered with nests of Easter eggs! She was out of sight supporting with her baby blanket hidden egg nests as her cousins Jamie and Chris were scouring the yard in a traditional hunt!

Bob's heroic fight to recover his body and build a career led to a job offer in Puerto Rico. Through all his travail, his marriage was not able to withstand the combined facts of pre-Salk vaccine polio, intense graduate school study, a challenging position, and a move from the United States. It ended in divorce.

After my brother Bob and his family moved to Arizona, my parents followed our dream by buying a home on Fanfol Drive in Scottsdale. Dad established a consulting business, Marketing Services, Inc., in Scottsdale but found Phoenix was not yet a ripe market for East Coast quality and price (just as we found the Phoenix market was not ready to buy top graphics design. Dad eventually moved his career, first back East, then to the cutting edge market of California.) It was while my parents lived in Arizona, where my brother Tom attended Scottsdale High School, that Dad sent the essay about the operation of the airlines to the president of American Airlines, and Tom received his American Airlines opportunity post Wharton School of Business.

Moving to Self–Build a Designer House

My and Woody's signing purchase of property and construction loan documents at the bank with Fred Eldean was only a baby step on a long journey! My husband's designs were innovative, incorporating many of the features T.P.Furrow's background, as a Frank Lloyd Wright builder, would be able to execute. However, we began from an existing structure so *before we could build we had first to tear down*. Our house would eventually be featured on the front page of the Sun Living section of metro-Phoenix's leading newspaper, *The Arizona Republic*, and in the features section of the *Scottsdale Progress* (precursor to the *Tribune* newspapers). However, in those early days it took a lot of vision to take a high dive into the work because our construction loan was for only $10,000!

Woody and I began our odyssey after Woody got off work from Arizona Messenger Printing Company by traveling each night all the way to Scottsdale from 29th Avenue! Boards from the stable walls would be removed and hauled back to our west side rental so I could sand and stain them. The boards would then be returned for installation in the 44-foot wide hallway of our new house. A naked light bulb would guide our work up to about midnight. Into this electric outlet I plugged a toaster so we had cocoa heated on a coleman stove and toast before we quit at midnight. One night a mouse jumped out of the toaster as I started the toaster! Another night, a not poisonous half-foot long scorpion walked through our work area, scaring me half to death! I knew by that time the tiny, narrow, segment-tailed scorpions were the truly poisonous ones, the ones that could cause death in a baby, and serious illness in an adult. The small, fat-segmented tailed scorpions caused a sting, but were not so dangerous. The big one I saw at our construction site was not dangerous. It just looked that way!

Jamie began to speak. Initially, his word for everything was "Dee Dee." This included cookies and eventually dogs which we saw on our walks. Our first dog, of course, became Dee Dee!

One day, coming in from the backyard with a load of laundry I'd collected from the line, I saw Jamie crawling toward a "panel-ray" heater inset in the wall (the heater was our only means of heating the space). Not able to physically rescue Jamie without falling on him with a basket full of clothes, I screamed "Hot!" I was too late. Jamie's little hand went up to touch the heater and he was burned. I consoled him with baby aspirin and burn medication, but it was a difficult night. The next morning crawling along the floor and looking at the panel-ray heater, not even red and activated, Jamie suddenly said *"hot"* with perfect diction, connecting his burn experience to a word for it, not unlike Helen Keller's moment when she said "Wah~Wah" for water, or when an actor speaks because he *must* out of his experience, environment and emotional trigger. It was an amazing moment, and I've told that story to the over one thousand actors I've since trained.

Jamie was plump and, our pediatrician, Dr. Phillips, prescribed non-fat milk for him. The biggest dairy in town went out on strike! I switched to powdered milk purchased in a box from the grocery store. When the milkmen and their employers finally reached an agreement our milkman asked me what I'd done during the strike. After I told him he rejoined, "O well, the dairy just takes powdered milk and adds vitamins to it when a customer orders non-fat milk anyway." I decided then and there I could make my own milk at eight cents a quart rather than use the services of the dairy at twenty-two cents a quart, saving our family several hundred dollars a year! A cement slab with plumbing lines foundation had been poured at the Jack Rabbit house by the time of Jamie's first birthday March 26, 1954. A snapshot shows him with his hand thrust into the middle of his cupcake, having a delightful time!

Moving to See My Baby Born

Good Samaritan Hospital in Phoenix was not on the cutting edge of "natural" childbirth which I had been a part of at New York Hospital. But, my

OB-GYN arranged for me to have a double room with no other patient there so I could have my new baby with me in the room and my husband could visit whenever he wished! I did not take any classes this time. I decided I would simply use what I'd learned before about nutrition, relaxation, and breathing. This time, God willing, *I would see my baby born.* I was not disappointed! Cheered on by Woody and my doctor, I saw Richard William Mizell born August 15, 1955. *"A baby is God's opinion that the world should go on,"*Carl Sandberg.

I was in ecstasy with a heightened sense of reality, colors, and love! So much so that I was out of bed right after I returned to my room to make certain my plumbing worked (which it did this time)! My "private" hospital room was air conditioned, so I felt like I'd gone to a nice motel for a short vacation! I did not think I could nurse (because I'd had mastitis with Jamie), so Ricky was immediately put on a bottle. He did well on a bottle at over eight pounds.

Bringing baby "Ricky" home and once again encountering Phoenix August heat of 110 degrees with no air conditioning [save evaporative cooling, which did not work well when the humidity was high in monsoon season) was a shock! But, things were going well. Woody worked at his job, then went to work on the house alone while I cared for my toddler son and my new baby. One day I walked out to the backyard to hang diapers in the hot sun and almost fainted! We decided it was mandatory that we splurge on diaper service. For increased income, Woody took a new job as sales representative of a successful graphics design studio and entered the loop of Phoenix's "Old Boys Club."

Work on the house was slow going. The typical top of barn cupola had been removed to create an angled roof with 44 feet of clerestory windows on the south side of the structure. Studs had gone in for the interior walls. The boards I had sanded and stained, many of which went back and forth between 29th Avenue in Phoenix and Jack Rabbit Lane in Scottsdale, went into the hallway facing the clerestory windows. Rolls of black insulation covered the exterior. One night, after Woody's workday at the printing company, Woody and I dug a ditch outside the house to implement the plumbing line from the kitchen and bath to the cess pool!

Days were long and the work was hard, but trips to the Eldeans to swim in their elegant environment on weekends made our weeks go by quickly. We were astonished when getting out of the pool at the Eldeans in the summer at the rapid evaporation which caused one to feel actually cold in 115 degree heat! Using my swimming teaching techniques that I had learned in Maine, I taught Jamie to swim so early he cannot remember learning to swim! Ricky was in the pool floating at six weeks old!

Woody and I still took our one night a week "vacation" away from children, sometimes going to a nearby hilltop overlooking Phoenix for a private picnic. The Eldeans invited us to our first ever experience with the Arizona State Fair held on the state fairgrounds in Phoenix. It was there that we ate Mexican tacos for the first time. Margie and Fred also treated us to our first visit at a Mexican restaurant, Los Olivos in Scottsdale, then Margie taught me how to make my own tacos and enchiladas at home. Thus another packed to the brim with activity year went by. Woody enjoyed his new job working with the top graphics talent in Phoenix. Jamie, blonde, tan and healthy, participated in a vacation church school program. Baby Ricky grew into a beautiful, rosy, beginning to walk toddler with blue eyes and dark hair! A photo shows Ricky (a déjà vu of his big brother Jamie) plunging his hands into his first year cupcake smiling and covering his face with icing!

To save money being spent on the Phoenix 29th Avenue house, we moved into the construction of our Jack Rabbit house. It was barely livable, filled with building materials, tools and paint cans but at least Woody would be spared the daily commute to work on the house after work. Moving day for me was a day of scrubbing the 29th Avenue house room by room from top to bottom while caring for Ricky, now one, and Dee Dee (our dog), plus loading boxes into our Jeep station wagon! Two-and-a-half-year-old Jamie was playing at the house of the Dan Davis family, our good friends who lived in Glendale, miles to the west. The Davis home was a warm and fun environment for him on a hectic day as Dan and Margie had a big rambling house with a large yard and tall trees.

It was August and very hot and humid. The water had been turned off at the 29th Avenue house, so even the evaporative cooler did not work! By four o'clock in the afternoon I was hot and exhausted but managed to squeeze Ricky and Dee Dee into the front seat of the Jeep around boxes, vacuum cleaner, buckets, mops, cleaning supplies, etc.—everything that remained in the old house on the day of the move. Traveling the speed limit toward Glendale, suddenly a large truck was stopped abruptly in the lane of traffic! Dee Dee jumped onto me in the front seat as I attempted to brake, but I hit the rear end of the truck—an accident for which I was at fault according to the law! What followed is a blur but, somehow, I, Ricky and Dee Dee emerged unhurt. Margie Davis came to get us, then Woody came to the Davis house for all of us. I was certain Woody would be furious about the damaged Jeep but, when we got to the Jack Rabbit house he kept saying how grateful he was no one had been hurt! How grateful I was for his loving and understanding attitude! Somehow, we found a used vehicle we could buy to replace the Jeep and soon after that we traded it for two small Fiats, a bug and a station wagon!

Moving to Meet Death

An April 8,1958 newspaper story written by Arizona Republic reporter Julian DeVries tells what happened next:

Anguished Parents Had To Watch Cancer Eat Little Son's Life Away
Did you ever watch a baby die?
Mr.and Mrs. W. G. Mizell, Jackrabbit Lane, Scottsdale, did. The baby was their 18-month old son, Ricky.
They watched, helpless and sick with grief while cancer ate the little boy's life away.
Up to [August) 1956 Ricky was a normal healthy youngster full of energy and high spirits.
[Five) months later he was dead.
Between those two dates, Ricky's parents suffered tortures beyond expression. Hopes were raised only to be dashed to the ground again. Ricky's pain was their pain, his anguish their anguish. And the best that medical science had to offer wasn't enough.
As soon as she noticed Ricky wasn't his usual sprightly self [he cried when he pulled up in his crib from obvious pain in his leg),Mrs. Mizell took him to the doctor. A careful check revealed nothing more than the possibility of a slight virus infection for which an antibiotic was prescribed [this diagnosis resulted after examination and being screened by a fluoroscope which pre-dates today's MRI). But the antibiotic didn't seem to work. A week after the first visit Mrs. Mizell and Ricky were back in the doctor's office. This time [after discovering a spot on Ricky's lung from the fluoroscope) the doctor suggested hospitalization and tests.

Four days of tests and a biopsy on Ricky's neck revealed neuroblastoma cancer present already in four places, the neck,the lung,the hip, and the leg. I can still see the pattern of the floor at St. Joseph's hospital as I eerily looked down following Dr. Phillips shoes into a consultation room following the biopsy.

And then they knew. Ricky had cancer.

Thirty days of daily cobalt followed. This radiation therapy aimed at each of the four places where cancer had taken hold had a devastating effect on Ricky's body, worse than the cancer had previously.

Test after test, treatment–all were to no avail. The cancer gnawed into Ricky's bones, so that he screamed with pain whenever he tried to sit or stand. It crowded into his little chest, making every breath a struggle.

At the end of the thirty days of cobalt, Ricky was x-rayed and we learned the cancer had honeycombed all his bone marrow. That's when we knew (it was before the days of chemotherapy) that Ricky would die. I elected to take him home to nurse him around the clock, giving him drugs and care night and day. Little Jamie was cared for every day by kindly church strangers. These thoughtful church people also brought us evening meals. Work on the house came to a complete standstill but, fortunately, the bank gave us an extension on our construction loan.

It struck him blind.

Christmas was approaching. Ricky's metastes had caused him to go blind. I could no longer quiet him at home. In fact, I was digging feces out of his little anus because he could no longer move his bowels. We put Ricky into St. Joseph's Hospital again. One evening at St. Joe's he appeared to be resting so I elected to go down to the coffee shop for a cup of coffee. As I entered, someone put a quarter into the juke box and "Younger Than Springtime" from the musical *South Pacific* (which I had seen twice on Broadway) filled the room! In my mind I saw Ricky as he had been, "younger than springtime, gayer than laughter," so beautiful and joyous, then I had a vision of his present little-skeleton-from-Dachau appearance, and I was raked with sobs right there in the hospital coffee shop. Ricky stayed in the hospital only four days because they could not do anything for him. When he came back home, Margie Eldean brought over a small record player so when he was awake I could play symphony music which seemed to soothe him. As we sat there, Ricky and I, I felt more and more like I should die with him.

On Christmas Eve, a member of our church who was a registered nurse generously volunteered to come stay with Ricky for a couple of hours so Woody and I could go to the Christmas Eve service. The following day, Christmas day, Dr. George Boss, our minister came out to Scottsdale with a Christmas card. Dr. Boss visited with us for awhile at a picnic table on our "back acre."

When he left we opened the card he had brought to find there an anonymous money gift, enough money, in fact, to pay for a required-by-law casket (even though Ricky's body would be offered for research then cremated). Prior to receiving that gift we did not know how we would pay for a casket because we were totally broke!

That night our baby's screams were worse than ever and Woody gave him an extra dose of his thorazine and codine while I groveled on the floor crying out to God to take Ricky because I could not watch him suffer any longer! Woody and I fell into an exhausted sleep. I awoke realizing I had not been awakened in the night by Ricky's cries, walked to his room, leaned over the crib and kissed him. *He was cold.* Ricky had ***moved*** from his ravaged body.

"We are made of elements forged in the stars and scattered through space. We are recycled stardust with the gift of consciousness," John Noble Wilford, *New York Times*, February 13, 2000.

His parents grew gaunt and hollow-eyed from lack of sleep. Worry and anguish were taking their toll of a once-happy young couple. Death finally brought merciful relief to the grief-worn parents and the pain-wracked little boy. Cancer had won another terrible victory.

When Ricky's disease was first diagnosed, Mrs. Mizell found it hard to believe. She thought babies didn't get cancer. But the physicians, surgeons, radiologists and pathologists who fought so hard in vain to save Ricky's life explained.

Cancer is a wild, uncontrolled growing of the cells which normally would become healthy tissue. The period of greatest and most intense growth of cells takes place in infancy, childhood, and adolescence. Therefore, the doctors told Mrs. Mizell, childhood is the most cancer-prone age of humans. Sometimes, the doctors pointed out, a cancer diagnosed in an adult actually began in childhood. Why such cancers remain quiescent, only to flare up and perhaps kill in later life, no one knows—yet.

But someday in the not too distant future, doctors hope to have the answer to the entire cancer riddle. Important breakthroughs on several scientific fronts have already been made. More will be made.

And then little tykes like Ricky will live, and parents will not be afraid.

I was aware, right up to the last day of his life, that *Ricky never stopped loving*, never stopped *trusting* us! Such a short time Ricky had the gift of life! Yet his joyous life (up to the time of the onset of the cancer) while living and heroic dying changed my life forever! What must *I* do with each moment, each hour and day to justify *being here* when Ricky suffered so much and died so young?

"There is a land of the living and a land of the dead and the bridge is love," Thorton Wilder

Moving to Live Again

I wrote about what happened next in an article published in American Express' *Travel & Leisure* magazine, May, 1979: "The Grandest Canyon: And Fourteen Ways to See It":

When I first saw the Grand Canyon on New Year's[Eve) over two decades ago, there was a mantle of snow on the ground. A deer greeted me at hand's length as I moved toward my room at Bright Angel Lodge Unaware of violating a National Parks regulation, I fed him the remains of a sandwich....

We had asked the mortuary following Ricky's cremation to fly his ashes into the Grand Canyon. After a simple memorial service at Phoenix's First Methodist Church chapel (we requested no flowers but rather gifts to the American Cancer Society), Woody, Jamie and I drove through Arizona's beautiful ponderosa pine and white birches to the Grand Canyon. On New Year's Day we arose before the sunrise where, at a lookout, we saw the sun rise from the South Rim. We watched 225 million to 510 million years of Earth's age gradually come alive in a blaze of ever changing shapes and colors. Then we drove home via Sedona's Oak Creek Canyon, marveling that a four-hour trip takes the traveler topographically from Canada to Sonora, Mexico!

When we got back home we had a huge problem to work through. We had our recent hell of grief to work through emotionally, a twice extended construction loan to pay in less than six months, plus an enormous amount of work to do day and night. We had run out of money to continue to use T.P.Furrow's services, though he completed installation of bathroom and kitchen equipment and, since the ceilings were angled with no space between the roof and the ceiling, the difficult to install wiring. Every day I painted (badly) the overhang and trim in the front and outside of the house. I stained the clapboard brown. When I had completed that I still had to paint every room inside. Every night after work and on weekends Woody intricately cut pieces of wood to conform to the angles in light decks and in walls.

It was a month after Ricky's death that I had the roller coaster nightmare, seeing Ricky looking like he did at the end of his life, shackled high on a rail but as hard as I tried, I could not reach him. I tried again and again to climb the narrow, slippery rail. I was helpless. I awoke screaming.

Finally, after Woody had laid all the tile floors in the Jack Rabbit house, the day came when the FHA inspector came to decide whether we had followed specifications closely enough to qualify for a much needed mortgage so we could pay off our Fred Eldean co-signed construction loan. I sat nervously at the end of the hall praying for a *win* now. Word came in twenty-four hours. We had passed FHA inspection—in spite of the unusual design of our house! However, *Woody's income was not sufficient to qualify us for a mortgage after all our work.* My parents came to our rescue again, agreeing to co-sign our FHA mortgage so we could pay off our construction loan and begin home ownership (they never had to make a payment in twenty-one years).

Moving Toward Melanie

During the first three months of this stressful time Woody was so full of grief he could not make love. I begged him. I had started volunteering at St. Joseph's Hospital in pediatrics as therapy for my grief. Finally, three months after Ricky died, my husband and I made love for the first time and again, I knew immediately I was pregnant! I wanted another baby so much. After seeing many more children die at St. Joseph's my spirits were so low I had to stop my volunteer work. I realize my expected baby probably saved my sanity. I began to concentrate on getting ready to welcome a new little soul due just after New Year's Eve, 1957.

We splurged for Christmas by buying a fifteen foot tree that reached all the way to the clerestory windows of our 44 feet long hallway. It was a loving expectant Christmas. I began to have false labor right after New Year's Eve. I knew caring for a new baby would mean Christmas decorations would still be up in March unless I got everything down and stored as soon as possible, so it became a race between my false labor and de-Christmasing the house! I'd also decided to make and freeze all the dinners Woody and Jamie would need while I was in the hospital. Finally, when all the un-decorating, cooking and freezing was done, after four days of false labor, I went to the doctor who gave me medication to start labor. Woody, Jamie and I celebrated this development by eating a gallon of ice cream! By evening I was at Good Samaritan Hospital waiting in the hallway because all the labor rooms were full. Shortly after midnight I joyously saw my baby girl born! As I was wheeled out of the delivery room, Woody asked what sex the child was and I answered "Melanie!"

Melanie Anne Mizell was born January 5, 1957. Having had two boy babies had not prepared me for Melanie's entirely different feminine essence! First, she was petite (six pounds rather than eight). I elected to attempt nursing again and this time it went well. Whereas my sturdy boys had spent an hour a day exercising their lungs on their tummies (fed, dry, clean and well Jamie did that daily just as Woody arrived at our Jackson Heights apartment after work, much to Woody's dismay! Ricky did that post our move to Arizona where, fortunately, I could escape to the backyard!) Melanie never did that. She just looked around at the world if she was awake! It was wonderful! She was a constant source of joy!

In fact, just as I'd brought Melanie home, Jamie was recovering from a case of chicken pox, a worrisome thing. Frightened, I called Dr. Phillips. Dr. Phillips said "Keep her fed, clean and dry!" Melanie got one pox and proceeded to sleep through what is usually a dreadful childhood disease! It's interesting short hand communication developed between a pediatrician like Dr. Phillips and me, a mother who has been through the hell of nursing a dying baby. We needed to say very little to one another and could manage most things without a doctor's visit. Melanie, cuddled and nursed, truly saved my life and made me want to live again!

Woody was doing well at his job representing a graphics design studio interfacing with the major banks, corporations and builders of Phoenix. He made a friend of the head of a major advertising agency and his Miss America wife. He spent time with the advertising director of the Arizona bank and began to go to social functions with an attorney, who was part of the law firm that did the legal work on the freeway I-17 and argued the Miranda law in the Supreme Court (the attorney, Neal Roberts, would figure greatly in my future story). We were invited to join a club, the Racquet Club, which is now John Gardiner's Tennis Ranch (first members got in a very low membership and monthly rate). I could now take the children *swimming* daily during the hot months of the summer while Woody was at work!

Moving Little Pieces of Ricky Into the Life Force

"...how to remain strong, no matter what shocks come at the periphery and tend to crack the hub of the wheel..."(*Gift From The Sea* by Anne Marrow Lindberg).

I still grieved for Ricky. Wondering whether I could honor his life in some way, I decided to write a letter to the American Cancer Society, offering my services as a volunteer. When ACS learned I'd been an actress I was invited to be a speaker. Soon I was being flown all over Arizona to speak about Ricky's heroic last months. Then ACS asked me to write a script that would be used in a film called *Four Stories*, the introduction to each story to be narrated by Ralph Edwards, host of television's *This Is Your Life*. After the script was completed it was filmed at our house and I performed its voice-over narration post shoot. I was asked to be the ACS's chairman for Scottsdale's door-to-door campaign. I supervised hundreds of volunteers who visited homes to give print matter about cancer's seven danger signals plus ask for donations. To learn what my volunteers would face I went door to door myself. I also organized a fund-raising event at the Racquet Club, inviting fine artists to donate their paintings for auction.

It was in the course of that activity that I met Don Barclay, specialist in clown portraiture and fine arts, caricature creator of all the famous people that adorn Scottsdale's Pink Pony Restaurant & Bar, Disney artist (Don created the burglars in the animated feature film *100 and One Dalmations*), and actor (he played the Bombadeer in *Mary Poppins*). Don drove a Rolls Royce but lived on Cattle Track in Scottsdale in a shack of "wall to wall dust," where a fine artist friend had painted a nude with a breast pointing down to his pillow on the wall. The land the shack occupied was owned by wealthy Walker McCune, whose mansion, with indoor ice skating rink, swimming pool, untold bedrooms and baths, adorned the west side of Camelback mountain! In future years Don's shack would become a fun destination to Melanie when she rode our horse Apache to visit him, which was then on to the desert which is now McCormick Ranch. Our entire family would attend Don's 75th birthday party, when helicopters would fly in dignitaries who partied outside his shack among hundreds of guests.

I was also asked to speak to a small group of socialites who were holding a ball to benefit the American Cancer Society at the home of Kax Herberger (she would later endow the Herberger Theatre in downtown Phoenix and the Herberger School of Fine Arts at Arizona State University). Maggie Savoy, famed *Arizona Republic* features writer, wrote a story about my talk, using a photograph of me holding a picture of Ricky in a full page cover spread. The women of Kax Herberger's "committee" raised more money for ACS in one night than had ever been raised in the history of ACS! Meanwhile, my volunteer activities for ACS continued for ten years, including ultimately the tracking of 200 seniors for six years, becoming part of a nationwide study of a million people to determine the effects of smoking. The study resulted in the Surgeon General's report on cigarettes as a leading cause of cancer and death in America.

Moving Into Local News and a Baby Boy

It was in the midst of all this ACS activity that the April 1958 story about Ricky (page 38-40) was published. And by the following April, an *Arizona Republic* front page Sun Living Section had published a picture story about the W.G.Mizell *self*-built designer home on Jack Rabbit Lane in Scottsdale! Photographs were of Woody, Jamie, Melanie, and me, pregnant again, and 7331 East Jack Rabbit Lane's, with its exterior unusual angled roof line and overhang, its interior 44-foot hall with clerestory windows, its angled glass facing the McDowell's four peaks, its bedrooms and kitchen, plus an Isamu Noguchi designed metal fireplace purchased from the Museum of Modern Art (Noguchi, born in Los Angeles, a Guggenheim Fellow, and student of both

Gutzon Borglum and Constantin Brancusi in Paris, had a large nine-part sculpture of pink marble in the Metropolitan Museum of Art).

The Scottsdale Progress (now the *Tribune* newspapers) followed suit with a Jack Rabbit house and family success story in the fall of 1959. Baby Gary Woodfin Mizell (later changed by Gary to Gary *Michael* Mizell—he didn't like the name Woodfin either), was born July 28, 1959. I had a baby boy again! By the time Gary was born, Good Samaritan Hospital had built a new "rooming in" wing for mothers who desired "natural" childbirth. Again I saw my new baby born and was euphoric about life! My room was lovely, freshly painted and furnished, with a small glassed-in room built into one wall for baby Gary. I had hardly returned home before Julia Kiene sent a hand-knitted Christmas stocking bearing Gary's name and the date of his birth in the stitches (which is displayed on his fireplace hearth to this day!). Melanie, two little widgets of blonde hair at the sides of her face, is pictured in our butterfly "sling" chair with baby Gary across her lap!

Moving to Win Over a Terminal Disease

Gary was six months old when Melanie's third birthday party was held January 5, 1960. Thinking it would entertain her little friends, I wore a white beard as the "Old Year" and put a "New Year" large red satin ribbon on Gary clad only in a diaper.

The following day, however, I realized Gary was very ill. In fact he was unconscious and *comatose*. I rushed him in the car to Dr. Phillip's office. We were immediately shown into an examining room. When Dr. Phillips examined Gary he elected to give him a spinal tap (a procedure usually done in surgery) to save time for the lab's diagnosis. This was a very courageous thing for Dr. Phillips. There is no margin for error at the point of a huge needle in a baby so young with a back so small. We waited for the lab report. It took only an hour because the lab was across the street. When it came back, I was again devastated—Gary had viral spinal meningitis!

Dr. Phillips would have to lie to get him into pediatrics at St. Joseph's hospital (the best hospital for children at the time), as by law only the county hospital could accept spinal meningitis patients (spinal meningitis is usually bacterial). Dr. Phillips signed Gary into St. Joe's stating he had to.be admitted for "tests." As it turned out the lab was never able to identify which virus Gary had! That meant *every four hours Gary had to be injected with four different kinds of antibiotics*! His little buttocks looked like a pin cushion at the end of two weeks but, the virus infection had been halted.

I was allowed to take Gary home with the warning to watch his fontanel (the soft tissue on a baby's head prior to bone formation) for any swelling because it would mean the fluid surrounding the brain could not circulate properly due to the formation of scar tissue in his healing process. Baby Gary had not been home forty-eight hours before I noticed the pouching out of his fontanel. My entire family was in bed with virus infections so I, having prayed all night and having received spiritual literature from a friend of mine who was a Christian Scientist, took Gary back to St. Joseph's Hospital emergency room. This time the hospital knew what Gary's illness was so a room had to be sterilized—floor, ceiling, walls, and furniture before he could be admitted. I stood with him for eight hours in the emergency room, focusing, as I'd been urged to do by my Christian Science friend, on God as Life in each of my baby's cells, a Force willing him to be perfect and healthy!

A great neurosurgeon, Dr. Hall Pittman, came to see Gary after he was finally admitted. Dr. Pittman decided Gary should have the fluid drained from his fontanel regularly to determine if he could heal that way. Gary was in a room with angels painted on the walls (the same décor I saw during Ricky's travail) for three months while this was tried. Some days I watched from a distance seeing Gary tied spread eagle to a crib with tubes coming out of him from many directions, unable to even touch and comfort him! Finally, it was decided Gary would undergo surgery by Dr. Pittman. Gary was taken off all fluids for twenty-four hours and given a prescribed shot to "dry up" his tissues. Unfortunately the nurse who gave the shot did not mark the chart, so it was given twice! By the time Dr. Pittman arrived to do the surgery Gary was screaming for hydration and his surgeon rightly refused to perform such a dangerous procedure under such conditions. Surgery could not be re-scheduled for four agonizing days (not just for Gary but also for Woody and me) and the hospital's error could not immediately be corrected regarding Gary until a new order to give him fluids was issued, which,unfortunately, took many hours because Dr. Phillips, in other emergencies, could not be reached.

Days later, the six hour surgery took place. Dr. Pittman removed a horseshoe of Gary's skull and laid it aside so he could operate on the membrane surrounding the brain. When the time came to replace the skull it was too big, a good sign, as that meant the fluid had been reduced. Gary's skull had to be whittled a bit to fit. Back on the floor, Gary had had so many caretakers, had gone through so many procedures on so many floors, that he stopped eating! Even though excess fluid was still present between his brain and its membrane, our doctors decided I must take Gary home to coax him into eating again. He had been at St. Joseph's three months!

A photo showing Gary with a huge bandage on his head surrounded by his family commemorates his return to Jack Rabbit Lane. Eerily for 48 hours he would not cry! If I had not known I had a baby in the house I never would have experienced him at all! *Gary had given up* believing his call for help would be answered! I kept going to him every three hours, giving him food, care and TLC. A miracle ensued! Not only did he begin crying for help normally, but in two weeks when we went back to St. Joseph's hospital emergency to have his huge head bandage removed he was pronounced cured! No more excess fluid was present!

Dr. Phillips prescribed a very high protein diet—jello water instead of milk, meat, egg yolks, yoghurt, cottage cheese, and vitamins five times a day before any fruits and vegetables were given. Amazingly, Gary, after having been tied down for three months, his spinal cord and membrane surrounding the brain damaged, having had countless treatments and eventually head surgery, in only three months actually rolled over, crawled, sat up, pulled up, stood and walked by his first birthday! Friends called Gary a "Miracle Baby" and indeed he was!

This time my prayers were answered! This time there was victory! My baby boy would live and grow to be an incredible man!

Moving to Make a Difference

Woody, having established his own graphics design studio called Design Associates, leased a just built office space in Phoenix, the interior of which had white tile floor and angled displays revealing his work done for Motorola, Honeywell, the Arizona Bank and most of the major agencies. He employed contract labor layout artists, illustrators, and photographers and had among his suppliers top printers and typographers (pre-computer word processing). Jamie had started pre-school at Paradise Valley Pre-School on Lincoln Drive in Scottsdale. With Margie Eldean's urging, we employed a live-in Native American teen as a babysitter, then later placed Melanie in an excellent pre-school, Little Scholar Day School, in a large house located in the Madison School District (one of the best districts in metro Phoenix). There at age four she learned phoenics and would skip kindergarten at Kiva School as a result. This child care allowed me to work for Woody part time as public relations-receptionist, payables, receivables, government reports-bookkeeper, interfacing with a CPA. We hosted parties at Jack Rabbit, made serigraphs and silk screen Christmas cards with Woody's attorney friend and his wife, and were invited among the "in"young married group of Phoenix to many events and parties. Woody was named judge of Phoenix's Rodeo Parade so we had grand stand seats for the parade year after year, allowing my "men," big and little, to dress as cowboys! By the time Jamie had entered kindergarten I was known in the community so, in addition to teaching church school, I was invited to be president of the teacher–parents group at the just built Kiva School.

Arizona was behind the times in education. Betina Rubicam (Broadway actress and wife of the founder of famed New York City-based international Young and Rubicam Advertising Agency) lived close by on Jack Rabbit Road east of Scottsdale road. She despaired when her child could not read, even after completing the third grade! One day she invited me, as president of Kiva's teacher–parent group, to her grand home where she told me she wanted to begin a campaign to re-introduce phonics into the public schools. Would I persuade, first, the teachers to teach both Scotts-Foresman [the look-see method of teaching reading) and *phoenics* in the same amount of teaching time, then second, the parents to privately buy additional text books. I had already experienced personally attempting to teach Jamie to read using phoenics. He could read words he'd learned in Scotts Foresman but would not even try to read new words!

Mrs. Rubicam's and my joint efforts were successful! When Kiva Elementary students were tested at the end of the year their scores were excellent in motivating first the Scottsdale School District, then the state of Arizona, to re-adopt phoenics as the way to teach reading. My volunteer work at the school also contributed to Kiva experimenting with "modern math." By the time a demonstration by five students for an audience of two hundred parents and teachers was held, my daughter Melanie, at just six years old because she'd skipped kindergarden, was one of those children chosen for the demonstration (a precursor to computers and abstract reasoning). That educational experiment also led to adoption throughout the district and the state!

Moving with Our Plants and Animals

Land around our FHA-mortgaged Jack Rabbit house was raw dirt initially! Again Margie Eldean came to our rescue! She gave Woody cuttings of numerous desert trees and cacti, including blue palo verde trees just a foot tall. They grew quickly, becoming towering trees ablaze with yellow-gold in the spring! One of the cactus cuttings she gave us, the Night Blooming Cireus, looked like a small snake when we first received it. It's a fascinating plant! It blooms once a year overnight, producing a gorgeous blossom, a cross between a white lily and a white orchid, that wilts as soon as the sun strikes it in the morning! Additionally, it has a heavenly aroma. Woody planted our little Night Blooming Cireus under our front yard blue palo verde tree. Year by year more cireus-snakes grew until finally the plant had a circumfrance of at least twelve feet! Still,there was just one bloom every year! One year, during monsoon season, huge rains came down from Camelback Mountain. So much rain, in fact, that houses along the canal were flooded. We had to sandbag our house to keep it from flooding, while Jamie, Melanie and Gary rode inner tubes down Jack Rabbit Lane! After the rains stopped, one night before sundown, buds appeared on the Night Blooming Cireus, not just one or two, but at least a hundred! We watched until the moon came out and suddenly our Night Blooming Cireus opened to an entire garden of at least a hundred glorious blossoms! We called neighbors and friends to come marvel and take pictures!

During another monsoon season, the wind and rain blew a tall palo verde on the east side of our property down! Woody could not bear to part with such a magnificent tree (and a tree surgeon told us it would cost well over $100 to cut the tree into sections and haul it away), so he experimented with covering the huge roots with soil. In answer to Woody's rescue, one of the *branches* became a new trunk! Along the ground the original tree trunk became a fantasy land of designer bells, including one from famed artist/architect Arcosanti. The new "branch"trunk eventually supported Jamie and Gary's tree house!

Jamie began collecting toads almost from the start of our residence on Jack Rabbit. At least a dozen of them would line up outside the angled glass facing Four Peaks at night under the outside flood light. If Jamie(as little boys will do)picked one of them up, it would immediately pee—so he picked them up often just to dismay us!

While we were still living in construction, Woody's and my bathroom shower floor had no cement floor, only a board placed over the drain. One night Woody and I woke because we heard invasion sounds coming from our shower! Inspection revealed a gofer had burrowed right up to the board and was attempting to come in! The next day, Woody somehow found time to pour the cement floor in the shower! Another morning we awoke to huge tapping of the clerestory windows, windows that ranged 44 feet across the angled roof to the south. We went into the hallway to witness a road runner attempting to peck its way inside through the windows! The road runner obviously did not realize he could not go through glass so he kept tapping away at each pane!

As Jamie grew more adventuresome in relation to the land around us, he and his friend Cable would go down to the canal (east of us on Jack Rabbit Lane) when it was drained and hunt for crayfish! He would then bring them home and put them in a galvanized tub as pets! The one wild thing I did not want as a pet on the premises was a baby rattle snake! Yet, one day a small but still lethal rattle snake got into the house! Of course, everyone was gone. As fast as I could I phoned everyone I knew but no one was available to come help me! I finally got James' butterfly net, threw it over the little rattler (which struck and struck through the net) then, gradually pushed it forty feet until I had pushed it out the front door! It must have crawled away because I never saw it again.

We eventually had thirty-six "pets" at Jack Rabbit (not including the wild denizens—toads, lizards, gofers, quail families and others outdoors) ranging in size from our horse Apache to a litter of tiny white mice, two goldfish and a turtle! We also had innumerable cats because the neighbor's female was unsprayed and kept laying her litters on our roof! Woody would take all the kittens back to the neighbor time and again only to have them all returned by the mother cat within twenty-four hours! It then became a race to get them off the roof before they became wild. Many trips were made to the Humane Society with dozens of baby kittens we could not possibly keep. Once Woody made the trip to the Humane Society because a little white rat pet of Jamie's had gone into convulsions. The vet insisted on test after test to be assured the creature did not carry a virus that would affect the children and the bill was $50!

After we remodeled Jack Rabbit with mediterranean white inlaid bricks for the floor, Jamie one day dumped his pet white mice out of a bowl and they scattered the entire expanse of the 44 by 30 feet central space of the house! They were indistinguishable from the floor! Can you imagine how we scattered looking for Jamie's "pets"? Eventually, Gary acquired a new and beloved white dog from the Humane Society, a purebread British pointer (though we were not allowed the papers) that he called Dutchess.

Off our land, just across Jack Rabbit Lane, there was a twenty-acre thoroughbred horse ranch. As a result, our children saw many mares foal. When the owner of the ranch died, the property, part of a large estate, had to be sold. The new owner put in twenty llamas (where the thoroughbred horses had been), ranging in color from burnt umber to pure white, so for many years we could watch their liquid, stately movement as we looked north! It was through these llamas that Gary's dog Dutchess eventually ran, leapt actually, like a gazelle, until she saw a flock of birds when suddenly she would freeze in a perfect point! It was graceful and magic to watch. One day I drove into our driveway and was stopped by a huge peacock with a deep blue, turquoise, green and white fan, that completely filled the breadth of the driveway! The Phoenix zoo would not come get the peacock. I learned later it did not belong to them. A private "zookeeper" from across Scottsdale Road on Jack Rabbit actually owned the peacock and I guess it found its way home!

Moving into Politics

If growth starts when there's discontent, restlessness, doubt, despair, and longing we were in for a period of painful growth. I was at Design Associates (Woody's design studio) on November 22, 1963, when President Kennedy was assassinated. I was stunned and in grief like the rest of the nation, then caught up in the funeral pageantry created by Jackie Kennedy. Though not a Democrat at the time, I watched the drama unfold on television day after day. Vice President Lyndon Johnson was not a John Kennedy! Arizona's Republican Senator Barry Goldwater was rumored to be the person who could challenge him. An "organizing committee" for Goldwater for President included the advertising director of the Arizona Bank (Woody's friend and colleague). One day, while doing my part-time daily stint at Design Associates, I was informed Goldwater for President's "organizing committee" wanted to meet in our design studio to start the ball rolling! The space of Design Associates, newly built and decorated, had (as already reported) a white tile floor which, on a regular schedule, was cleaned and waxed with a rented machine. I did not like or trust Lyndon Johnson. Because the Goldwater for President meeting was a hurry-up event just twenty-four hours hence, I ended up spending the good share of a night scrubbing and waxing Design Associates' white tile floor on my hands and knees! My pro bono effort helped launch"Goldwater For President"! Goldwater was soundly defeated by Johnson in '64. He, however, continued as a distinguished United States Senator from Arizona for many, many years until his retirement.

Woody's Arizona Bank advertising director friend was a good "birddog"for Woody and usually we were very grateful for his referrals! However, as a result of his colleague's referral, Woody gained one extremely "bad apple"client, a man who was "planning a factory in Phoenix." The client required "the whole nine yards," a complete promotion and sales start-up campaign! The Arizona Bank had loaned the gentleman $50,000, so Woody thought it safe to put our staff artists on the job. He also sub-contracted with layout artists, illustrators, photographers, typographers, and printers on behalf of the client. Having completed a logo design with letterhead, cards, invoices, sales brochure, print ads etc., Design Associates' receivable for that one client reached $10,000. Then we heard! Woody's Arizona Bank friend called to say the client was "kite-ing" checks (writing bad checks state to state). It wasn't long after that we learned the man had fled the state. This meant we would not be able to collect the $10,000 due for services but, we, having already paid salaries to our employees, still would have to pay contract labor and suppliers hired to do that client's job. *That one client closed down Woody's studio in Phoenix.*

We had to move Design Associates to a room on Jack Rabbit then, to satisfy creditors, I spent three years negotiating payments, working hard to create minimum thirty-day collectibles, while Woody, now out of the central Phoenix loop, had to double and triple his effort to sell Design Associates services. We had no money to buy a vacuum, so I spent many more hours on my knees doing the same thing I did for the Goldwater For President in Jack Rabbit's 44 feet entryway!

Four-year-old Gary, who had gone to the excellent Little Scholar Day school while I worked in Phoenix at Woody's studio, came home too. On Jack Rabbit, therefore, we ran a business and held forth with child care; provided space for my soon-to-be-established coaching of actors, rehearsals of shows, building of mobile set pieces; hosted youth group church meetings (to one such meeting in the early '70s, at the time of the first Fiesta Bowl, Woody invited the entire Florida State football team for cocoa and cookies and they *came*!); committee meetings; parties (including an annual Christmas brunch for one hundred neighbors, clients and business associates); and had road runners, quail families, lizards, an occasional peacock in the driveway, a horse, dog, cats, and twenty llamas outside!

It had become time to ***move*** my life again, back to who I am.

Part Three

Morning

1963-1975 – Assassinations, Vietnam War, Back to My Roots

Moving Back to Who I Am

"The future belongs to those who believe in the beauty of their dreams." Eleanor Roosevelt

Though hampered in a desert environment, as far as work for actors is concerned, it became very clear to me the whole family must attempt to create income! Serigraphs and silk-screened Christmas cards added to Woody's graphics design income at his studio on Jack Rabbit were not enough. We had too great a debt load and too many financial responsibilities!

Soon Woody would opt for a salaried job as art director of Blood Services (one of the largest multi-state providers of blood products based in Arizona) for which he designed a sleek but simple image campaign! In 2004, Woody's logo image is still being applied to all Blood Services vehicles, signage, packaging, print, collatoral and promotion materials!

Elementary school age Jamie took on a paper route and on rainy mornings I was up by 5a.m. to drive him around on his many miles route. I, became a "hyphenate"(multi-tasked regarding my chosen theatre-film-literary work) by first writing a whimsical children's story, *Cowboy Doots, Little Squaw and Pokey*, which I sent back to New York City pitching Stewart Beach, Editor of *This Week* magazine. The below exerpt is from his letter:

"I was awfully interested to read your story Cowboy Doots, Little Squaw & Pokey. *But, the children's stories we have been running occasionally are all condensed versions of new children's books, using the illustrations prepared for the book...Nevertheless, I read your story through and enjoyed it thoroughly...A book publisher might be interested in it. The story has a sense of the wonder of a new world to a child...."*

The story never was published but Mr. Beach's letter motivated me to attempt to write for publication and income. *I ultimately did after I returned to finish my undergraduate degree.* I took courses in magazine writing and play writing at Arizona State University. One of the prerequisites of the magazine writing course was that I must *publish* to pass! I have since been published in thirteen magazines over three hundred times, plus written plays, screenplays and a book for the head of the Los Angeles Dodgers!

I also started directing, coaching and teaching actors. I was hired to direct a children's theater show at Phoenix Little Theatre (directing there Sarah Rice, who would later star on Broadway in *Sweeney Todd* with Angela Lansbury). In addition, I began enlisting acting students at Jack Rabbit, students that would include over a period of six years Dianne Kay, who became a principal in the *Eight Is Enough* series.

I became a producer too. Young Players was the name of my privately owned company. In short tours of children's classics, i.e. *Tom Sawyer* and *Hans Brinker*, Young Players gained audiences in many metro Phoenix schools. Woody utilized his creative design and building skills again to create back-of-a-station-wagon put together set-pieces that could create a show in any space and could be struck in less than an hour.

A superb choreographer, Judy Chruma, who each year for eighteen years organized auditions and rehearsed all the local dancers for Ballet West's "Nutcracker" at Frank Lloyd Wright's Arizona State University Grady Gammage Auditorium, worked with me as contract labor, doing amazing things with the bodies of untrained-as-dancers youthful actors. As a byproduct of my work with Judy, soon my young daughter Melanie was taking ballet at the Phoenix School of Ballet owned by Kelly Brown (a former American Ballet Theatre soloist). Judy Chruma, along with other colleagues of Kelly, taught his classes prior to his untimely death.

"Sadly, Kelly Brown... [who worked in Hollywood in *Seven Brides for Seven Brothers* in 1954, *Daddy Long Legs* in 1955, and *The Girl Most Likely* in 1957) *died just about two weeks before his son Ethan Brown joined American Ballet Theatre in 1981...*[His wife) *Isabel says that the film* The Turning Point[1977), *the story of a dancer who gives up her career to raise a family...one of whose children rises to ballet stardom is closely based on the Browns."* Doris Perlman,Dance Magazine, June 1999

The Turning Point starred Shirley McClaine (as the fictional Kelly Brown's wife), Anne Bancroft (as the ballerina Nora Kaye character), Leslie Brown (as the young ballet dancer) who is, in real life, Kelly Brown's daughter, having trained at his studio, and Mikhail Baryshnikov (Russian soloist with

Kirov Ballet, American Ballet Theatre [ABT], New York City Ballet, considered to be the leading male dancer of the early '80s). When the Shirley McClaine's character becomes pregnant (based on Isabel),she leaves the ballet to follow her husband to help found a dance studio in Phoenix, Arizona(following the advice of her rival). The film couple's daughter (Leslie Brown) aspires to be a ballet dancer and is accepted for ABT's summer season in New York City by now a ballerina (Anne Bancroft). The daughter falls in love with ABT lead dancer (Mikhail Baryshnikov). Mentored by the ballerina, the daughter appears to be a rising young star. Jealous of her former rival's interference, the mother erupts with long pent up hostility based on her forsaken career! *"Leslie Brown claims it's not really their family at all but that screenwriter and playwright Arthur Laurents used their input for the script because they were a useful source of information"* (Dance Magazine, June 1977*).*

James Edmondson (today a leading actor and director of the Oregon Shakespeare Festival) was already doing brilliant work in Phoenix, and later would become my instructor at Arizona State University. Jim directed Lorca's *Wool, Red Wool* at Phoenix's Little Theatre. Kelly Brown and I sat with each other to watch the exquisitely moving Judy Chruma as the featured dancer in the show! The production brilliantly utilized only a fifty foot by five foot swathe of red wool as a set! What a curious coming together of energies was that moment watching James Edmondson's *Wool, Red Wool,* in which Judy Chruma danced, while sitting with Kelly Brown!

My children were bona fide talents, too as child actors. Melanie and Gary, competing with a hundred other children, won an audition for a Kool-Aid commercial which was to be shot during Christmas week. Unfortunately, it rained all week and the commercial shoot moved to Florida. The residuals would have paid for Gary and Melanie's college expenses! Melanie was cast in a melodrama for the Scottsdale Players and all three of my children did several Young Players shows. Today, Gary (who is vice president of Key/ Select Sales and Service Aetna/USHealthcare Arizona, Utah, Nevada) says "Acting taught me discipline and concentration!"

Phoenix (incorporated in 1881)was *less than a hundred years old* when we first arrived in 1953!

But Phoenix was **moving.** It would become the sixth largest city in the United States by 2003! *"Be the change you wish to see in the world."* Ghandi Why else would *I* have left New York?

The rapid development of Phoenix and Arizona post–WWII is due to the miraculous bringing of water to the desert via an elaborate series of reservoirs and canals! Part of the canal system comes from the east of Phoenix Verde River, on which our family rode inner tubes for fun one day! The phoenix bird symbol is momentous—a symbol of resurrection, the phoenix bird, when it reached 500 years of age, burned on a pyre, from which a new phoenix bird arose). Phoenix was begun by an entrepreneurial one-arm Civil War veteran, who utilized irrigation ditches constructed by prehistoric Hohokam Native Americans to raise hay, that he could sell at a profit to the nearby Fort McDowell's military as feed for their horses.

One of the reservoir lakes that feeds Phoenix irrigation system canals is Saguaro Lake, east of Phoenix. Melanie, Gary and I were hired to do Salt River Project(SRP)'s *Working Water, Playing Water* television commercial, billboard and print ad campaign. The SRP shoot was done in the winter at Saguaro Lake. Saguaro's water was icy cold the day we worked in swim suits, yet we had to play in it *as if* it was a frying-an-egg-on-the-pavement day!

Moving to Direct a Superstar Before He Became Famous!

I became the director of an Ernie Pyle (famed WWII reporter) short play *Weep Twice* at the Scottsdale Players then created the opportunity to videotape the work for local CH5 television (using the three camera techniques of *Studio One* in New York City). Needing a young leading man I found Nick Nolte(then starring as a prince in a Phoenix Little Theatre show!) Thus I became the *first person ever to direct Nick Nolte for the camera*! Nick would experience the emotional triggers of facing death for the taping. I used close-up shots on his charismatic and handsome face. It would be a short William Inge play, *The Last Pad*, first produced in Phoenix then in a 99-seat Los Angeles Equity waiver theater that would launch Nick into the "Big show." Because Inge committed suicide the day Nick's play opened, it received front page press in major newspapers. Everyone in Hollywood came to see the show out of deference to Inge (*Picnic, Bus Stop*,etc.). Nick was *ready* to be "discovered"! He had been perfecting his craft in Arizona and California for almost ten years. He went from his starring role in Equity Waiver's *The Last Pad* to star in *Rich Man, Poor Man* and soon became a household name!

Moving to Gain Inspiration from a Theater Innovator

Joseph Papp, theatrical innovator, founder of the New York Shakespeare Festival (NYSF), at first produced free-to-the-public professional actors in Shakespeare classics on the back of a truck in Central Park. Papp, meanwhile, continued to earn a salary doing production at CBS. NYSF, a tax–exempt organization, then gained for a dollar a year an old structure from the city of New York, the Public Theatre, which was renovated into several theaters, rehearsal and administrative office spaces. Prior to 9-11, Meryl Streep starred in Anton Chekhov's *The Seagull* produced by NYSF. The production's million dollar cost was assured up front even as it *played to millions free of charge* in Central Park! How was this possible? Joe Papp had by that time produced the first Public Theatre production of *A Chorus Line*.After the show's short smash hit run at NYSF, Papp cut a contract with the show's choreographer so the show could go to commercial-Broadway. With that contract, NYSF would gain residual *earnings from every future production of "A Chorus Line"!* Therefore, the tax–exempt New York Shakespeare Festival has benefited upwards of $100 million by 2003! *"Life in the twentieth century is like a parachute jump; you have to get it right the first time,"* Margaret Mead.

Papp's outrageous, innovative production of *Hair* played the Phoenix Orpheum in 1967. Pickets formed outside the theater protesting *Hair's* sensational nudity. (The clothed scenes were actually more pornographic than the unclothed ones!) I walked right through the pickets to see an artistic, lit-like-a-painting nude scene in the precedent breaking show and was fascinated with Papp's staging, which began in the audience.

Moving Through Possibility of Death

After seeing Papp's *Hair*, I took the opportunity to go to New York to revive my professional contacts. My dad paid the hotel tab so I could stay at the Canadian Club in the Waldorf Astoria and my brother Tom (by that time VP of Thomas Cook in London and New York City) treated me to a ticket to see Papp's hit *Two Gentlemen From Verona*. The Papp *Verona* production starred Raul Julia and Janelle Allen. It moved back and forth between frenetic rock dance, comic '60s street-smarts and classical Shakespearian speeches! It was joyous, colorful and delicious!

I left Papp's *Two Gentlemen From Verona* at a theater just off Broadway, walking into hundreds of theater goers emerging from other Broadway theatres. Thinking I'd do better hailing a cab if I started walking toward Broadway itself, I arrived at a corner about two blocks from the theater. *Suddenly I saw three mounted policemen with guns drawn, moving directly toward the sidewalk I was about to walk on*! It took only a split second but I made the decision to keep walking! *I walked right through an ambush* as the horses moved toward the the building to my right! I didn't run, I just kept walking. It wasn't 'til I was safe in a cab riding to the Waldorf Astoria that the death threat I'd just passed through hit me! I got really scared, yet, as before in Harlem when I took the wrong subway in the middle of the night, I felt I must have an angel bubble protecting me.

Moving Again to Work with Great Artists

In Phoenix, word about my directing made the grapevine. The Orme School, located about seventy-five miles north of Phoenix, is a private preparatory school. It attracts the rich and the famous, i.e. James Stewart's children, Ronald Reagan's(Patti Davis and Ron Reagan seen in June, 2004, at the Reagan funeral in Washington, D.C.), Mary Tyler Moore's, plus John Paul Getty's niece, William F. Buckley's nephew,etc. Students at Orme, in addition to superb academic standards (Charles Orme,Jr., Orme Headmaster when I worked there, is a graduate of Stanford and sat on the USA College Entrance examination board for many years), have ranch chores to do, cattle round ups to participate in, caravan trips to take through the southwest and Mexico. Sometimes they go on Native American artifacts digs.

I was hired to cast, story board and direct one hundred and twenty Orme student-amateur actors for an industrial/fundraising film, *Orme School Revisited*, which was to be narrated by famed actor James Stewart! The film won Columbus Film Festival's second place among a field of four hundred, including Hallmark and Ford! Then it went on to build buildings and recruit students for Orme for many years to come as Orme's Buck Hart took it around the United States and the world!

Following my work on *Orme School Revisited*, I was invited to be the theater workshop director of Orme's innovative, experimental, *first* Fine Arts Festival (which has become a highlight in the Orme students' curriculum). Students were taken out of academic classes for a week and given the opportunity to participate in workshops of their own choosing. As theater workshop director, I enjoyed *ten one-week-jobs over a decade at Orme*, in the company of artists like John Waddell (sculptor of the ballet statues at Phoenix's Herberger Theatre, leader of the Sculpture Workshop), Francoise Gillott, leader of the Painting Workshop (fine artist wife of Jonas Salk, who at one time was mistress of Picasso, a story told in a 2003 television feature *Surviving Picasso*, which starred Anthony Hopkins), Jeb Rosebrook, Writing Workshop leader(screenplay writer *Junior Bonner, Miracle On 34th Street*, episodes of *The Waltons*, for which he won an Emmy nomination), and Francis Smith Cohen, Dance Workshop leader(artistic director of Dance Theatre West that plays the Herberger Theatre in Phoenix).

Moving to "Find Joy as it Flies"

I drove my children to my parents' home in Rancho Santa Fe, north of San Diego, for the chance to go to the beach and deep sea fishing. Increasingly, however, balancing our survival-stressed lives pushed both Woody and me into"Zerriscenheit." Zerriscenheit is a German word meaning torn-to-pieces-hood.

"For it is not merely the trivial that clutters our lives, but the important as well."(Anne Marrow Lindberg, *Gift From the Sea*)

It was in camping that Woody and I began to "*...start at the center of ourselves* (to)*discover something worthwhile extending toward the periphery... some of the joy in the now, some of the peace in the here, some of the love in me and thee which go to make up the Kingdom of heaven on earth*"(Anne Marrow Lindberg, *Gift*)

Leaves color us
Scarlet
Chocolate

Gold.
Air prickles us
Robin's egg blue.
Now, here *in this moment*
I'll be *real*-me!
You be *true*-you!

Woody's WWII experience tramping hundreds of miles across France and Germany helped our family embark on innumerable camping trips throughout Arizona, the southwest, and eventually across America to the East Coast, then across America to the South. We began camping by taking Melanie, when she was only six weeks old, on a camping trip to beautiful Oak Creek Canyon in Sedona. Woody borrowed a tent and though it was a typical frying-an-egg-on-the-sidewalk weather in Phoenix, it was freezing at night in Sedona! We did not have sleeping bags and ended up covering ourselves with newspaper, we were so cold under blankets. Melanie, meanwhile, in a white-with-white-fur "trundle bundle," looking like a little white and pink angel, was snug in a little wooden cradle Woody had built. Nevertheless, she woke every three or four hours. She would cry a little, causing me with frozen fingers to mix formula with evaporated milk from a can and hot, sterile water from a thermos. Congealing with cold, I'd give her the prepared bottle, she'd take a few gulps, and fall back to sleep. This was repeated until morning, when her cradle was lined on the outside with barely drunk bottles! I was totally exhausted and expected her to sleep all morning so I could take a nap! That didn't happen! She was wide awake, entranced with the clear Oak Creek water flowing over the stones, the shimmering leaves on the trees, the birds flying about! In fact, she was wide awake when I couldn't take it any longer and fell asleep in the tent while Woody took over!

We made two cross-country camp trips—one to New York City (we rode the Statten Island Ferry to the Statue of Liberty and went to the top of the Empire State Building) and one to Atlanta, Georgia's cyclorama. But, our most spectacular two-week-long-trip was embarked upon during a summer when we were *stone broke*! I persuaded Woody we had to eat at home and our only expense, which we could put on a credit card, would be gas. Ah-h-h youth! We had a big Ford station wagon at the time. With each person's belongings packed in a separate, small, stryofoam container, a coleman stove, a tent, sleeping bags, pots, cuttlery and food (most purchased along the way), we went first to the Apache reservation in northeastern Arizona's gorgeous White

Mountains, where Woody, Jamie and Gary fished. Then we went to Canyon de Chelly (home of the Navajo tribe) to see towering Spider rock. From there we camped overnight at Monument Valley (I scarcely wanted to sleep, seeing first the sun set over the monuments, then the starry sky with the monuments appearing as inky designs, and finally the rosiness of a blazing sunrise!), then went to Lake Powell's Wahweep Marina to swim in clear blue water. Incredible!

We drove to picnic at Bryce Canyon, then camped one night each at Sequoia and Yosemite National Parks, visiting the world's largest and oldest trees. We drove north to camp on Bannon Lake, above San Francisco. Dressing in our good clothes by crouching in our tent, we drove back across the Golden Gate bridge to dine at Joe DiMaggio's (up close and personal for the second time in my life as he stopped by our table to chat!) restaurant on Fisherman's Wharf (where the women were wearing fur coats). Finally, we drove down the Pacific coast highway to camp at Big Sur, a state campground that overlooked a private beach so we could watch a glorious sunset over the Pacific ocean before crawling into sleeping bags! Finally we camped at the Calabassas home of one of Woody's Army buddies, outside of Los Angeles. *Pretty amazing stone broke vacation!*

We soon found as summer getaways primitive rental cabins at Mountain Meadow Ranch, a privately owned property of one hundred and twenty acres with thirteen hunter's cabins, backed up to national forest along Christopher Creek (close to the recent devastating Arizona forest fire) on the Mongollon Rim in pine-covered central Arizona. The property had its own fresh water spring amid a cluster of fresh mint, where we collected our water for drinking, cooking, bathing and washing clothes. There was no electricity, no TV, no telephone, not even a bathroom! It was like stepping back in history a hundred years! Melanie became my "potsie pal" to the outhouse.

One night, on our way there our flashlight's beam caught a skunk a few feet ahead! Usually strong light causes a skunk to run the opposite direction, but this one came toward us! We ran back to the cabin deciding we could "hold it" a little longer! At Mountain Meadow Ranch I could read seven books a week. My days were not wall-to-wall full like they were in Scottsdale. So, with a wood stove fired up at night for fresh fish and camp coffee, with sleeping bags for bedding, with a broom for cleaning, and wild flowers and pine cones for décor, there was little or no house, office, or professional work to do. I could read! Childcare took care of itself too, since we were in the forest. Melanie would make "fairy gardens" down by the creek as her brother Jamie and Woody walked up the the "crossing" to fish.

One day, when Gary was just a small boy, possibly only four years old, his dad put him on a rock below the cabin, gave him a rod, and told him to sit there until he caught a fish. I was, as usual, busy reading, smelling the heavenly aroma of evergreens, watching leaves backlit in the sun. Three hours after Woody had put Gary on his rock, all of a sudden I heard a yell! Running toward Gary, I saw he had caught his first fish! He had patiently remained on his rock until he scored! His dad was a couple of miles up creek, but a kind fisherman helped Gary get the fish off his line. My youngest son was so proud he carried the fish, head up, around Mountain Meadow all day, showing and telling everybody, "I caught a fish!," "I caught a fish!" Gary was a natural fisherman. After he caught his first fish he was up by 5 a.m. every time we went to Mountain Meadow. He dressed quickly, grabbed his pole and bait and walked a mile down to the pool fished by Christopher Creek old timers. He had caught his limit before breakfast!

Occasionally, while at Mountain Meadow Ranch our family would drive up on the Rim to the father of the American western Zane Grey's cabin (which has since been destroyed by fire). Zane Grey would figure in my professional future.

Moving into Space in Mountain Meadow's Barn

John Glenn had circled the earth three times in *Friendship 7* (Mercury-Atlas 6) in 1962. One day at Mountain Meadow Ranch, (after the Kennedy assassination during the Goldwater For President campaign)we were invited by the Walkers, the owners of Mountain Meadow, to come up to the barn to sit on haystacks to watch a film of John Glenn's historic flight! The Walkers had set up a projector powered by a generator (since there was no electricity at the ranch) in the most rustic environment imaginable, with haystacks in a U for audience seating! The generator broke down at one point. But there we were, imaginatively in the midst of America's first *space* flight, though actually in a place filled with turn of the century and early twenties equipment, with a difficult to make function generator! What fun it was! It would not be long before we, and the rest of the world, watched televisions raptly as on *Apollo 11*, July 20, 1969, Neil Armstrong and Buzz Aldrin would step on the moon to say *"One small step for man, one giant leap for mankind!"*

One time, after walking a mile toward the "crossing" of Christopher Creek, I found myself deep in the ponderosa pine forest with no sound except the soft crackling of twigs under my feet and the cool breeze caressing wild flowers and underbrush. I flung myself face down on a bed of needles. Soon tears flowed as I reflected about the grief and financial difficulties our family had already faced in our chosen Arizona. I was worried because these stresses had taken a toll on Woody's and my relationship and I couldn't understand his change of personality after he'd had a glass of wine (naively I did not know the early symptoms of alcoholism). As I lay there my eyes were at ground level. When I opened them I could see in bas relief the pine needles backlit in the sun. They sparkled like Christmas ornaments! As I looked closely at the space around me, space I had never really *seen* before, I observed industrious movement not more than a foot away! *Alive* creatures were *moving* and looked big and busy! They didn't even notice *me*! They were a steady stream of reddish-brown ants, carrying without stopping bits of forest food toward their kingdom underground. I remained very still for many minutes so as not to disturb them. All of a sudden it became very clear to me: *The kingdoms of ants ride our space ship earth just as I do! Perhaps, in God's master plan of things, ant kingdoms may be as important to the whole as I am!*

It was a wonderful, freeing revelation! I sprung to my feet feeling light and gay. (This experience happened years before Steven Spielberg immortalized ants in an animated film.)

Moving into a Dispirited America

But, already the post–WWII "cold war," with its twenty-nine mile(47 km)Berlin Wall built in Germany in 1961, plus the Vietnam War(1954-75 America fighting with South Vietnam against the communist guerilla Viet Cong of North Vietnam) was changing the face of "Born On the Fourth of July"America (interpreted brilliantly by Tom Cruise in his Academy Award nominated performance in the film). International events—the Beatles, the fall of Khrushchev, coupled with the national civil rights act, the Surgeon General's warning about cigarettes, the rise of Muhammad Ali, the free speech movement at Berkeley, the KKK's murders in Mississippi, the '68 black ghettos rioting—were beginning to cause domestic turmoil, violence and protestor demonstrations all over America.

In 1968 we watched our televisions as Robert Francis Kennedy ("Bobby," who had served as his brother's U.S.Attorney General) was assassinated after winning the Presidential primary in California. In Memphis, on the heals of RFK's assassination, was that of clergyman-civil rights leader Martin Luther King (who led the non-violent march on Washington in '63 and won the Nobel Prize in '64). Was this America?

When Nixon became President in 1969 (I actually voted for him) he was a fan of George C. Scott's *Patton,* screening the Academy Award winning film and performance innumerable times in the White House. Nixon made the decisions to bomb Cambodia (1970) and Laos(1971). *Over three million people were killed in the bombings! Where was America's "humane" face now—America being, thus far, the only superpower that has unleashed a weapon of mass destruction on its enemy, i.e. the atomic bombs on Japan?*

The Vietnam War's reality became clear to me after America withdrew from the Vietnam conflict. I coached a couple of Vietnam War veterans as actors in workshops where they were asked to do "private moments," i.e. non-verbal-behavioral-self-experiences. (The "private moment"[a term used in Actors Studio sessions to connote something experienced that no one else is expected to see] exercise contributes to an actor's pallet of easily available "triggers" for performance). One male actor crawled through the jungle in Vietnam (reliving his intense experience), reacting to every sound, every motion of fauna around him, until he was hit by a Viet Cong sniper. The actor's terror and tension were palpable! So strong was his "trigger" we acting colleagues *experienced with him* the horrors of Viet Cong guerillas ever present but out of sight in the jungle! We agonized with him in the pain of his grave injury(much as we have in episode after episode of 2003 Spielberg-Hanks HBO *Band of Brothers* mini-series). Even though he was in a remote and safe *workshop space,* his experience was *real* to us! Another actor did moments from his capture as a Vietnam POW, conveying his torture, hunger, emotional anguish and pain from physical injuries.

In a prayer group I belong to, another Vietnam vet, Paul W. Estes, Veteran-First Infantry Division Vietnam, 1969-70, told this story: "When police attack dogs are 'retired' they are re-conditioned, separated from other dogs, separated from people, carefully observed, re-trained and positively reinforced to behave differently, prior to being reintroduced to the civilian population. Yet, when a military man is released from the service, one day he's a killer and the next, he's expected to be a peaceful, productive, free and law-abiding citizen!"

By 1972, the Watergate scandal had descended upon the American psyche. America's disillusionment was palpable in Nixon's tangle of lies, impending impeachment and resignation on August 9, 1974. What was happening globally (including the USA) was played out locally as *drugs became rampant among youth,* reaching all the way down to James and Melanie's tony, northeast Scottsdale, Arizona Saguaro High School. Though James worked as a photographer for his yearbook, at CH5 television studios with broadcast cameras via Junior Achievement, as an intern in photography for the *Scottsdale Progress* (the local daily newspaper), on a role in his school play, in his own rock band, he already had become involved with the drug, rock and hippie culture. James would graduate from Saguaro High school in '71 with a drama scholarship at Scottsdale Community College at the same time he received his draft notice. After much soul searching he persuaded our minister to write him a letter of the conscientious objector but, during his year at Scottsdale College we almost lost him twice as surely as if he had gone to Vietnam! He was given a Karmann Ghia for his high school graduation and one day was broadsided coming out of a side street, throwing the car 20 feet.… Miraculously he walked away from the accident. James actually got himself to and from the emergency room where they found him essentially unhurt, but, *he lost his college transportation.*

A few months later, Woody and I returned home from a movie to find the studio, given to James for his college "pad," that was attached to our house, on fire! James' roommate (who provided James with added income) had stuffed dirty clothes in the light deck where a bulb had ignited the clothes! The entire structure was burning to the ground! The gulf between James and his family widened. Finally James, making a student film for one of his classes, borrowed without permission his father's prized gun from WWII. Somehow the gun was stolen during the shoot. An horrific fight between my husband and my son resulted in James (penniless) leaving home to live as an *itinerant musician hippie for a decade*! During those ten years, James became a very talented rock and classical guitarist, a composer and arranger while he played small clubs in Arizona and Los Angeles. However, he lived for years with no outside wall or windows.

Melanie, senior class secretary, a member of Saguaro's honorary drama group, president of her church youth and of church youth for the state of Arizona, graduated with honors midterm at age 15, but had already become involved with marijuana and sadly an abusive boyfriend. She opted to go down to the University of Arizona , a giant step for a girl so young.

These family facts exacerbated progressing symptoms of alcoholism in Woody. He still had the "burr" haircut of a WWII G. I. (in sharp contrast to his son James' popular hippie-culture long hair). My husband, with the long-lanky-"down home" quality of a Jimmy Stewart in *It's A Wonderful Life*, honored veteran of the "just" war, man who had helped liberate Buchenwald, designer and builder of our designer house, businessman to the best and biggest clients in Phoenix, Arizona, "natural"childbirth support, was becoming final-stage-dysfunctional as an alcoholic. (I have since learned this was not uncommon among those who went into France over Omaha beach.) It took feeling queasy at a play (about a character who could "hold his liquor" but was spiraling downhill into addiction) to make me face my husband's symptoms, symptoms that had been there since the first year of my marriage, but I did not see the "danger signals."

Then one day, I walked into the unfinished building Woody used as a studio. The walls had only insulation, no paneling or drywall, because for many months we had a lack of funds to finish the structure. The walls had only open insulation. From a crack in the insulation I saw an empty wine bottle and when I examined closely I found an entire wall filled with wine sacks and bottles! I began to confront Woody's illness in myself by attending AlAnon meetings, and informing him about where I was going. We, as a family, began using avoidance behavior, i.e. having our evening meals isolated one from another, because a "sit down" dinner always produced verbal abuse by Woody toward one family member or another.

When Woody's boss and wife came to dinner (this was during a time when entertaining meant serving alcohol) I suggested we serve screw-drivers, vodka for our guests, mere orange juice for us (telling Woody no one would know the difference). Orange juice in a tall glass of ice was what I got but Woody fixed his own drink with double shots of vodka(I could tell by his behavior shortly after cocktails had been served). Midway into our festive dinner (which I had taken great pains to prepare) suddenly Woody's voice stopped as he was telling a story. His eyes became glassy. He stared into space. *He'd had a blackout in front of his employers!* His boss was forced to help me carry Woody to the bedroom and I, horrified because the incident would affect his employment, had to serve dessert to our guests (whom I scarcely knew) attempting be a gracious hostess!

Several months later I was cooking in the kitchen. Woody'd been drinking and he could *no longer walk or talk* (typically now, just a little wine now would cause the change) so he backed away from me after entering the kitchen. He staggered. He mumbled. Then he disappeared around the corner and I heard him fall! When I went to find out what had happened he was lying spread eagle in the middle of our 44 feet hallway. *He had no pulse.* I screamed to little Gary to call 911. Gary was only nine years old but he got help! Firemen were at the house in less than five minutes and in another two minutes had pumped Woody's stomach and taken him to our bedroom. They learned he had taken *prescribed tranquilizers with his alcohol.* The combination almost killed him!

In 1969, as student protests over the Vietnam war infiltrated the Arizona State University campus, I realized our family's Titanic—Woody—*was going down. I must get out the life boats if the rest of the family would survive.* That's when I decided to go back to school. I did sixty-eight hours in twenty-one months!

Moving to Finish My University Undergraduate Degree

Below was written about me at the end of my BFA Theatre degree from Arizona State University, the letter on Arizona State University, College of Fine Arts letterhead.

> *To: Alfred Thomas, Registrar, Arizona State University:*
> *...With this letter I am sending you a carbon copy of my response to Mrs. Mary Mizell, one of our superb students who graduated at the spring commencement with a bachelor of arts degree in the field of drama...She ...graduated with a 3.51(GPA).*
> *....She resumed her studies after her family was mature enough to not miss her at home, and in two years did a fabulous job of catching up and proving her eminent value.*
> Sincerely yours,
> Henry A. Bruinsma, Dean

To wrap an undergraduate degree from Arizona State University as quickly as possible, I transferred my general studies credits from Goucher. I also tested for as many credit hours in theater as I could get. The opportunity to test was based on professional teachers at the core of American theater with whom I had the opportunity to study (Sandford Meisner, Joseph Anthony, Martha Graham, Merce Cunningham) plus performing as a union actress in Connecticut summer stock, Off-Broadway and live CBS television drama. I sat for the test and received six hours credit immediately. Then, in the rain, I stood in long line after long line during ASU's (population then—48,000, today 58,000) registration, only to learn that my desired required classes had closed, a process unknown to me when I attended small, private Goucher College for women in Towson, Maryland, population 1000 (acceptance in desired classes at Goucher had been a given)!

To find parking in the always full lots at ASU was also a challenge. Because I continued to be responsible for a home on an acre and an eighth, three dependent children, thirty-six animals, part-time work and an ill husband, *every second counted* (as Lance Armstrong would write in his 2003 book *Every Second Counts*)! I carried a full course load each semester. *I found I could drive to the ASU stadium, park, then run across the street to a dorm where I locked my bicycle. I'd hop on my bike and zoom like the wind to each class! The whole process was timed perfectly from the moment I left my driveway on Jack Rabbit Lane in Scottsdale until I double-step-climbed the stairs to class at seventeen minutes!*

The teacher who drew me to Arizona State University's drama department was the before mentioned James Edmondson (today a leading actor and director of the Oregon Shakespeare Festival). "Jim" taught exciting classes using five senses and movement exercises, scene and monologue work. His work re-connected me to my great New York teachers—Sanford Meisner, Joe Anthony, Martha Graham, and Merce Cunningham. Jim also *straddled the professional theater and the academic world successfully* (I have come to believe the only true *teacher* of theater and/or film must do this). I used as my final monologue in one of Jim's classes a great piece from *Come Back Little Sheba*. (I'd seen *Come Back Little Sheba* on Broadway performed by Shirley Booth). Performing the tragic wife in *Sheba*, I had plenty of personal "triggers" to create the character! The play is about a woman who becomes attached to a little dog because *she has an alcoholic husband*. James Edmondson awarded me with an A!

Fortunately in my minor field—Mass Communication—my professor was Eldean Bennett, Ph.D. candidate. Eldean Bennett had spent twenty years in CBS News in Minneapolis so he *knew* television in addition to performing well in the academic world. Courses in Dr. Bennett's department included TV production (during which I operated broadcast cameras at KAET, the local PBS affiliate), plus magazine writing (for which, as already mentioned, I had to *publish to pass*!). A few years after I got my BFA in Theater degree with Mass Communications as my minor, Dr Bennett invited me to teach at ASU, but by that time I was ready to try my luck in Los Angeles. Dr. Bennett later became head of Arizona State University's Telecommunications Department, bringing Walter Cronkite to ASU. Cronkite had agreed to allow his name to be used for ASU's just established Telecommunications Department.

Since I went to school every summer I had to find child care for little Gary (Melanie and James were old enough to have productive activities, including church camp). So Gary spent days at the Boys Club where one of the counselors "adopted" him for One on One basketball games (leading in part to his high school athletic prowess). *I was always late to pick him up from the Boys Club.* Though still a little boy, Gary got so tricky-clever he informed me Boys Club sessions were over an hour earlier than they actually were! He figured rightly that I'd be *early to pick him up* and he wouldn't be the last person waiting for a ride home!

One of my hour-long plus commuting time classes was at 7 a.m. I thought to leave Gary with his fishing pole at a little city park en route because the park had a small reservoir lake. It also bordered a nine hole golf course. Instead of doing much fishing Gary spent hours watching people on the golf course play golf. When I came to pick him up he begged to be allowed to play golf! So we went to a nearby Yellow Front (a now defunct surplus chain that emerged out of Army-Navy stores) and picked up two golf clubs, a putter and a driver. With these two clubs in a little over night bag I left Gary with enough money to play nine holes of golf. When I returned to pick him up he was nowhere to be seen! I drove around the golf course and found him on the fifth hole. "Haven't you finished the course yet?" I asked.

"Of course!" he piped. Apparently, when he finished he just started again(without paying)! He begged me to come back in an hour which would allow him to complete the course a second time. When he hopped in the car, tossing his little overnight bag with its two clubs in the back seat, he announced "That's the most fun I've *ever had in my life!*" Gary went on to play the difficult Phoenix Papago public course with scores in the 80s. He later was included in a Junior tournament playing all the elegant, prestigious metro Phoenix golf courses including the Paradise Valley Country Club, the Phoenix Country Club, Litchfield Park, etc., before he entered high school, where he earned a letter in golf. Other letters earned were in baseball and basketball!

(This was my "miracle baby"!) Because he had been featured in the *Scottsdale Progress* sports section as having pitched a "no hit" game in Little League, he was courted by a coach at Chaparral high school upon graduation from Kiva elementary. Coach Dawson eventually gave Gary a ride to and from Chaparral High for almost a year. Gary, a member of the "King's court" in his senior year there, dated classmate Lynn Cassidy, a cheer leader, who was ranked fifth in their class academically.

One of the required courses I had to take for my degree at Arizona State University was a science course. I chose rat behavioral psychology. The course was taught by a professor who had been "conditioned" in South America to treat people the way people treat rats! Therefore, in addition to lab work (water reinforcing the rat to press a lever over seven experiments) students had twenty-one tests. Each test had to be passed with 100% before a student could progress to the next test. If a student did not get 100% when tested the first time the test had to be repeated, written or aurally, until a perfect score was achieved.

Midway in my fifth semester (including two summer semesters) I got a grant from the Arizona Arts & Humanities to do a PBS special with actors "holding book" for Dickens *A Christmas Carol*, at KAET, ASU's PBS station. I simply did not have time to spend hours in the lab conditioning my rat so I took "withdrawal" from the class that semester. Thinking I'd not want to start all over from scratch on experiments with my rat, I brought him home with me! Woody in a sober moment built the rat a cage which we kept in our bathroom! Meanwhile, I got so busy both working and carrying a full load I never finished my required science course until the *last two weeks of my last undergraduate semester* at Arizona State University! By then my rat had grown much too big for his cage and a couple of times had escaped! It required tall boots and thick gloves to capture him without being bitten(which I was a couple of times)! I carried twenty-one hours my final semester(double registering on the computer, of which six hours with Dr. Bennett's help, were independent study) because *I had decided I must either get my BFA that semester or stop!* I *had* to take my rat back to the lab! He'd lived almost a year and a half in the bathroom! Picture me: I crossed busy College and University on the Arizona State University campus with my now huge rat in a portable cardboard container hanging from the handlebars of my bike! He was gradually chewing up to my fingers! When I finally got him back to the lab, however, and attempted water reinforcement to get him to press a lever, he wouldn't do *anything*! I finally decided it would be easier to "condition" *me* than the rat! So every day I studied in the Memorial Union(MU) from 7 a.m. until 4 p.m., went to take a test between 4 p.m. and 5 p.m., got 100%, then repeated the process the next day eleven days in a row until I had passed all twenty-one tests with 100%. I, therefore, went into the final with an "A" on the tests and must have aced the final because I got an "A" in the course! I also aced all the rest of my twenty-one hours giving me 25 hours in one semester! Considering my circumstances, that was a triumph!

After I graduated with a BFA in Theatre in 1971, I went on job interviews and the only job I was offered that paid a decent salary was that of executive director of the Maricopa (the county in which Phoenix lies) Mental Health Association (MMHA). My job included supervising a staff of five, working with a men's board, supporting the women's board busy with Ball activities, redecorating the office, raising money from corporate employee groups, and producing an event that featured the actor Barry Sullivan, who had starred in a fundraising film about mental health.

Barry came over from Hollywood. I brought him first to Jack Rabbit for lunch, then shepherded him through publicity at a banquet where his film was screened for mental health VIPs.

I also had the opportunity to attend in Tucson a meeting of the state's top psychiatrists and psychologists where "television therapy" was demonstrated by a Wisconsin clinic. Videotapes of a suicidal patient were shown. The tapes revealed the severely ill patient watching herself on a video monitor every day for a week. Each day she modified her behavior so by the end of the week she had dressed neatly, had her hair cut, re-gained the care of her small child and gone back to work. Astounding! In only one week she was functioning! I approached the speaker from the Wisconsin clinic to ask whether he'd ever heard of the great Russian theater innovator Stanislavski. He said "No," but, I couldn't help thinking about what similarities there are between mental health therapy and acting techniques I'd been teaching for years!

One of the MMHA board members was Jack Stewart, Jr., founder of *"in all the world only one"* Camelback Inn, a unique southwestern resort on Lincoln Drive in Scottsdale, now owned by the Marriott corporation. Below is a letter he wrote to me during my employment as Executive Director of Maricopa Mental Health Association:

> *Congratulations on your good work in raising money from business concerns.*
>
> *In my several years with mental health this is the first time a really great drive has been staged to secure contributions from*

companies....
Cordially, Jack

Jack Stewart was already in the process of assembling a group of colleagues to create the Fiesta Bowl (which is today one of the most prestigious of American post football season bowl games). His wife Louie was on MMHA's women's board and would, in the future, become my landlady.

I continued my studies at Arizona State University, completing fifteen hours on my master's degree in theater with film as an emphasis. The fifteen hours were in independent study, since ASU did not have faculty in film. ASU, however, did have superb archives.

It was during that brief time when our family, for a very brief period, actually had two paychecks, when Woody was fired due to his alcoholism! There was no employer-"intervention" at that time in Blood Services, no urging Woody into a recovery program. The term "alcoholism" was hush–hush and shameful. Woody's parents in Ozark, Alabama, were so in denial they threatened me when I attempted to connect them with Alanon. How could they be so in denial when Woody's sister (who had been a WAVE in WWII) had been hospitalized with DTs and I was in anguish over my beloved mate in the most acute stages of alcoholism!

I found myself completely alone, knowing my paycheck must support five people. Every night Woody's demons caused him to threaten a suicide by driving into the canal with our only means of transportation. Meanwhile, I worked all day in a difficult executive position.

"The only limit to our realization of tomorrow will be our doubts of today. Let us move forward with strong and active faith," Franklin D. Roosevelt.

I knew I must ***move*** (after twenty-one years of being a *two*)to being *only one.* I would go forward with $20,000 in community debt, no child support, and the annual real estate taxes on our house unpaid. Proceeds from the eventual sale of the house in a community property state had to be split. I left my marriage of twenty-one years on October 24, 1973, with only 5,000 dollars, a lacerating decision. I grieved not just for myself but also for Woody (who loved his family and the home he had created) because he would lose *everything.* Three years earlier, we had received a home improvement loan and completely remodeled the house in Mediterranean white, adding a screened-in porch between the studio and the main house with slanting glass walls, replacing all kitchen and bathroom equipment, gaining a splendid new roof (the original roof had begun to leak in many places during monsoon rains) and white brick floors. Equity in the house was very small as a result. I was forced to take the first offer I got on the Jack Rabbit property, an offer for a fraction of what the property ultimately was worth (one recent owner put $250,000 into the interior of the house, utilizing its beautiful interior design features). My 5,000 dollar share of the equity seemed small indeed after 21 years of marriage!

The Titanic(Woody) had gone down and I and the children were in the life boats. But, even my lifeboat had sprung a leak! The Women's Board of the Maricopa Mental Health Association protested that I was spending too many of my professional hours on the business of the Men's board. Not surprisingly, based on my emotional state at the time, I was fired!

I was also lonely. I began dating and would spend the next six years fixated on a prominent man in Phoenix who, though handsome, talented, and financially stable, had already been married and divorced four times. He did not find *me* (as poor as I was and with as many dependents) "a good catch"!

Melanie, Gary and I moved to a three-bedroom home south of Shea Blvd. in Scottsdale on Beryl Lane. It had a large backyard for Gary's British pointer dog, Dutchess—a dog accustomed to running free on twenty acres among llamas on Jack Rabbit. One time after we moved to Beryl Lane she ran all the way to South Mountain before she was found and returned! The night I moved to Beryl, I was grateful to be visited by long-time friend attorney Neal Roberts (then one of the most sought after solicitors in Phoenix) and his beautiful second wife, Antje. Antje, who had been a German model, was a lovely person and a knock out beauty. We became close friends.

It was from the Beryl Road house that Melanie, Gary and I had a funny experience with my little Karmann Ghia sports car. It was the only vehicle available for *all* our commitments. I worked many different free lance jobs. Melanie, meanwhile, had a job with the Palo Alto Preschools (having returned home from the University of Arizona following the mumps as a freshman). Gary was active in sports with practices every day after school plus games. Our little Karmann Ghia was driven almost sixteen hours a day but, *no one person was responsible to fill it with gas!* We belonged to Triple A at the time. *We had so many emergency calls due to running out of gas, AAA wrote us a letter terminating our membership(probably unprecedented in the history of that organization)!*

Gary brought me up short one night about dinner time when, after a full school day and many hours of sports practice, he arrived home to find no food in the refrigerator and no food in the cupboards. "Dad cares more about us than you do!" he shouted (his father, still unemployed, was hurtling downward toward death from alcohol addiction, so Gary's accusation hurt me very much). Gary slammed out of the house to spend the night at his girlfriend's house. I caught up with him at school the next day, confessing that though I was stressed out working and waiting (sometimes thirty days or more) to get paid for freelance work, I had been lax in my first priority—my family. *I promised to apply for food stamps(which I did, finding it an humiliating experience) so he'd never have to come home hungry again!*

I still acted once a year as the theater workshop director at the Orme School Fine Arts Festival job. At one of my final workshops, an Orme student asked to be my "assistant." Tony Shepherd, son of one time head of Metro Goldwyn Mayer Richard Shepherd, great-grandson of legendary L. B. Mayer, and grandson of Mayer's daughter Edie Goetz (owner of a priceless collection of Impressionist paintings), post-Orme attended Amherst College in Massachusetts, where he directed in Amherst's civic theater. When Tony left Amherst he asked my help to secure a job in Phoenix. I introduced him to Plaza III's Helen Ross (a stunning lady who had spearheaded models for an "Artists and Models" event I produced for the American Cancer Society). After Tony had worked at Plaza III for awhile, he produced a Phoenix actors seminar which featured his dad (Richard Shepherd, above) and Lyn Stalmaster, the famed casting director of Academy-Award-winning *Coming Home*, which starred Jon Voight and Jane Fonda. I attended the seminar.

Just as the attendees at the seminar were given a break for lunch, Mr. Stalmaster said, "I will see monologues performed by any of you who want me to see your work after the break!" None of us had been pre-informed of this opportunity! To meet this test depended entirely upon our *readiness in our craft*! I went to a Circle K, got a cup of coffee and an apple, and sat in the car to run lines in my head for the character Beverly from the play *Shadow Box*. Beverly is the ex-wife of a dying man who is living in a homosexual relationship. In the monologue, Beverly confronts her ex-husband's lover's selfishness when he complains about the mess and work involved in caring for a dying patient.

My turn came to perform the piece for the great Lyn Stalmaster! He directed me to do it right to his eye (the viewpoint of the *camera)*. I did and was happy to get an ovation from the members of the seminar! What I did not expect was Mr. Stalmaster's critique. "I saw the play on Broadway and I wish I'd seen you in the part"! he exclaimed. Music! His critique fed my spirit for many years to come!

Meanwhile, Tony Shepherd's next job was in casting at the short-lived but brilliant California Shakespearean Festival in Visalia, California, with artistic director Mark Lamos, who later won the Tony for his work at Hartford Stage regional theater. While at CSF, Tony got me a job teaching interns and wrote the following about me:

> *I have known Mary Mizell for a number of years, and can say without any reservation that she is an exceptional talent of both high caliber and extreme dedication.*
>
> *She has proven her gift of the theater in any number of instances as an actress, director and instructor. I've seen her perform such difficult roles as Lady Macbeth and other classical roles as well as such modern parts as Beverly in The Shadow Box. She gives life and breath to all such performances, and is an absolute joy to work with.*
> *Tony Shepherd*

Gary, after going to school all day during his senior year, then giving up his sports to work all night at a self-serve gas station in a move to help us financially, had graduated and gone to live at a dorm at Arizona State University his freshman year. He not only carried a full course load there, he also worked every weekend and every vacation as head of a department at K-Mart. Melanie returned to Tucson to work for a pre-school there. She later went to work for the Tucson school district as a teacher's aide in special education. She danced through her classes to communicate better with the children. She had a teacher-pupil ration of one to five, so among other innovative projects, she spearheaded a "trot" program where handicapped children could go horseback riding! She did so well at her school district job the city of Tucson employed her to administer a summer camp for handicapped youngsters (the camp occupied an entire school plant)! There she directed teachers with master's degrees!

Finally I was on my own! No children! No animals! Jack Stewart had died and his widow Louie agreed to allow me to rent a guest studio under her multimillion dollar home overhanging Camelback Inn. Built on Mummy Mountain Road, the studio's fifty-foot plate glass wall overlooked to the south three hundred and fifty miles, including what appeared to be a little toy of downtown Phoenix skyscrapers and all of metro-Phoenix's outlaying mountain ranges and residential areas! The sunsets and sunrises were awesome, the desert denizens numerous—giant saguaro, prickly pear, century, ocotillos, and desert wild flowers were everywhere. One night I almost stepped on a Gila monster going down the path to my entrance! Fortunately I saw him first, because Gila monsters are protected by the state! They are poisonous and do not let go once the bite you! The frosting on the cake at my "bachelorette pad" was the fact that just a step up from my balcony was a heated swimming pool so I could swim under the stars year round!

My fancy environment as an eligible single didn't last long! Gary developed hepatitis as a freshman from eating something contaminated at the ASU dorm and he "hated living in a dorm." Because he carried a full load plus worked all weekends and vacations full time, he had to save while attempting to recover. "Would be possible to move home to the garret?"he asked. The garret on Mummy Mountain was a walkway to the bathroom under the main house, featuring exposed plumbing and basement shelves full of assorted stored items. Gary agreed to pay a portion of the rent and we somehow fixed him up a bunk in the garret (occasionally there were mice and other denizens in residence with him). Superstar Gary stuck it out for a year and a semester, largely because he had no choice. His only perks were study in my studio with its 50 feet of plate glass overlooking Phoenix and on the 4th of July he could invite his friends to watch city wide fireworks and have a steak cookout around a heated pool with the most glamorous view in the city! Still, it took persistence and courage to each day rise above that environment through the three semesters. Finally Gary (who had gained many scholarships plus government loans in addition to his job at K-Mart) found a little house to rent in Scottsdale for a year.

Gary became a superb honors student at the university. He and his high school sweetheart, Lynn Cassidy, married during the New Year holiday of his senior year. The ceremony was held at the First Christian Church in Scottsdale. A beautiful Radisson resort reception was hosted by Lynn's parents, Earl and Colleen Cassidy. The bride and groom each had nine attendants, including siblings and friends. A flower girl and ring bearer plus musicians(one had cut an album in Los Angeles, plus Gary's brother James, who had performed at clubs) came from other cities. The Oliver family came from all over the United States and gave Gary and Lynn a lovely bridal supper the night before the wedding. In a surprise moment during the reception, *Gary sang to his bride!* He had written a song and enlisted his high school buddies who were musicians, plus his brother, to back him up! He took a handheld microphone and walked through the crowd with a surprisingly great voice! It brought an ovation! Gary and Lynn spent their last semester in an apartment near the ASU campus (Gary had rented it the semester prior to their marriage). The newlyweds wrote a market research study which was outstanding among all in the business school graduating class. They graduated members of the honorary business fraternity, their GPAS: Lynn 4.0, Gary 3.8! Gary has since earned a 4.0 MBA!

This is what my dad wrote to Gary and Lynn upon their graduation:

St. Patrick's Day -1980
Dear Lynn and Gary:

It has been said, though I do not remember who said it, that achievement is its own reward. If so, you two are sharing a rich reward, for yours is a rare and magnificent achievement. The fact that you have accomplished it together makes it all the more impressive and meaningful.

We are inordinately proud of you and share the joy that both of you must feel.

Scholastic honors auger well for the future that you will have together. They constitute a solid foundation upon which to build. But happiness and success go far beyond competitive laurels.

That you find and enjoy both together is our fondest wish.

As I write this, Gary, I am thinking back to the courage, sacrifice and perseverance which your mother has poured forth unstintingly to help you to live and to accomplish those things which will mean so much to you as you travel forward on life's highway.

Of all the people I have known in my lifetime, few, if any, can match the manner in which your mother has faced hardship, incredible sorrow and obstacles which would have defeated most ordinary individuals.

You have given her profound joy and I am sure that this must mean as much to you as it does to your grandmother and me. Perhaps more.

Love to you both. Grandfather Oliver

Among my multiple contract labor jobs were publicist campaigns for a series of clients which included the Palo Alto Preschools, the Albuquerque Cooperage 10K, the Arizona Association of Industries, the Merit Selection of Judges and the first "Northbank 10K."

I was referred to Dr. Art Mollen, a superb "spin master,"on the crest of the fitness wave that would spread across the nation. Having arranged to bring champion distance runner and Olympic gold medalist Frank Shorter to Phoenix to do a 10K, he got the Northbank restaurant as a sponsoring venue. The Northbank was just north of Camelback Road, adjacent to the canal (from which it got its name), at 40th Street in Phoenix. Art hired me to do the 10K's first publicity campaign, calling the event the Northbank 10K (it has since become the Phoenix 10K, sponsored by the *New Times* weekly newspaper.)

I sought and procured famous 1936 Berlin Olympic gold medalist, African American Jesse Owens (a resident of Phoenix), to pose for pictures and attend a kick off breakfast press conference at the Northbank restaurant. Jesse (who had single handedly destroyed Hitler's "Aryan" theories by setting world records in the board jump and the 200 meter race, then equaling the record in the 100-meter race) brought Phoenix press corps to gales of laughter when he confronted Frank Shorter, saying, "I've never been able to figure out why anyone would want to run more than 100 yards!" Needless to say, the event got maximum picture story publicity! What followed was an unprecedented front page of the *Arizona Republic* (Phoenix's prime daily) aerial picture story showing runners stretching to the entire length of the page! By the time I had done the campaign six years, I could count on a minimum of six press helicopters covering the event! Dr. Mollen wrote following my first success: *"...my sincerest gratitude for the most amazing job that you did on the run. I am quite sure that without your enthusiasm and expertise in promoting the run it would not have been nearly as successful."*

Following my Northbank 10K success I was hired to do the publicity for the Cooperage 10K in Albuquerque, New Mexico. In just one week on location I had to conceive of a press "handle" that would automatically gain the Cooperage 10K a nightly news feature and front page coverage. Albuquerque had a star favorite son in Maxie Anderson, the first person to make a successful balloon flight across the Atlantic ocean. I contacted Maxie and proposed that he launch his famous balloon at the front of Albuquerque's first 10K. He agreed! The Albuquerque press did not have helicopters so I arranged with the United States Army to provide one. The day of the race it was an up again, down again sharing of the Army helicopter by major press photographers and television cameramen! We got it all! Front page coverage in the major daily plus features on all the major television news channels. Jim Schumaker, chairman of the event wrote: "*...It's no surprise to me you're the successful person you are when you create such enthusiasm in people. You are a truly inspiring person.*"

Tom Larsen, vice president of Valley National Bank, and a personal friend, was one of the founders of the Palo Alto Preschools, a multi-state chain. Tom thought highly of the visible results of my publicity campaigns, so again and again he hired me on a contract labor basis to work in Phoenix, Tucson, Los Angeles and San Diego. Innovative thinker Tom had purchased a million-dollar curriculum in association with a Stanford University Ph.D. The Palo Alto Preschools therefore attracted many talented early childhood educators. Surprisingly, my "soft news" Palo Alto Preschool campaigns reached the second front page (features) in most cities, plus the evening news!

One of my campaigns reached the front page of the Arizona Republic (an unheard of publicist accomplishment since such placement was not possible even with very costly paid advertising). Palo Alto had successfully "mainstreamed" handicapped pre-schoolers into regular classes so the picture feature highlighted a little boy who was legally blind clambering up difficult climbing structures with sighted youngsters.

The story was titled:

"Preschool is no drag for blind 5-year-old by Cecelia Goodnow"

"Five-year-old Cecil Carlin jingles a bracelet of bells as a phonograph record blares out a lively tune. He twirls to the music and then joins his preschool classmates in imitating ferocious monsters..."

One of Palo Alto's teachers had begun a bold and daring experiment. I decided to pitch a story in New York City to the Editor of *People* magazine. *People* took my bait, hiring me as a "stringer," to cover the students' extraordinary learning experience. Below is the text of my story:

> The View from the Top Was Grand, but the Climb out of the Canyon
> Nearly Floored the Tempe Tykes!

> Seventy years ago, President Teddy Roosevelt set aside the Grand Canyon as a national treasure. 'Keep it for your children, your children's children,' he told Americans....

> Predictably, there was drama. Justin Decker, 6, lost his mitten in the campfire and then suffered an upset stomach. Shanda McDonald, 8, got dizzy, fell off the path, rested and went on. Mandy

Barger, 7, found she had a fear of heights. Ben Peterson, 6, turned green, and 5-year-old Ryan Hales toppled into a creek. Still, on balance, "the whole trip was a high," says (Connie) Anderson, 27.

Their trek began in the chilly pinon and ponderosa pine groves on the canyon rim and went 3,500 feet down the Bright Angel Trail through the balmy climes of cottonwood trees and cactus. As planned, the youngsters ended their descent at Indian Gardens, a little more than halfway to the bottom—nine of them anyway. Seven kids turned back early, some just a half mile short. The others faced the grueling climp up the canyon- a round trip total of 8.8 miles. The hikers sometimes had to be kept going with promises of a rest at the next shade tree or every 10th curve. (The Grand Canyon mules respond to a similar carrot-and-stick formula, working for 20 minutes, resting for one). Besides Connie and her teacher husband Rob, six other adults accompanied the expedition, which first entailed a 260-mile drive from Tempe to Grand Canyon National Park. For the descent, the group was divided into three sections and down they plunged—from an Earth age of 225 million years at the rim to 510 million years in the canyon.

By 6:30 p.m. they were all back at the campfire and, while dinner was being prepared, Gary Semmel, 6, gathered stones of all sizes and arranged them in a loop. Soon other kids joined in and a kind of rocky shrine took shape. The adults were invited over, and Gary read a report which he had written on two sides of a paper plate: 'We made a Grand Canyon and it is very wide and deep it is big and long. We hiked it today. Now it is afternoon it is getting dark. We are resting now.' As she listened, Connie Anderson's blue eyes brimmed with tears. Teddy would have been proud too.

The night before the hike, bedding down at Bright Angel Lodge on the south rim of the Grand Canyon, I thought I'd seriously overestimated my physical ability to do the story. *People* had sent a photographer who regularly ran five miles per day, the little pre-schoolers had been training for months with their mile runs! I, on the other hand, had been writing magazine stories, acting/ directing/coaching in theater, doing publicity campaigns sandwiched between managing my minor children and maintaining a home. When I finally climbed the last grueling steps out of Bright Angel Trail, putting one foot in front of another thinking it would never end, I wasn't sure I'd make it to the top! But, my story ran with wonderful art on several pages of *People* magazine's Adventure section.

Mr. Warren Joyce Ayers, Chairman of the Board of the Ayres and Associates,Inc. Advertising of Lincoln, Nebraska (Palo Alto President Tom Larsen's hometown friend), wrote to Tom:

" My goodness!', as Paul Harvey would say, 'you sure know how to get great news coverage.' Really, it's some of the best I have seen."

I also did campaigns for the Arizona Association of Industries and the Citizens Association on Arizona Courts. President of Arizona Association of Industries Thomas L. Frankovic wrote:

"Congratulations on the completion of a very imaginative and constructive "Support Arizona Industry" Campaign......You did a splendid job and it was a pleasure working with you."

It was at an Arizona Association of Industries press conference that I first met Bill Denney, the beloved Phoenix former major league baseball player who would become a sports broadcaster for both Phoenix CBS and NBC. For three years before he died, Bill served as President of Actors Workout,Inc., the tax-exempt theater corporation I founded in 1992. President Sturdivant, of the citizens group to create the Merit Selection of Judges, wrote: *"Your Sue Lofgren story was 'right on target. We are reproducing and mailing it to 11 Arizona dailies, 55 weeklies and 10 other publications..."*

These campaigns went a long way toward keeping my family going since I received no child support. My little Karmann Ghia, my family's only transportation, was taxed to the limit along with me. Someone had to put gas in the Karmann Ghia! Other ways had to be found to earn our keep.

My course at Arizona State University in magazine writing (the course that required students to publish to pass) had led me to a weekly magazine, *Arizona Living* (now extinct) edited by Moyca Manoil, an extraordinary woman journalist who had worked for the *London Times*. Arizona Living paychecks were very small but life enrichments were very large! I got the opportunity to both write a column called "Resorting" and to do feature stories. In addition, I sold advertising to increase revenue for the sleek but financially beleagured weekly. I had kids to feed, rent to pay! I needed the sales revenue to survive and the tear sheets to market myself to other publications.

One assignment, that evolved from my work on the Northbank 10K, was from *Arizona Host* magazine. The story was about a young girl named Kathy Miller. My copy (in part) follows:

Love Will Find a Way
Update Kathy Miller in Havasu Canyon

The stereo speakers of Larry Miller's car radio blared Pablo Cruz's "Love Will Find a Way" as we drove the 66 miles of Colorado Plateau from Hilltop to Peach Springs after an enervating two-day, twenty-mile hike to and from Havasu Falls at the bottom and west end of Grand Canyon. Crumpled up on the seat beside me was Larry's daughter Kathy, recipient of "Great Britain's Victoria Sporting club International Award For Valour In Sport." Cyril Levan, founder of the award, has described it thus: "You see the face of valour in every sphere of the human act. It is uniquely in the pathfinder, the one who dares the first step. It is most dramatically seen when the spirit shows its face on the slopes of Everest, in the Marathon, on the playing fields, in motor racing—in fact, in any sporting activity where the human race seeks to excel." Kathy won the award over Los Angeles pitcher Tommy John, British racing driver David Purley and many other outstanding professional and amateur athletes. She accepted her award from Prince Michael of Kent in view of a satellite television audience of fifty million people. She appeared on Good Morning, America. She was featured in Seventeen, Us, Family Circle and other magazines. Yet at that moment in the car, fifteen-year-old Kathy looked like any typical American teenager after such a rigorous hike, with the possible exception that she slept with her legs twisted around her head.

My own body, especially my legs, were in massive painful rebellion, after the twenty-mile, 3000-ft-drop hike, where twelve hundred million years of geologic history are revealed. But, Kathy's overcoming America's Shangri-La Canyon is another in a long line of miracles (never mind her aches and pains).

Seventeen months ago Kathy Miller was struck by a car near her Scottsdale, Arizona, home and her nearly destroyed body endured massive brain damage, and a compound fracture of the femur bone(which twenty years ago would have necessitated amputation). She went into a deep coma for 10 weeks and nobody thought Kathy would live. When she finally emerged from the coma and was released to her parents' care, she weighed only 55 pounds and could not walk, talk, eat, speak, read or write. She could not remember events from one day to the next. She regressed to the second grade level academically. When her parents lovingly redecorated her room for her return home she could not recognize the room and begged to be taken to her "real home." Against physician's orders, Kathy's mother Barbara put Kathy in the swimming pool her first day home, and force-fed her vitamins and mega-powerful nutrients.

One day, Kathy announced she wanted to run again. She'd finished third in a City Girls' Cross Country Meet against 75 competitors prior to the accident. Eventually Kathy crawled, stood, and walked, but, when she tried to run she stumbled and fell, breaking her nose.

However, one step at a time, she kept at it and only five months after her return from the hospital she ran Phoenix' Northbank 10,000 Meter Run (6 ½ miles) and finished! The Arizona Marathon Society awarded her the Most Courageous Runner Award; her story made the front page of the Arizona Republic, was picked up by International Newswire, and was seen by the Victoria Sporting Club's executive director, who solicited Kathy's nomination. The rest is history.

Learning Kathy would attempt the Northbank 10,000 Meter Run again in November, immediately following two minor surgeries— one to straighten her toes, the other to cosmetically fix a hold in her leg—I became intrigued with one part of her training plan—the hike in and out of Havasuipai Canyon in two days. Most of the journalists and photographers of my acquaintance who backpacked and explored Havasu Canyon rested for many days at the falls before returning. I wanted to watch Kathy take the first and last step in her newest challenge. So I signed on.

We embarked at 5:00 a.m. from Scottsdale and drove north via Prescott, Seligman, and Peach Springs to Hualapai Hilltop, then on foot plunged down through Coconino Limestone, Supai Sandstone, Supai Sandstone, Redwall limestone and Muav Limestone. The red walls became progressively higher until only a strip of blue sky could be see above. Kathy, who had some pain in her toes, hung back at first, partly out of concern for a family friend who had short legs. Then, in spite of increasing fatigue, she frequently ran ahead to catch her dad, former Los Angeles Dodgers and New York Mets pitcher Larry Miller. Larry carried the heavy pack with our food supplies, but remained in the front line along with Kathy's brother, Larry Jr., who plays baseball for Scottsdale College.

When we finally reached the fields, gardens, and homes of the Havasuipai Indians in the late afternoon it was difficult for any of us to… take one more step! I had wrenched my knee during the first mile down and had begun popping aspirin about every half hour to keep going. After signing in with the tourist manager we went to the affectionately called "Havasuipai Hilton"—two dorm rooms, a kitchen, clean sheets and hot water—great luxuries for the circumstances. That night under stars that blazed with a brilliance unseen in metropolitan areas, we determined the plan for the following day. The thought of hiking four miles to and from the falls PLUS ascending the eight miles we'd just completed seemed impossible. But, we agreed on the plan.

(Description of trek to the falls.)

Two miles back and eight miles up! Legs that already felt like rubber bands stretched to the breaking point.(With the exception of Kathy's brother Larry, who with the energy of a gazelle, had walked the two extra miles to Mooney Falls{in Havasu canyon} and back and finished the trip up to Hualapai Hilltop a full hour ahead of everybody else, we were all hurting.) Yet, Kathy Miller, painful toes notwithstanding, frequently led the pack.

At one point, watching Kathy run ahead, Larry, with a catch in his throat said: "If I'd known a year ago what I'd be watching today, I'd never have believed it."

Love, indeed, found a way. Kathy Miller took the last step to the top of the trail at Hualapai Hilltop ahead of us.

POSTSCRIPT: On November 5, 1978, Kathy Miller completed her second Northbank 10,000 Meter Run (6.5 miles). In the year between the two Northbank events. Kathy has advanced to the tenth grade level academically.

To date I have been published in *My Weekly* (London), *On Location* (Los Angeles production film trade), *Travel & Leisure* (American Express travel publication), *Arizona Living, Easy Reading, Arizona Highways* (famous for its photography), *People* (the Palo Alto preschool story), *Dramalogue* (Los Angeles actors trade), *the Arizonian, Arizona Arts & Lifestyle, American Premiere* (Los Angeles film magazine), and the *Phoenix Sun Papers*, including flying in a balloon with Bob Sparks, who attempted to fly over the Atlantic ocean only to ditch midway!.

Moving to *"Counterpoint Peru"*

One exciting "stringer" assignment for *Arizona Living* magazine sent me with twenty travel journalists from all over America on what turned out to be *one of the major experiences* of my lifetime! I flew to Peru from Los Angeles (think flying to New York *and back* from L.A. *without stopping*). Housing was at the luxurious Lima-Sheraton, at Paseo de la Republica 170, across from the new modern civic and convention center. From Lima we flew to Cuzco (capital of the Inca civilization, 10,000 feet above sea level in the awesome Andes), and from Cuzco we went down the Amazon in a dug out canoe to visit the headhunters! On September 7, 1973, the following excerpt from my story appeared in *Arizona Living*:

> Color it turquoise, robin's egg blue, shocking pink, lime green, sun yellow; add the snow-capped Andes, Inca ruins, tropical jungle and the Amazon River; stir generously with people—women bearing babies in blankets on their backs, little girls balancing bowls of fruit on their heads, llamas, guinea pigs, piranhas; dub in traffic noises and constantly blowing horns, the sounds of espanol and Qechuam (pronounced KECHwum), the roar of jet engines at takeoff, the click-clack of train wheels on single gauge track, the steady slosh of a paddle in a dug-out canoe, top with gleaming golden artifacts from pre-Columbian times, glorious handwoven *tapices* (wall hangings), alpaca and llama blankets, rugs, panchos× and what have you got?
>
> Sit back sip your pisco sour!
> You're on a Braniff Airlines tour of Peru!...

All land arrangements were made under the auspices of the Ministerio de

Industria y Comercio (the department of Tourism of the Armed Forces Government)with whom Braniff enjoyed cooperative relations. The *Revolutionary Government of the Armed Forces of Peru* marked its fourth year in office in 1972. They were committed to social and agrarian reform, but restricted all press, television and radio programming to "socially useful," thus prohibiting newsmen from publishing or broadcasting anything that could be construed as derogatory to the regime. However, it was impossible not to be repelled by the poverty that coexisted with the opulence. Everywhere I saw gutters strewn with papers, trash and garbage, torn-shredded posters and Spanish graffiti defacing buildings.

Stench and muck are painted robin's egg blue and shocking pink by the indomitable dwellers of the ever present slums. The Lima-Sheraton, a gleaming modern structure, however, was resplendent with many stories high *tapices*, 830 in all, in a spectrum of colors—violet, indigo, peacock blue, tropical green, oranges and magentas. Viewed from ground level in our hotel atrium they bedazzled us. (The tapices are woven by Quechua-speaking inhabitants of San Pedro de Cajas, a small town in the central Peruvian highlands about three hours drive from Lima. Almost every one of the town's 11,000 people work at the craft using 6000 looms [*tolares*]; they have not changed their method of weaving since the days of Inca Pachucutec, in the 14th century).

Our host, Victor Cabrel, 33-year-old manager of the Lima-Sheraton, had the unique custom of sending plates of fruit, cookies, crackers, cheese and wine to the rooms each day at the cocktail hour. His custom carried one's hunger pangs over nicely until dinner, which is late in Peru—10 p.m.! However late we ate and partied, we were summoned early the morning after arrival to the beginning of a *life and death experience* when we journalists were *flown by the Peruvian Armed Forces* over the spectacular snow capped Andes toward Cuzco. Just as we were approaching our destination we learned the Inca capital city was "socked in" with zero visibility. Our pilot elected to backtrack toward the coast where he put the plane down and instructed us to disembark. We found ourselves at a scruffy, tiny, desolate air strip. We had not been milling around more than twenty minutes when a loud speaker announced *we must get back on the plane and land in Cuzco* (never mind that the pilot, controlled by the military, could not see the airstrip!) At that point two journalists from San Francisco decided to abort the tour, electing to stay in the absolute wilderness of the tiny airport (on terra firma). Knowing I was the sole support of minor children, it was difficult to make the choice about whether to board the plane or not to board the plane. I elected to board because it seemed to me the danger was about equal—the danger of staying in the strange, perhaps hostile coastal airport and the danger of trying to land in totally socked in Cuzco. And so I *moved* the second time through possible death.

We landed safely, but were told to go immediately to bed for a couple of hours to adjust to the high altitude and thus avoid *altitude sickness*. We noticed immediately the colorfully clad peasants, who, though small in stature, had unusually large chests. Informed this is nature's way of accommodating the body to store more oxygen at 10,000 feet, everyone on the plane but one person, a journalist I did not know, and had not even had a chance to talk to (*Arizona Republic* investigative reporter Don Bolles [already famous in Phoenix for his stories about the Emprise Corporation, considered to be the "mob"]) took to their beds.

We gathered for lunch at our Cuzco hotel. We began eating and suddenly Don Bolles *collapsed*! Typically he had not obeyed the admonition to go to bed for a couple of hours. Instead he had "investigated" Cuzco's streets, shops and people! While we were still at lunch we learned Don Bolles was near death and that a priest had been summoned for last rites! No attempt could be made to fly him out of Cuzco because the airport was still "socked in." Don would be flown out of Cuzco as soon as it was possible. Oxygen was brought in. A small group of us filed into Don's room that night to cheer him, then retired to our own rooms because we knew early in the morning we would take the train to Machu Pichu, the revered worship-center-Inca ruins high in the mountains. About midnight a commotion awoke me and I looked outside my room to see Don desperately crawling on his stomach down the hall! Apparently, his oxygen tank had run out and he could not breathe! Everyone called for help at once. By the next morning before we'd taken the train to Machu Pichu, Don had been flown back to medical care in Lima. However, this would not be the end of the drama I shared with Don Bolles.

Our journalist party climbed into awesome Machu Pichu, explored the ruins, then were transported to the Amazon jungle, where we were loaded into primitive canoes and paddled down a muddy feeder stream to the Amazon River, and thence to a small island decorated with human skulls! Many sparcely clothed natives stood about. We did not land but were informed the small tribe had been *cannibals*. I shot a short (very good actually) Super 8 film while riding in the canoe. The next day the party flew down from Cuzco, stopping at an elegant resort in Arequipa (midway between Cuzco and Lima) for a beautiful many-course luncheon. I photographed a white-faced Devil dancer, whose costume and makeup represented the conquering Spaniard there (the photo was used with my published story). Wc did not know as we ate the sumptious, many course meal that we were being served a dish containing food poisoning. We got back to our 5 o'clock plate of crackers, cheese, fruit and wine in our hotel rooms looking forward to dancing and dining at the elegant Lima Braniff restaurant at 9 p.m.. However, by 7 p.m. I knew I would not wine, dine and dance that evening! I was sick—vomiting without ceasing. During the night I took one small bite of banana and one small bite of cracker every two hours and by dawn managed to convey on my hotel phone to the hotel management (sans Spanish)that I was *very* sick. A nurse arrived. I demonstrated in action (I knew about body language!) the degree of my sickness and I was given some medication. Later, when our party assembled for the flight home, I learned I was the first of almost the entire party of journalists who succumbed to the food poisoning!

The flight to Los Angeles was uneventful. At LAX, however, I discovered I would be the only person in the group along with Don Bolles who would be taking the shuttle flight to Phoenix. Of course we sat together for that hour. During the flight we talked of what happened to him and he defended his wish that I not say anything to his wife (a nurse) who would be waiting for him at Sky Harbor Airport along with his little deaf daughter. I, of course, promised to say nothing and learned he'd taken the Peru assignment because he needed to get out of the danger of reporting on the mob (not dreaming a travel story would cause him to almost die in Cuzco,Peru). He also told me the shocking fact that when the Emprise Corporation sued him for $1 million, he was served at his home in front of his family and neighbors and his "boss," the *Arizona Republic*, had not offered financial or legal help! I asked why he didn't move with his career to another city. Don replied it was because his "young daughter was in an excellent school for the deaf in Phoenix." Before we disembarked in Phoenix we pledged to meet to share our Peru stories after they'd been published. I'll never forget the sight of Don being encircled by his wife and daughter at the gate.

A month later, we did meet for a drink and gave each other tear sheets of our Peru stories.

I told Don I was fascinated with the possibility of becoming an investigative reporter myself. But Don strongly discouraged me (knowing I was the sole financial and emotional support of minors). He shared with me even more shocking stories about his tenure with the *Arizona Republic*.

He told me he'd spent almost a year doing research for a story about Arizona's judges. He took the story to his publisher, Mr. Pulliam, who read it, told Don it was *"great"* but *"too hot to publish"!* A year's work! He also told me he was always assigned his Emprise stories "accompanied by an Arizona Republic colleague." It wasn't until he'd been accompanied by the same person for almost a year that he learned his *Arizona Republic* colleague was somehow "connected with Emprise!"

Don felt beleaguered from inside his job and endangered from those he wrote about. Perhaps, his choice to go alone in 1976 to a hotel at the corner of 3rd Avenue and Clarendon in Phoenix was predicated by his lack of trust in the *Arizona Republic* man assigned to him.

It was on a frying-egg-on-the-pavement day in the parking lot of that hotel that a bomb exploded under his car, killing him by inches over the next several days.

As the story unfolded I found myself at its vortex because Neal Roberts, the attorney who flew John Adamson (the suspected murderer) out of town the night of the murder, had been a longtime friend of my husband and me (first with his first wife Lois, when we made silk-screened Christmas cards on Jack Rabbit Lane, then later with his wife Antje at the time of my divorce). I would not see or talk with Neal for ten years following my realizing I knew not only the victim of a horrible murder but, also a person implicated though never indicted with the murderer.

Ten years later I willingly *moved* right into the story again!

Mary Daisy Moving Through Bodies

Mairy Daisy at age 3

Mairy Daisy at age 10

Mairy Daisy as a young actress in New York City

*Mary Daisy (adult) as Ana in George Bernard Shaw's
"Don Juan In Hell"*

Mary Daisy as a senior bike commuter

Part Four
Noon

1976-1986 – Phoenix Car-Bombing, Iran-Contra, Creative Growth

Moving on Assignments in the UK and Europe

I knew financially I must, so after Peru I patched together an amazing group of assignments in the United Kingdom and Milan, Italy, and squeezed in a weekend in Athens, Greece. I boarded British Airways flight over the poles, which delighted me as I heard the music of various British dialects all around, plus I sat next to the former business manager of the Beatles, now business manager of the Bay City Rollers. "Where is Arizona exactly?"he asked me.

The headline of the story that ran in *Arizona Living* magazine was:

WHERE'S LONDON?

"Ladies and gentlemen!" the bus driver barked in thick cockney. "Straight ahead is the new London Bridge. There's been a bridge on this site since Saxon days. The last bridge to occupy this site was dismantled block by block and rebuilt in Arizona, which is in the United States."

Thus the only state in the U.S. to be mentioned on the Round London Bus Tour was pigeonholed by a put-down. Don't the people of the United Kingdom *know Arizona is in the United States?*

Little did that bus driver know a *resident of Arizona* was riding on his bus! Thus the satiric thrust of my published piece excerpted above!

Moving up close and personal to theater greats was close at hand! I had arranged pre-flight(with the help of a show business friend, Ros Sistrom, who had married the producer of Olivier's *Hamlet* and worked as an actress on the West End) to interview Sir John Gielgud back stage at the Wyndham Theatre. My story eventually ran in the Los Angeles actors trade Drama Logue (now merged with Back Stage West) on the front page.

JOHN GIELGUD: An Actor's Actor

LONDON-Sir John Gielgud, who can speak Shakespeare better than any living classic actor, has flipped his coin to play Spooner in Harold Pinter's *No Man's Land* in the National Theatre production which opened at the Old Vic, then transferred to Wyndham's Theatre on London's West End. He slouches in garish, slovenly clothes, skips in disreputable sandals, coils around expensive booze, and speaks in short sentences and,monosyllables(a la Marlon Brando). Often he doesn't speak at all. He looks like a small man.......

When I saw Gielgud after watching his Actors Studio type performance in *No Man's Land*, I was dumbfounded to discover how virile and tall he is! His voice physically struck me like a gust of wind—all glorious tone, pitch and articulation.

"I was brought up in the classics, but I am very fortunate these past eight years to be doing new things," the nephew (Gielgud) of actress manager Ellen Terry announced happily. "This is a black play. Spooner stays positive, but he's a monster, really....."

My story continues.

Gielgud scored his first "hit" as Richard (Old Vic '29). At the time he said, "It gave me a wonderful sense of power to feel I was beginning to control the lovely language which, at rehearsal time, moved me so tears sprang to my eyes." But, the great classic actor has not been seen in Shakespeare in London since he played Wolsey in 1958....

"...Olivier said of Gielgud in an interview with Kenneth Tynan... 'we were the reverses of the same coin; the top half John, all spirituality, all beauty, all abstract thought; myself all earth, blood, human...the baser part of humanity without the beauty.... I was trying to sell realism in Shakespeare....'"

My back stage impression of Sir John matched Olivier's precisely. He was a strikingly handsome man with a voice that bowled me over with its richness. The great British director Peter Brook (author of *The Open Space* who directed John in *Measure For Measure*) said of him "[John's] professionalism and his enormous experience are a virtue and a vice. Even an audience cough would cause him to sense audience restlessness and produce a brilliant but well tried stage trick to catch audience attention."

A few years after I did the interview with Gielgud, I also did a story for the front page of *Drama Logue* on Sir Peter Hall at Sardi's in New York. Sir Peter had directed Gielgud, plus most of the other great British Shakespearean actors of the era, so I specifically asked him what he thought of "method actors" (referring to Stanislavski). He replied without hesitation *"All great actors are method actors!"*

Amen! Even Olivier, who openly scoffed at Stanislavsky–trained actors, especially Dustin Hoffman while filming *Marathon Man*, spoke of being like a "telephone operator" who could "plug into one experience and emotion or another." Gielgud's reality–based film performance in *Arthur* won him an Oscar as Best Supporting Actor!

While in the UK I also had the opportunity to go to Glydeborne, the estate outside London that hosts the opera attended by the royal family in the summer. Royal parties have champagne picnics on the beautiful lawns prior to and after performances. The BBC was filming *Play of the Month* on location there, directed by Cedrick Messina, who would eventually direct the British Shakespeare plays for television. I was allowed in the control room and marveled over the shoot, which utilized eight cameras! Sir Cedrick edited as the takes progressed from what seemed like an enormous number of monitors! From one of the producers I learned BBC cameramen are expert at shooting drama because, as opposed to American television cameramen, they shoot soccer, for three days per week, then drama the remaining four days all year! Thus, the BBC is able to achieve fifteen minutes of usable tape *per day* on such shows as *Masterpiece Theatre*, whereas American film companies consider three minutes of usable film to be a successful shooting day! The BBC is incredibly cost efficient in leasing locations. The Glydeborne location I visited, which included a grand mansion, outbuildings, acres of lawns and gardens, was leasable to the BBC for only $500 rent per week! Add extraordinary British actors (who train for a decade in the provinces prior to work in London) and the result is productions of exceptional quality!

Next I flew to Milan, Italy, capital of Lombardy and Rome's Western Empire, the economic heart of modern Italy. I had been hired by an Italian comic book writer/artist, creator of a character not unlike the Lone Ranger, to be a consultant for a film (based on his Italian cowboy character) to be produced in Arizona. I was entertained royally by my host beginning the first night when I was given a hip-high long-stemmed red rose to carry to an elite

Italian restaurant where we had a dinner for the gourmet! After we were seated I was informed by my host that, "Everyone in the restaurant knows you are I American!"

"How?" I inquired.

"It's the way you walk" he said. "You are so sure of yourself!"

The following day a lovely young girl, an Italian-English translator, took me to the Galleria Vittorio Emanuele, the shop-lined hall that remains Milan's traditional meeting and people-watching place (built in the late 19th century). The Galleria's glass-and-steel dome is spectacular! It was under the dome at a sidewalk table that I was entertained by the translator at lunch, then taken by car to see Leonardo da Vinci's *The Last Supper* (created circa 1495-1498 and recently made controversial via Dan Brown's best selling *The Da Vinci Code*, which claims Mary Magdelaine was Jesus's wife). *The Last Supper* is a fresco in the Church of Santa Maria dell Grazie. Its superb spiritual content plus the power of its invention mark it as one of the world's great masterpieces! Everybody's seen *The Last Supper* in reproductions, but *I* was not prepared for the richness of its colors and its radiant-life-like beauty! Leonardo, while creating the great piece, experimented with the new form, fresco, which partly accounts for the work's damage though I learned from my hostess of a WWII miracle! The Church of Santa Maria dell Grazie was bombed to ruins! *All the walls except the wall upon which the great* The Last Supper *dwelt were destroyed!*

I was then taken to a meeting with Italian filmmakers, some of whom were winners in the International Film Festival. They questioned me about Arizona, especially the weather, which they were surprised to learn was well over 100 degrees hot in the summer. That was the season they expected to shoot so they were very disturbed. My firsthand account of the weather in Arizona in June, July and August must have derailed an Arizona shoot. During the meeting via my five years of Latin and my acting training (body language, emotions), I understood what the filmmakers were saying though they spoke in Italian *before* the translator spoke to me quietly in English!! It confirmed what I'd always taught actors—that audiences understand intent (if the actors are doing a great job) *without words!*

My hotel was in clear view of La Scala (the world famous opera house). That night I had a front row center seat at La Scala where, surprisingly, I was only a few feet away from a guest conductor from America, Zubin Meta, of the Los Angeles Symphony!

Moving into a Past Life Unexpectedly

I had a spare weekend so, on a quest, without hotel reservations and little money, I elected to fly to Athens, Greece. The decision to do so turned out to be one of the best decisions I ever made! My luggage decisions before I left the United States helped this last minute choice. Regarding wardrobe, I used the"layering" principle. I did the entire extreme-weather-change trip with only an airline travel bag and a purse, carrying, in addition to clothes, cosmetics, a Super 8 and still camera and a script! I had a wonderful, long A-line velour black coat with faux fur cuffs and collar, over my arm if not worn. I wore black pants and boots and added blouses, turtlenecks, sweaters, scarfs, and jewelry (depending on the occasion), plus toted a compact umbrella, and a faux fur trimmed black knit hat. However, when I disembarked in Athens in weather not unlike that of Phoenix in the summer, I changed into a black A-line halter with my black pants and boots! I went to the center of the city there Athens had a student travel center. I needed to find a doable(money-wise) hotel or hostel immediately! My English got me three possible choices and a cab. The cab drove around to two dark and dirty "bed and breakfasts" then took me to a sidewalk-fronted hotel which I could see (without speaking Greek) was just opening! I went inside and found, to my amazement, everything was sparkling white! An already registered Canadian guest told me the owners had a room available but that the owners(a husband and wife), had been up all night painting and were now sleeping! I dismissed the cab!

Soon I was being guided by a small Greek girl with thick black curls, all shy smiles, to an elevator. She carried a pile of white sheets. The elevator stopped on the second floor and she led me to a door which opened onto a room that was totally immaculate and white—white walls, white floors, white draperies, white new-simple furnishings—with a single bed, a desk and chair, and wonder of wonders, a door to a *private bath with a shower* (unheard of in Europe at next to nothing rates) also white! Together, laughing and smiling, we took the sheets and made the bed. Then the small beautiful Greek child parted the drapes on a sliding glass door and led me out onto a balcony that was one and a half the size of the room! I turned and looked and there was the Parthenon, the Temple to Athena on the Acropolis, directly in front of me, not more than a mile's morning hike away! I was beside myself with glee to be so close to the masterpiece Greek architects Icinus and Callicrates had created in 447-

432BC!

I ran down to the small street in front of the hotel and quickly found a shop where I got green grapes, cheese, and a small bottle of wine, took the chair from my room and sat above terraced homes where I could watch multiple families' activities below me. People watered flowers and trees, had late afternoon coffees, hung out small lines of wash, and played with children. Soon the sunset blazed to the west, making the Parthenon golden. In perfect peace I sat there until I found myself watching the light and sound show against the night sky, eating my private picnic on my own private balcony! The next morning, after a wonderful hot shower and a continental breakfast in the dining room (part of the room cost and delicious), I took my Super 8 camera and hiked up to the Parthenon. The magnificence of 46 Doric columns plus statuary (335 feet of the original 525 feet still standing) depicting the birth of Athena and her contest with Poseidon, caused me to run around and pan my camera! There was so much to see! So much to capture. (The end result of the Super 8 film was un-editable—too much panning!) What a wonderful day I had, toting the remains of my last night's picnic for a midday respite!

Finally, in the late afternoon, I hiked down the hill to the Theatre of Dionysus (the Greek god of fertility and wine, later considered to be a patron of the arts). It is believed, from the music, singing, and dancing of the Greater Dionysia in Athens, came the dithyramb and ultimately Greek drama. I found myself standing where Euripides, Aeschylus and Sophocles presented *Medea, The Trojan Women, The Oresteia, Oedipus Rex* and *Electra*. This was an open space theater, *free to all*. In the center of the arena, I turned and faced the throne chairs, and the strangest sensation came over me! I was most certainly thousands of miles from Phoenix, Arizona, USA. I had gone for over a week conversing in English only briefly with the Canadian lady at my hotel, yet I had the child's Christmas morning sense that *I was home*! I had **moved** into a reincarnation experience! I had been in the Theatre of Dionysus before!

Fortunately, my carry-on luggage policy saved me from being stranded at the Athens airport the next day, because the shuttle I took from my magic hotel overrode my terminal, forcing it to come all the way around again while I lost an hour pre-flight time to check in! I carried my airlines travel bag and a purse, running through check-in, and made it into my plane just as the flight attendant was closing the door!

The next day in London was cold and drizzly and I felt the flu coming on, so I found a bed and breakfast (sadly passing up the chance to meet Alan Bates backstage!) and just huddled under the covers from the time I got in til a breakfast tray was laid at my door. Then I got up and went to the Tate Gallery before boarding my plane at Heathrow, so I could see Rodin's famous *The Kiss*, a massivily erotic yet spiritual piece of artwork I love!

Flying home to America over the poles, there was severe turbulence. A Slovic lady sitting next to me clutched me sobbing. I found myself comforting her while I had a serene sense of **moving** exactly as I should through mind, time and space. When the lights of Los Angeles, USA appeared below, I wept with joy and pride about coming *home* to America!

We **move** in and out of many bodies in our lifetimes. Our bodies are not solid. They are 70% water with atoms migrating all the time. The *I* of me continues to exist in ghost form in those many bodies and places (we are ghosts, out of body, in our own time in addition to after we've left our material bodies!) One of the amazing things about the camera to the art of drama is the way it preserves great artists *in-bodies*. And, of course, one of the most amazing things in all of human history are libraries, buildings and museums preserving mankind's "little grey cells" (Agatha Christie), civilization really. The newborn infant body my dad saw, when he named me for the mother of Jesus, is not the body that could scarcely see a root beer float glass over the edge of the table because it was so tall. Nor is it the body riding atop my 5th grade boyfriend on a sled through snow drifts in Mansfield, Ohio. It is not the body that played Mary (mother of Jesus) in the junior high school play, nor beat the current Librarian of Congress in the public speaking contest in 8th grade then played Penny in *You Can't Take It with You* in the high school senior class play. *I* was in all those bodies, of course. It is not the body that learned swimming in college, nor the body that studied acting in the professional classes of famed coach Sanford Meisner and Broadway director of *Rainmaker*, Joseph Anthony, while performing in New York City's CBS live television drama *Studio One* in the early '50s. It is not the body of the bride in Mansfield, Ohio, nor the body of the mother of four babies by "natural" childbirth. It's not the body of the woman who helped build a house in Scottsdale, Arizona, nursed her baby with neuroblastoma cancer to his death on Christmas day, scrubbed the white floor of her husband's studio in Phoenix for the first organizational meeting of Barry Goldwater for President. It is not the body of the actress in classes with Shelley Winters at the Actors Studio in Los Angeles in the '80s. Nor is it the body of the woman whose 501©(3) theater corporation received an environmental award from the current Mayor of Phoenix Phil Gordon.

From Walter Isaacson's 2003 best selling biography *Benjamin Franklin*, Ben's own epitaph confirming the above, was written when he was a "fledgling printer":

The body of
B.Franklin,Printer;
(Like the cover of an old book,
Its contents worn out,
And stripped of its lettering and gilding)
Lies here, food for worms.
But the work shall not be lost:
For it will,(as he believed)appear once more,
In a new and more elegant edition,
Revised and corrected
By the Author.

All my different looking bodies *miraculously worked* without much help from me!

However my **moving** body by June 2,1976, had developed a troublesome fibroid tumor in the uterus. I carried the fibroid for a couple of years, unable to lose freelance income which I always sorely needed. I was assured by my uncle Verne (my mother's brother, an OB-GYN in Boise, Idaho, co-founder of a cancer research center and head of the Idaho Medical Association) that if the tumor was watched and did not cause me undue trouble I could ignore it. However, my menses had become embarrassing hemorrhages as I hurried between many contract labor jobs. I elected to go to Surgi Center to have a therapeudic and diagnostic "D & C." That's where I was when I came out of anesthesia to hear on the radio that a bomb had exploded under a car killing Phoenix, Arizona, investigative reporter Don Bolles.

"Investigative reporter….has been rushed to the hospital in a critical condition after a bomb exploded under his car!"

"I know him!" I cried out. Don was on my trip to Peru, the colleague who almost died of altitude sickness! It was Don I watched have a touching reunion with his nurse wife and young deaf daughter at Sky Harbor Airport!

From behind a colorful drape at Surgi Center, a patient with the voice of a woman said "I know him too! I have been his stenographer. He has been working on stories so secret we work with a security guard protecting us at a secret site!"

My son Gary came to take me home from Surgi Center and later that night I watched horrific news on television, learning my Peru journalist colleague's body had been shattered in the explosion! Don was fighting for his life. However, he had uttered one name before losing consciousness—"John Adamson."

What the announcer said next astonished me! He said "Neal Roberts [friend of my husband and me, my friend along with his beautiful wife Antje at the time of my divorce] *"had flown John Adamson to Lake Havasu City and had been with John Adamson and additional murder suspect Max Dunlap shortly before the bomb exploded under Don Bolles."* Didn't that make him guilty by association? Wasn't he an accessory to the crime? *My friend?* Why do decent men commit or abet evil acts? And once they have done so, how should we interact with them?

How do they live with their consciences? How do small, sequential decisions necessitate and compound one another? And how can our faith in our own good intentions and our ignorance of those around us undermine our objectives?

> Neal Roberts in 1976 was a respected 47-year old civil attorney whose dashing good looks made heads turn. His success was visable in the Eldorados he drove, in the Spanish complex at 90 W. Virginia where his offices wrapped around a swimming pool. He liked to play a whist variation called "pitch" at the Arizona Club in the afternoon. The private club atop a downtown high-rise seemed a lofty and proper setting for socializing with businessmen and state senators. Few knew he often started his day at 8AM with Irish whiskey in a dark midtown bar known as the Ivanhoe, where he delighted in introducing his friend John Adamson as "your friendly neighborhood assassin." (*The Don Bolles Murder: A New Times Special Report*-June 1986)

The realization that I was the friend of both victim and a possible accessory to the victim's *murder* threw me into a deep depression.

I would not see Neal Roberts again for another ten years. Neal Roberts retained his famous colleague and friend John Flinn (who argued the Miranda decision before the Supreme Court) to strike an immunity deal for him so he could never be indicted. The Phoenix car bombing was followed in Tucson by the supposed shotgun suicide of Judge Thompson's daughter Lynn (the judge who presided over the Don Bolles' murder trial), a University of Arizona pre-law student! My daughter and son, living in Tucson at the time, were astonished! Insider buzz had Lynn looking forward to a successful future. Had Lynn been murdered to influence the beleaguered Judge Thompson's decisions? It seemed a circle of evil had **moved** into my life!

But, I had to keep **moving** away from the evil! My survival and the survival of my family depended upon it! After covering a small jet air race to Mexico in 1976, I did a major bicentennial piece for *Arizona Highways* which was illustrated by famed southwestern illustrator Ted DeGrazia, and had the following poem by Harvey Shahan as a preface:

"Only a fool walks on the edge of a cliff.
Only the man who has walked there knows what's behind.
Only the man who has walked there can see where no man has been
And where no man has been is where some men must go."

It struck me as singular that on July 2, 1776, Fray Francisco Garces entered the Hopi villages in northern Arizona. My opening paragraphs convey the "handle" of my story:

The Spirit of Arizona—1776

If the story of 200 years young United States of America is one of people believing all men are created equal, with rights to life, liberty, and the pursuit of happiness, building from a vast wilderness a great nation in an unbelievably short time, then the story of Arizona 1776 is All-American!

With religious fervor and benevolence, contempt of danger, curiosity, and resoluteness of the 1776 principle, Arizonans in that year match in sheer guts and style all that is best about our nation's Bicentennial heroes.

Meet Fray Francisco Tomas Hermengaldo Garces, instinctive supporter of "all men are created equal." Intrepid Franciscan Garces, accompanied by a lone Mojave guide and a horse, discovered an overland route from San Gabriel Mission (near Los Angeles) to the Hopi villages in northern Arizona.

Meet the Hopis themselves and visit their village of Oraibi, believed by many to be the oldest continuously inhabiated community in the United States. Pottery shards indicate occupancy at Oraibi since A.D. 1150. The Hopis, undaunted by the Christians, held firmly to their ages-old religious beliefs and remained obedient to their own unique "bill of rights." They played unwilling hosts to

Fray Garces on July 3-4, 1776.

On those same historic days 3,000 miles away on the East Coast, representatives of the 13 English colonies adopted the Declaration of Independence from Great Britain. The ringing of the Liberty Bell at Philadelphia tolled the end of colonialism on the East Coast while on the West Coast, colonialism, fed by the vitality of an all-American melting pot, was just beginning....

I wrote and sold many Arizona stories in addition to the *Arizona Highways & People* magazine stories. A story about speedboating to Rainbow Bridge marina, houseboating 90 miles to Bullfrog marina, then speedboating up to the headwaters of Lake Powell, was published in *Travel & Leisure* magazine. So was my story, "The Grand Canyon and Fourteen Ways to See It." I was invited to go on the river raft trip through the Grand Canyon with pioneer explorer Georgie White. Georgie founded the pontoon barge used by all the rapids trip companies today. A prototype of the sausage pontoon she created is featured in the Grand Canyon South Rim museum. Part of my story published in *My Weekly* in the UK and other magazines follows:

Queen of the Colorado

To Georgie White, athlete, adventuress and river runner, now in her 70s, the Colorado river of the Grand Canyon is home.

No one would deny this is so for she is the mighty Colorado's only woman pilot and has made more trips through the Grand Canyon than any person, male or female, living or dead.

Georgie is an amazing woman. She.... swam 185 miles of the Lower Colorado during the time it was "big" water before the Glen Canyon Dam opened in 1963, and she was first to photograph at the site of the 1956 double airline disaster at the junction of the Colorado and Little Colorado on Chur and Temple Buttes.

Georgie is also the only person to be lowered over the rim in a bucket at President Harding Rapid when the site was being considered for a dam.

In fact, Georgie has spent more than six months on the river every year for over 30 years.

Can you imagine feeling "at home" on the mighty, charging, surging, seething, unpredictable, cutting Colorado river? Georgie, who sleeps with one leg up over the 'sausage' of the large pontoon barge she pilots downriver, insists, "I'm married to the river an' I ain't getting' no divorce!"

I and Georgie were the only single women on the river raft trip I covered (one other woman traveled with us, but she was with her husband). I was fascinated by Georgie during the six nights and days we camped out on the banks of the Colorado river. I could not perceive how a woman with menses could function on the river as she did. I got her alone on a walk one day and asked her that direct question. She replied, "I got a hysterectomy right after my daughter was born. It was the only way I could be equal with and compete with men." Sadly, Georgie's only child, a daughter, was killed in a tragic automobile accident when the young woman was in her early twenties.

Everyone on the trip knew I was on a magazine writing assignment, so from day one I was teased unceasingly by a group of men traveling with us. We camped on a Colorado River sandbar every evening. Around a campfire we shared cocktails and dinner. The men claimed they worked for the city of Los Angeles "garbage department."

"Los Angeles' garbage department is so good, all the cities of the world send their garbage to Los Angeles to be recycled!."

It wasn't 'till the third night on the river that I learned they were actually from the Los Angeles District Attorney's office. They had been first at the site of the Manson murder of Roman Polanski's beautiful, pregnant actress wife, Sharon Tate! (New York City in 1967) William Manchester (the author) remembered haunting Grateful Dead concerts in the Avalon Ballroom that summer was a bearded little psychotic who liked to curl up in a fetal position right on the dance floor…Later he would be well-remembered in Ashbury. His name was Charles Manson'"(*New York Days* by Willie Morris).

Each rafting person had but one very small rubber container for all their clothes, vitamins, toiletries, extra sneakers, etc. Engineered for the rapids, the pouch was around a foot and a half square and each day was strapped with heavy ropes to the side of barge so it could charge down the rapids without losing our possessions. At the end of one day my container went missing! A huge blister now adorned the bottom of my foot, so searching for my waterproof sachel was difficult. To tease me, the guys from the D.A.'s office had hidden it! All the teasing and prank playing, however, was balm to a single mom's psyche. I had dependent offspring and lived below the poverty level, so I felt very vulnerable to each man's daily propositions, though I accepted none!

After the campfire each night I found a little place of privacy hidden by desert flora where I could unpack a "ground cloth" piece of plastic. I blew up my air mattress (which, unfortunately, got a leak in it almost immediately!). On top of that I placed my sleeping bag and crawled in. One particular night I took the time to wash my few clothes using water from my canteen, so I had items of clothing hanging on bushes. Tempting fate and the weather, I crawled into my sleeping bag naked. There I was, only a few yards from a thunderous, roiling Colorado River, pushing tons of sand and tree branches as it cut ever deeper into the Grand Canyon! I slept exhausted till I was awakened by a great noise and the pelting of a huge thunderstorm! I managed to pull the plastic of my "ground cloth" out from under me up and over my sleeping bag. I took the plummeting rain on my face and head all night long with only my "ground cloth" between me and a torrent moving down the monuments. In the morning, feeling like a soaked rat, all possible glamour was gone!

What did that matter? It was incredible to rush by the oldest geological formation on the face of the earth, the polished black ebony-looking Vishnu Schist, rising many stories high above our heads, like a great black mirror! The most difficult rapid was at the end of the trip, Lava Rapid. We reached there late in the afternoon when everyone was tired from continuous exposure to the sun and water. Georgie beached for a half hour, explaining we had to do the Lava Rapids yet that day due to the decreased water level of the river which would occur the following day (water flow is now controlled by Glen Canyon Dam). To assure we were all game she passed around a bottle of tequila and everyone took a swig! Then we strapped ourselves to each other then to the barge and descended 50 yards into the hole of an extinct volcano, actually submerged under water for at least 30 seconds! Fortunately, with Georgie's survival techniques, we all came through!

Among the story ideas I pitched to *Arizona Highways* magazine (one of the highest paying markets in Arizona) was a story about Zane Grey, father of the American western, whose cabin I had visited during the years our family cabin-camped on Arizona's Mongollon Rim. The "handle" of that story would be Zane's dependence upon his wife Dolly for the success he achieved. Pearl (the name on his birth certificate) Zane Grey, a newlywed, *un*successful dentist-would-be-writer, lived in a small cottage on the banks of the Delaware where the snow came through the cracks in the winter. He wrote "*unwearyingly-romances, short stories, verse....After my savings had melted away we were forced to live on my wife's money..."*(Zane Grey. *The Man and his Work. An Autobiographical Sketch* 1928). Zane's wife Dolly contributed her entire trust fund to the couple's survival as Zane struggled to become a writer. Dolly would ultimately edit all of Zane's books as he became a best selling and famous writer, make his film deals (more movies have been made based on Zane Grey's books than on any other writer in the history of films!), and via her innate financial brilliance, became America's first lady banker. In the process of writing the piece I interviewed Zane Grey's son, Loren, a professor at U. C. Northridge. Loren wrote the following after reading my story:

> *I have read your article about my father, and think it is great.*
> *You have our authorization to go ahead and sell it anywhere*
> *that you feel appropriate.*
> *Sincerely yours,*
> *Loren Grey*

Dr. Grey, whom I interviewed at his home in Woodland Hills, California., north of Los Angeles, told me crime writer Mario Puzo had taken the theme of his best selling *The Godfather* directly from Zane Grey's *Heritage of the Desert*! I decided to send my story to Mr. Puzo(to gain the right to publish the relationship of *The Godfather* to *Heritage of the Desert*)and received a complimentary letter about my writing!

> *Enjoyed your article very much. Thank you for letting me*
> *read it.*
> *Sent the release to the magazine also.*
> *Best,*
> *Mario Puzo*

Moving to Have an Oscar in My Lap!

Loren, meanwhile, confided to me that Puzo was "shopping" (seeking to get a film deal) his *Heritage of the Desert* screenplay (he was unsuccessful, even after the blockbuster Academy-Award-winning *The Godfather*), and that Grey Frederickson (one of the producers of *The Godfather*) would produce Puzo's *Heritage of the Desert*.

I called Mr. Frederickson from Phoenix. He graciously invited me to call him the next time I was in Los Angeles. I planned a trip to L.A. immediately but first I hurried to Arizona State University's fine library but was unable to find Grey Frederickson in the film encyclopedia. Therefore I arrived at Grey Frederickson's Beverly Hills gate unarmed with information about who I was about to interview (this "homework" was my responsibility)! Mr. Frederickson had a speaker phone at his gate. When he unlocked it there stood an extremely handsome, tanned, friendly man with a towel wrapped around his bathing trunks. He informed me he had just returned from the way-over-budget-and-time (over a year instead of scheduled months) *Apocalypse Now* shoot in the Philippians. A bevy of beautiful model-looking women mysteriously disappeared as we went into his study. I mumbled apologies for not being able to find him in ASU's film encyclopedia. He merely said, "What would you like to drink?" When he returned with my screwdriver he put a tall, gold statuette in my lap—his Oscar for *The Godfather*! Cuddling the revered show biz trophy, I felt a *very green* Hollywood person indeed, but mustered the courage to ask Grey questions about Mr. Puzo, *The Godfather*, and Mr. Frederickson's most recent time in the Philippians (it had been horrific apparently).

Grey became a wonderful mentor to me in Hollywood, arranging an audition for me with *Godfather* and *Apocalypse Now* director Francis Coppola's casting director. The audition went well, but Screen Actors Guild (SAG) struck for residuals on commercials. The strike went on for a year and a half. Therefore, I could not work despite the good auditions. The Writers Guild of America (WGA) joined the actors in the strike. Had the Directors Guild of America (DGA) joined the actors and writers the entertainment industry(the #1 source of the economy in Los Angeles) would have closed down completely with dire results. The entire industry was saved within a day by legendary "Godfather to the film industry" and head of Universal studios, Lew Wasserman. I had my first picketing experience in front of the entrance to Universal Studios.

On Friday, June 9, 1978, *Arizona Republic's* entertainment journalist Kyle Lawson(a director in theater from Omaha, Nebraska, therefore a knowledgeable, passionate writer who would contribute greatly to the growth of live theater in metro-Phoenix) wrote the following about me:

> Mary Mizell [my married last name]
> Directing a farce is no laughing matter
> In the current issue of *People* magazine, there's an article about

Valley youngsters hiking the Grand Canyon that was written by a local woman.

To some of her friends, that reveals an unexpected side of Mary Mizell.

They know her only as one of the finest acting teachers and directors in the Valley, a woman who has given a helping hand to a substantial number of young talents.

Those who have either been in her classes or part of her casts include film star Nick Nolte; Dianne Kay, part of the family on TV's *Eight Is Enough*; Blair Farrington, Scottsdale dancer with Juliet Prowse's Las Vegas revue; Sarah Rice, ingénue in New York's *The Fantasticks*; Penny Metropulos, one of the stars of "Vanities" at the Scottsdale Center for the Arts; Dan Witt, ASU professor who recently co-starred in Phoenix Little Theatre's *My Fair Lady* and Arizona Civic Theatre's *Equus*; Jim Edmondson, an actor-director with the Ashland Shakespeare Festival and Nancy Gregory, who danced with Gene Kelly on tour.

To name a few.

It should come as no surprise to see Mizell's name in print either. Among the famous people she has interviewed for local and national magazines have been Mario Puzo, author of *The Godfather*; Sir John Gielgud; tennis player Bobby Riggs; Jean Marsh of *Upstairs, Downstairs*; Gordon Davidson, artistic director of Los Angeles' Mark Taper Forum, and screen writer James Lee Barrett(*Shenandoah*).

One of the handful of Valley women to be recognized as a director of merit, she has helmed several Valley productions, the most recent of which, is *A Flea In Her Ear*.... She has also directed James Stewart in an award winning industrial film.

...Impressed? Even if you are, Mary Mizell is not. She's just doing what she has to do. "When you have this love of the theatre—this passion, really—you've got to share it or you'll explode," she said.

The explosion started when a "very, very tiny girl" acted "between the sheets hung on a line in my grandmother's back yard." It continued in high school when she played the leads, and in New York, when she broke into the Golden Age of Television playing opposite John Forsythe and Beatrice Straight on Studio One....

"As a woman you're constantly proving something……But I've found that once you do prove you have a genuine contribution to make—based on knowledge and a track record, of course—things work out...."

Does she regret the move to Arizona? "Sure. Everyone dreams of the big break. And there's just not enough work here...."

One of the asides of directing *Flea In Her Ear* was the fact that I was cast as a nun in Brooke Shields' *Wanda Nevada*, which was shot in northern Arizona, but had to turn the job down because *Flea In Her Ear* was in final dress-tech rehearsals at the Phoenix Performing Arts Center. Little did Kyle know how little work there really was for me and my family during those years when the Triple-A cut us off due to too many running out-of-gas emergency calls! I had too many careers because I needed many streams of income.

Kyle mentioned the 1979 Bobby Riggs piece in his story about me. I interviewed Bobby post his cocky tennis match against Billie Jean King (Ms. King was the first woman to defeat a male champion). Bobby was doing a lucrative circuit of speeches following his defeat, including Phoenix's Ramada Inn. After my story had been published and a copy sent to Frederick P. Osborne, Vice President of Ramada Hotels, Mr. Osborne wrote this to me:

> *....Mr. Riggs may be seriously training for his next tennis match; however, he seems to have met his match with you!!! Your well-written, fast-paced article clearly exemplifies one woman's expertise with words. My compliments to you!!!...."*

This is part of what I wrote:

> Opportunist-buffoon in true American standup-comic tradition he may be, but 'Official Male Chauvinist Pig' Bobby Riggs is *not*! He's playing the part for hire. I sensed that the minute he sized me up when I interviewed him prior to a luncheon address of the ladies luncheon of the Ramada International Association convention.
>
> Bobby's eyes twinkled as he replied to my comment, "Since you only play women, you must really *like* women" with the speed of a real tennis pro. His answer was not really a put-down. It was his next line in the script. "I *love* women. I think every man should have at least two!"

If jester Bobby's prostituting of male tennis has been a boon to women's liberation, it's also brought about the emancipation of his vendible 55-year-old "sex symbol" image. He's found selling his wares from place to place not only extremely profitable, but a pile of fun as well. The Billie Jean "Catastrophe" reputedly brought him $900,000. Talk shows and honorararximus, in Paul Dean's [Phoenix *Arizona Republic* reporter] words "have him weeping all the way to Fort Knox." He's been offered a Burt Reynolds' centerfold but he's holding back on accepting *that* until the offer goes up to $50,000!

My son had primed me to ask him if he prepared for the match. He replied emphatically "No."

Bobby knows how to train. He started early. He was California singles champ by the time he was 16, and by 1939 he had won three Wimbleton titles.

Formerly cocky, Bobby claims he found beating Margaret Court "so easy," and the Hollywood starlets "so tempting, even though tennis is the only way I can still make love" that he came into the match totally unprepared. He also blames his failure on Billie Jean's youth versus his age, Houston Astrodome's fast carpet surface, and an overdose of prescribed pills for a battered elbow.

…Henry Miller says if you live by reason, life is a comedy; if you live by emotion, life is a tragedy. Bobby seems to have the Miller idea. Fun isn't such a bad thing to have these days.

But, I'll bet that "sawed off Tarzan"(who looks a lot taller on TV than in person) trains more seriously for the next one.

Moving Back to Pro Acting

Delbert Mann, the Academy-Award-winning director of *Marty*, which starred Ernest Borgnine, was in town casting a movie of the week. The film, *To Find My Son*, would star Richard Thomas. I auditioned for Delbert himself and won a small role which enabled me to join the Screen Actors Guild (SAG). My son James worked in the mail room at Capital Records in Los Angeles and had taken an apartment in North Hollywood. He invited me to "share the rent" there, which gave me a base for straddling two states, Arizona and California, in my work search. I began *bi-monthly commuting between Phoenix and Los Angeles,* sometimes working all day in Phoenix (where the lion share of my income still came), driving all night, then auditioning and looking for work in Los Angeles all the next day. The bad news happened whenever I had a flat tire in the middle of the desert because, always on the edge financially, just one tire would often cost $75.

One time during this period I drove from Arizona direct to the Mark Taper Forum at the Music Center to see a play. I parked in a parking lot near the theater. At midnight, a stream of theater patrons moved toward their vehicles paced by a couple of policemen. When I got near my car I saw all the doors were open and the overhead inside lights were on! Moving closer I saw the side window was smashed, the dash board was ripped out and my clothes, which were in the rear of my hatchback, were gone! Sadly that stash included items I'd collected for over a decade, none of which probably brought more than ten dollars when they were "fenced." They were, however, invaluable to me, i.e., the long black coat I'd taken on my jobs to the UK, Milan, Italy and Athens. Eventually I moved my career entirely to Los Angeles.

Ronald Wilson Reagan, actor then governor of California in 1967, was the president of Screen Actors Guild (SAG)for two terms until1975. During the time Reagan was California's governor, he severely cut state welfare, medical services and education funds (i.e. my local branch of the library in North Hollywood cut back its staff several jobs and was open fewer hours and days). The crime rate in California continued to rise, the welfare caseload doubled and welfare costs tripled while state taxes and spending were up by 100%. Reagan had been an active participant in creating Hollywood's unsubstatiated communist "black list" for Senator Joseph McCarthy and his young aide Roy Cohn (Cohn's evil was recently portrayed in HBO's *Angels In America* and McCarthy was condemned by the United States Senate in 1954). I, naïve and unaware regarding political beliefs, had odd connections to Reagan beginning with Nancy Clark Reynolds(President of Goucher College's Athletic Association). I was GCAA's Secretary and thus pictured with Nancy in a brochure. Nancy, later a lobbyist in Washington during Reagan's years as President, became Reagan's administrative assistant while he was governor.

Of Reagan as President, the day after reported June 6, 2004 the day after he died: "He did not know enough. And he did not know how much he didn't know. Because of Reagan's knowledge gaps, his presidential news conferences became adventures in the uncharted regions of his mind"(*Reagan* a biography by Lou Cannon, 1982).

"Most of the time he was an actor reading lines who didn't understand his own programs"(Former House speaker, Thomas P. O'Neill). I met Reagan's mother-in-law, wife of famous neurosurgeon and ultra-right political activist, Loyal Davis, one on one during the years I was a motivational speech maker and special event chair for the American Cancer Society. Mrs. Davis was on one of the ACS fundraising committees. Meanwhile, more connections came while I was working as theater workshop director at the Orme School Fine Arts Festival.

I had Reagan's close right wing political friend and advisor William F. Buckley's nephew in one of my theater workshops and Richard Kiley's niece, who was best friends at Orme with Patti Reagan. Before Ms. Reagan's book was published (telling of her flight from home the day her father received "Father of the Year" award), I heard stories about the dysfunctional relationship the Reagans had with their children. So when I became active in the Screen Actors Guild (SAG) as a conservatory workshop leader at the American Film Institute and attended meetings in the SAG board room (which features a Reagan portrait) it was with an eerie feeling. After the election of Ed Asner as SAG President in the late 80s I accepted Reagan's handshake at Patti's Orme graduation but it was well known in the entertainment industry that Reagan "sold SAG out" by allowing MCA producers a special waiver to escape making major residual payments for reruns of TV shows to screen actors.

Fortunately for me, during the 1981 strike I (picketing with SAG outside Universal Studios) expanded my magazine writing client list to include *Premiere, On Location*, and *My Weekly*, in addition to regular assignments for *Drama Logue*. I had *some* source of income. My *Drama Logue* story featured actress-director Lee Grant.

I began my first full length work too, a screenplay titled "Reaching," the story of my family's struggle with my husband's alcoholism, before the therapy of interventions practiced today. The protagonist of the screenplay is a teenage boy named Mike Manning. The character is based on my son Gary's heroism.

I worked on "Reaching" for a year. It sold as a Movie of the Week (MOW) to producer Hank McCann at the end of the strike. However, when I went to collect the check and sign the contract, in reading the fine print of the contract I discovered the producer could bring in a listed writer approved by the major networks, a writer who could *change or add one line and get full screenplay credit while I would get only "Story By" credit!* Naive as I was (many successful Hollywood writers have emerged via this practice) this *seemed wrong* since the characters and lines had emerged from my gut and personal experience! I gave the check back and refused to sign the contract. Later I received from the Director of the American Film Institute Alumni Association's Writers Workshop, the following:

> *I had the opportunity of meeting Mary Mizell through the AFIAA's Writers Workshop. During this time I have been very impressed with her astute comments on other writers' screenplays. Her screenplay "Reaching" I feel clearly demonstrates her exceptional talent as a writer.*
> *Sincerely,*
> *Willard Rogers*

Later, Willard arranged for me to direct a performance holding book of "Reaching" at the American Film Institute. The producer of *Sophie's Choice*, Robert Ralyea, was the moderator. The performance elicited the comment that *"...if 'Reaching' were packaged with the right stars it would win not only all the Emmys but also all the Christophers* (humanitarian award)."

The industry, at the tail end of a major strike that almost caused the demise of Universal studios, was not in the mood during its recovery to test itself on an untried writer, especially one who wrote a "relationship" film. Willard Rogers, however, invited me to become a member of the AFIAA's Actors Repertory (a group of working Hollywood actors who performed regularly new screenplays holding book at Hollywood's major studios and in the AFI auditorium). Moderators included Richard Dreyfuss (winner of the Academy Award for the first film of Neil Simon's *The Goodbye Girl*) and Robert Wise (director of *The Sound of Music*, and Chairman of AFI's Center for Advanced Film Studies). I was testing my skills as an actor/writer/director with working professionals of Hollywood in this group! I felt very lucky!

Very shortly after gaining a California driver's license that read "ACTWRI" (a special-issue plate with letters meaning actress/writer) I got lucky again. I met and entered into one of the greatest love relationships of my life with actor/director/coach Dan Mason. It was and is a *platonic–collegial love*, almost spiritual, based on mutual joy in actors performances, superb productions, exquisite films and industry personalities with whom we have associated. It endures to this day, more than twenty years later! Dan truly took an interest in my career just as I, like a magnet drawn to metal, took a natural interest in his!

When I first met Dan he was working as dramaturg for the Los Angeles Actors Theatre (LAAT). LAAT was founded by Ralph Waite (the father in *The Waltons*)and was the precursor to a thirteen million dollar Los Angeles Theatre Center in downtown L.A. I took Dan a copy of a play written by my then-boyfriend which he rejected. However, he invited me to perform in readings of new plays, which he periodically staged on the top floor of a Bank of America building on the NW corner of Santa Monica and Western Avenues. LAAT was gifted the Santa Monica and Western office space by B of A as a grant in kind for $1 a year! I performed one script via Dan's invitation where I met and got a huge crush on the extremely handsome, tall Bill Whitehead, a USC PhD candidate in social ethics, who was writing a book for Random House. Bill's play *And If That Mockingbird Don't Sing* was produced in L.A, Equity Waiver. It starred Marcia Rodd (who was in Neil Simon's Broadway company of *The Last of the Red Hot Lovers*). The play was also produced at LORT(League of Resident Theaters) Alley Theater in Houston, where Bill was named "Best Playwright In Texas." Meanwhile, with Dan, I **moved** mentally and emotionally into shared work, time, dreams and heart!

Dan Mason left a successful on and off Broadway, television and film acting career (*Star Trek: The Next Generation*, *White Mama* with Bette Davis, *Anthony & Cleopatra* with Lynn Redgrave, *Backstairs at the White House* directed by Michael O'Herlihy) to direct plays in Dublin, Ireland. Beginning with the acclaimed Irish premiere of *Spoon River Anthology*, he went on to stage Marguerite Dura's *Days in the Trees* and Cather McCallum's *Lizzie Borden in the Late Afternoon*. Returning to New York, Dan became Artistic Director of the Shelter West Company and directed the American premieres of Gerhardt Hauptmann's *The Rats*.

I first saw Dan shortly after we met as Rennie Davis in the Los Angeles Odyssey production of *The Chicago Conspiracy Trial*, the year and a half long running Equity Waiver production (union actors work without salary to showcase their talent). "Everyone in the company got feature films, series, or legitimate theater jobs," Dan claims. However, it was not until I saw him in *Hamlet* that I realized the full dimension of his talents. The *Drama Logue* gave him a "Best Actor Award" and its critic wrote: "Daniel Mason is a superb Hamlet holding back in the first act then slowly building the seething passion of this melancholy Dane. With thin, gaunt face, chiseled cheekbones and a mane of unruly locks, Mason's profile rivals Barrymore's; his rich, textured voice and agile movements express the anguish, sensitivity and grace of

Hamlet."

I next saw him as the definitive Jimmy in *Look Back In Anger* at Los Angeles' Fountain Theatre, where his sensuality and sexuality vied with his passionate rage. When Charles Marowitz directed *The Petrified Forest* at the L. A. Theatre Center, Dan, as understudy, took over an Alan Squire performance for Rene Auberjonois. (Though Dan had no rehearsal time with the cast, the *Petrified Forest* company declared Dan's creation of Squire to be superior to Rene's!) I thought Dan amazing in the role! What followed were Equity Waiver productions first in *Hedda Gabler* as Loevborg at the Cast Theatre, then *The Seagull* as Trigorin at the Richmond Shepard Theatre. His close friend and colleague Guy Giarrizzo(Guy co-wrote with May Sun, then staged and directed the 1990 Los Angeles Festival's *The Chinese Chess Piece*) directed Dan as Professor Peter Feeney in Ralph Hunt's LIT 305, a one-man tour de force for which he won his second "Best Actor Award." Reviews were spectacular:

"Mason is memorably intense and mordantly funny" (*L.A. Times*).

"Mason is marvelous…spellbinding. It's a terrific performance" (*L.A. DramaLogue*),

"Dan Mason is quite extraordinary: His voice is like an instrument that is filled with dissonance and harmony, his timing is acutely wrenching and his person is indeed the failed, ever unrequited romantic…"(*L.A. Review*).

Dan's performance affected me viscerally as few performances have. He decried the loss of poetry to the universe, the loss of poetry to *me,* the desecration of education in universities so focused on athletics. When I became Artistic Director of Actors Workout, Inc. in Phoenix, I brought Dan to play Professor Feeney at el Pedregal, the Boulders in Carefree, Arizona. LIT 305 was later performed at the Edinburgh Festival to similar reviews.

In the '80s, Dan and I became audition scene partners at the major studios and at the Actors Studio in Hollywood where I had been accepted as a member of the Playwrights Unit. I was attending sessions moderated by Shelley Winters (who gave us actors great coaching advice including her techniques for quick memorizing). During sessions I worked alongside Valerie Harper (featured as Rhoda on the Mary Tyler Moore show).

Almost weekly for eleven years in Los Angeles, Dan and I would meet for coffee, lunch or an occasional dinner to dream our next major project together! My association with Dan led me to go to work for the Los Angeles Actors Theatre. I would enthusiastically help build the founding audience of a thirteen million dollar historic building renovation in downtown L.A. It would be called the Los Angeles Theatre Center(LATC). The new theater center would have four separate theater spaces, surrounding a huge domed lobby. I worked the phones for referrals, ultimately bringing at least a half million dollars in subscribers to LATC. Part of this success in selling came from performing back to back monologues for groups of seventy-five to a hundred prospects for memberships, i.e. Who's Who International in Rolling Hills Estates and for a smaller but wealthier group at the pent house of Chase Manhattan Bank. I also performed and solicited founding members at the downtown stock exchange and at the Grand House in San Pedro (near the Queen Mary and Howard Hughes' Spruce Goose). Owner Marilyn Ginsberg became a friend and I loved her gourmet menus seated in a courtyard built around a giant old tree.

The grand opening day of LATC brought on an extremely funny family story. I invited my mother to drive down from Garner Valley to attend one of the play openings. Thinking LATC was located at Santa Monica and Western Avenues, the site of Los Angeles Actors Theatre (LAAT), parent of Los Angeles Theatre Center (LATC), where I had been working, Mom got off the freeway at that exit and began searching for the new theater center. In her searching, *my very conservative mother went naively into a porn shop* on Santa Monica Blvd, around the corner from LAAT! She was confronted with a large poster featuring a young woman's genitals! *My* mother! A man, sensing correctly she was in the wrong place, came to inquire what she wanted and was kind enough to help her with directions downtown! We connected and saw the play.

Mom told that porn shop story many times at dinner parties! My mother had many out-of-the-ordinary adventures. Another famous story happened on day when she and my dad were expecting guests for dinner. One hour before her guests were to arrive, with the table set with her loveliest china, linen and fresh flowers, food cooking, hors d'ouvres on tables, bar at the ready, mother went into her shuttered off laundry equipment which lined the wall of her family room and found a large snake! Making a quick decision she hastily shut her decorative shutters (manufactured at her son Dick's Steiner & Mateer in Whittier), which had zero space beneath the doors, so therefore the snake could not slide through. Mother, the gracious hostess, had her party and after the guests left, dishes were washed, she cautiously decided to check on the snake! She opened the shutter doors. The snake hid behind her washer/dryer. Mother decided to take couch cushions and lay them in a double aisle all the way to an open sliding glass door, optimistically thinking the snake would oblige and "follow the yellow brick road"outdoors. The next morning she saw no trace of snake so she decided her brilliant scheme had worked. She drove my dad down to San Diego airport so he could fly to his consulting job in Palo Alto south of San Francisco.

A couple of days later she opened the door to one of the upstairs bathrooms and there was her friend the snake! This time he was coiled and not too friendly, so mom got *bug killer spray* and sprayed him which really made him mad! He struck at her, scoring a bite(not poisonous fortunately). Mom got mad too! She went for a shovel which she used to kill the reptile! Mom had other wild animal adventures in Garner Valley which I will relate later.

Coaching in Los Angeles became an important source of income for me. I was listed as one of the top coaches in the actors trade *Drama Logue* to which I contributed articles. After working with actors for some time I began to hold showcases. One evening I held a showcase at my own apartment in North Hollywood and invited my brother Dick and his wife Dorothy as audience. The actors had developed monologues that became the basis for a show, *Female From Crash to Cable*, at Alan Miller's Back Alley Theatre in Van Nuys. Dick's wife Dorothy was a fan of estate sales in the Whittier area and one day bought a "box" with unknown contents for $25. Included in the box was a black leather jacket that fit Dick but it was not something he would normally wear in his run of the mill business activities. However, the night of my showcase, thinking the black leather jacket looked "Hollywood," he slipped it on. He and Dorothy thought the actors "great" and on the drive home he happened to put his hand in the pocket of the black leather jacket. Astonished, he pulled out $300 in cash! The jacket had been hanging in his closet for over a year!

Meanwhile, speaking of cash, my brother Tom had propelled himself from being the youngest vice president American Airlines ever had, to being in 1978 the Senior Vice President of Federal Express (after a tour of duty at Thomas Cook, the worldwide travel-organization, based in London). Tom's job was "to make sure that the volume of Federal Express business [continued] to compound at 50% annually—and he [did] that in large part with an advertising and promotion investment that [kept] pace with anticipated sales growth. Sales in fiscal year 1982 [would] be over $800 million and the promotion budget [would] be about $25 million…" (*The Memphis Connection*, Marketing & Media Decisions, May 1982).

FedEx was begun by Fred Smith, a native of Memphis who parlayed a Yale term paper (on which he barely got a passing grade) into a multi-billion dollar bonanza.

Subtitle of the May 1982 article explains my brother Tom's vital role in the company:

The secret to Federal Express's fabulous success is the connection its planes make in Memphis. But that's not of much interest to its broad customer base, so its advertising concentrates on customer problems, on promises of solutions, and adds a a touch of humor. The man who created the Memphis connection is Fred Smith…. The man who spends $25 million a year to sell it is Tom Oliver, Guest Editor of this issue.

An August, 1985 Profile story in Management Pac was entitled *"Tom Oliver, the Man Behind the Funny"* had the subtitle *"Some of my best decisions have been made when I'm all wet."*

Tom explains he uses 80% of his time communicating, talking, listening, and traveling to customer service centers, field stations and sales offices…endless meetings then the interviewer asks him how he spends the remaining 20% of his time: "…TRO: About five percent of the time, I try to do nothing but sit and think something through or figure out a better way. Most of my creative thinking doesn't happen when I'm in my office. In fact, given the time in the office and the amount of time I spend traveling, it is difficult to sit down and do much meaningful thinking at the office. I stand to do it in places away from the office, like when I'm out on a plane or in a call center, or sitting in my easy chair at home…or when I'm in the shower. My division calls them "shower ideas." Something has been on my mind, and suddenly it hits me! Right there in the shower! Some of my best decisions have been made when I'm all wet."

Continuing to earn my shekels any way I could in Los Angeles, I staged actors workshops and seminars at prestigious venues, i.e., the theater in Laguna Beach. The seminar for actors there, which included performances of actor monologues, was titled "Way To Grow." It was videotaped with broadcast level equipment via a feature film technician friend and sponsored by a SAG signatory talent agency. Featured in the Laguna press with a full page picture spread "Way To Grow" was co-led by me with Tony Shepherd (my former assistant at the Fine Arts Festival at the Orme School). Tony was now VP of Talent for Aaron Spelling.

One of the panelists I invited for the Laguna event had been the subject of a story I did for *Drama Logue*, Jim Byrnes. Jim had attracted *Godfather* producer Al Ruddy to his work via a screenplay he'd written while he was still driving a truck! However, with Al Ruddy as a mentor, plus his quite considerable talent, Mr. Byrnes(at the time of the Laguna seminar)had written not only episodes of the *How the West Was Won* series, but more than sixty episodes of *Gunsmoke*. Jim invited me to have a showcase at his Encino home. It was full of *Gunsmoke* memorabilia plus a giant photograph of James Arness as Wyatt Earp. A film audience was invited to view the actors regarding possible work. It was a showcase I almost didn't hold.

I would soon move out then back into my own body. "For everything there is a season...a time to die..." Ecclesiastes 3:2

Why can't **moving** out of this body happen with less de-humanizing stuff, machines, tubes coming in and out of bodies from everywhere, indifferent caretakers? Grim, horrific, shocking, putrescent, morbid, ghoulish death, especially in hospitals and hospices so cold and gruesome! Death should be an adventure! *Why can't we just de-materialize like* Moses did? Or (as my daughter Melanie believes) like the millions of birds that circumnavigate the earth annually. "You hardly ever see a dead bird!"Melanie exclaims.

My Grandfather Fred, who lived in my parents' home ten more years than I did, passed away in a union printer's home in Colorado Springs because he had become too ill to be cared for in my parents' home. It was 1969 (during the time I was sprinting to a degree at Arizona State University). My dad was the only family member at Grandpa Fred's bedside and the last words (the man who bought me a root beer float taller than my head so many years earlier and sang at my wedding reception) said to his son were: "Goodbye. And God bless you."

Meanwhile, my youngest brother Ron, born late in life to my mother in her 50s, was in ill health all his life. He struggled with too many schools and too many homes during my dad's career moves to establish meaningful relationships. With my mother's constant encouragement he did manage to attain an AA degree from a junior college, but died of mysterious causes in August 1980. The family was summoned to view his macabre remains.

This was followed closely by my ex-husband Woody, always in denial about his alcoholism, who spiraled down to his death in the Veteran's Hospital in Tucson, Arizona, October 26, 1982. Alcohol had gradually consumed his vital organs. I returned to Arizona to be with my sons James and Gary (and Gary's wife Lynn) for Woody's flag-draped casket funeral at the Veterans Cemetery, on I-17 north of Phoenix. The cemetery is in a beautiful, open desert location.

Thus, the saga of my WWII GI was finished.

Woody's death caused me to have a dream. I was in the back of an open garage. Woody was driving into the driveway at freeway speed. I got out of the path of his oncoming car and woke up as he crashed, killing himself against the wall. After that I knew I had done all I could to save him, including getting out of his way at the end.

Then, R&Ring at my parents home in Garner Valley, which overlooked the spectacular San Jacinto Mountains near Idyllwild, I experienced a strange foreboding sense of death for myself during a restful weekend. As I was leaving I announced to my parents *"I will either be dead soon or I will live to be eighty and do great things."* My dad was shocked and pooh-poohed my statement, telling me to not say such ridiculous things. But, the sense of death continued.

As a routine matter I went to Planned Parenthood for the first Pap smear I'd had since my earlier D & C at Surgicenter. Lying on the table, I was surprised when an obstetrician was summoned! She examined my belly and announced I had a tumor as large as a four-month-old fetus! "If you don't have surgery immediately it could cut off the ureter connecting the bladder to the kidney!" she said. "You could end up on a kidney machine for the rest of your life!"

I had no health insurance but the doctor arranged admission for me at USC Women's Hospital (a county hospital connected to the University of Southern California). I was scheduled to have surgery in 48 hours *if* I could find four blood donors (required pre-op). My son James came to the rescue, rounding up three of his friends in addition to himself to donate the blood.

Meanwhile, I was on deadline for a magazine story which I completed and delivered. The actors showcase at Jim Byrnes Encino home was held successfully. Within 48 hours, as directed, I waved goodbye to my parents seated in the waiting room as I was wheeled into the operating room of USC Women's Hospital.

That's the last I remember for two weeks!

Fulfilling my prophesy to my parents, just prior to the surgeon's cut I had a heart arrest, was "dead" for five minutes, received heart resuscitation, then had amnesia!

I watched the action of the heart when, in physiology lab at Goucher College, an experiment required my dissecting the chest of a small white rat. Ever so carefully I removed the rib cage to watch the little animal's heart beating. Never again! That experience plus watching medical staff while my baby Ricky was dying and my son Gary with his spinal meningitis necessitating head surgery convinced me I will never go into medicine!

Today I marvel at my niece Cheryl, who is a cardiac nurse and has assisted in open heart surgeries!

The heart is an amazing thing! Think about it—my heart *muscle* has steadily *moved* almost seventy-five years, with each year three hundred and sixty-five days, of twenty four hours, of sixty minutes, many times a minute, and has never stopped to rest except those five minutes when I "flatlined"!

Actually I don't even abuse my heart the way some people do. I don't take alcohol, cigarettes or cholesterol-laden junk food! I have been vegetarian and a bicycle commuter for over five years and I continue to swim laps daily six months out of the year. So why had *my* heart stopped?

I awoke expecting to have an incision and pain in the area of my uterus only to have instead pain over my heart. I was being driven up to Garner Valley by my dad. I gradually perceived I had either been allergic to the anesthesia or had received insufficient oxygen. Either way, my heart had stopped. I would yet have to undergo the surgery but, strangely, the sense of death was gone . Instead I felt joyous! Before I turned eighty I would do great things.

I wrote the following short poem in celebration:

MY POEM IS COMING
You
Who have never died
On the operating table
Due to insufficient oxygen
Or maybe an allergy to anesthesia,

Been pounded and shocked,
Shocked and pounded,
Come alive and hurting
After amnesia
Don't understand.

I was kept alive for a reason.
My poem is coming.

When I got back to my apartment in North Hollywood (my son James drove up to Garner Valley to drive me down), I called my friend Dan Mason who invited me to drive to Hollywood's Old World restaurant on Sunset Blvd.to celebrate. We had a wonderful reunion! After all, I was still alive!

The Old World restaurant is located on a steep hill and when I hugged Dan and bade him goodbye I drove out of the parking lot onto a busy fronting street. Suddenly, the brakes of my Datsun failed! I managed to nurse the car back into the parking lot without getting smashed only to discover(I had been so out of it for so many days) I had no money except one quarter to call for help! I tried the operator, hoping she would summon the police, explaining I had just had a heart arrest, just been released from the hospital! The operator, citing rules, said she could not help. My show biz friends had answering machines. I dared not spend my *only quarter* calling just one friend in Hollywood who might not be home. I finally elected to call a friend likely to be reached. He lived in Northridge (site of the most recent large earthquake) many, many miles north of Los Angeles. Bob Redfield (a friend dating all the way back to Bala Cynwyd Junior High School in Pennsylvania) and his wife Jan drove all the way to Hollywood to drive me home! The next day Bob came back with a U-Haul hitch and towed me to my mechanic in North Hollywood! Talk about being lucky to have such friends!

When my car brakes had been fixed the mechanic informed me on the phone he would not take a check or a credit card due to a small turndown in the economy. So I began a continuing episode of "Perils of Pauline"! I got on my bike to ride four miles to and from my bank for $400 cash to get my car out of hock. However, after only a couple of blocks my bike had flat tires, so at every gas station along the way I had to stop to fill my tires(fortunately air was free in those days)!

When I finally rode the distance(the pain around my heart still great), and successfully got $400, I elected to stop at a grocery to get some items I needed. Without thinking I locked my bike to a rack in front of the store only to come out and discover I did not have the key to the lock! I fetched the grocery store butcher to came out with his giant hack saw to break the lock! I would continue to the mechanic and there retrieve my car. By that time I was laughing and crying! It was a wonder I was not dead! How could one person have so many crises, each topping the other? It was like a Mack Sennett Keystone Cop movie!

Mack Sennett's "Hollywoodland" real estate offices and café are in the Hollywood Hills on the climb to the Hollywood sign. The original sign had thousands of light bulbs (a man had to be employed full time year round to change the light bulbs) and was the beacon for planes reaching America pre LAX lights! The original sign went into ruin and was eventually demolished, pieces of it sold as memorabilia framed and numbered. I purchased one of the keepsakes and gave it to my brother Dick. Curious to get up close to the landmark that had been the scene of a disillusioned actress's suicide, I climbed the wild underbrush hill to the Hollywood sign. Each letter is almost four stories tall!

After my heart arrest, back in my North Hollywood apartment, still groggy I ***moved*** again close to death. I forgot to lock my window on the ground level of my apartment house (common anti-burglary practice in L.A.). I awoke at 3 a.m., walked into the living room and realized my TV, TV game, a set of knives over the stove, plus the contents of my purse were missing! I later realized a tape recorder and my diamond pendant which had been at the foot of my bed were also gone. *A thief must have stood at the bottom of my bed armed with a knife!* Police investigating assured me I was lucky I had not awakened because I would surely be dead or seriously wounded! My natural inclination would have been to blurt out, "What are you doing here?"

Soon I was summoned to USC Women's to be examined by a team of the top doctors who could not determine what had caused the heart arrest. "You look ten years younger than your chronological age!" they said. "You must have an extraordinary amount of natural estrogen!" I had never taken supplemental estrogen so I guess they were right. *What would be my body's next **move**?*

Sixty days later I would undergo surgery awake. The sense of death was no more. Pre-op I was mandated to have a chest x-ray. The technician doing the procedure remarked "Haven't I seen you somewhere before? Were you here recently?"

Part Five
Afternoon

*1986-2001 – Whittier(L.A.) Earthquake,
Persian-Gulf War, New Start*

I cheerily rejoined "I died here two months ago!"

He looked astonished and declared, "That's where I saw you! I was there to x-ray you right after you 'died'! You sure do look better!" People always look better alive and *moving* than dead!

This time there would be only a spinal. I told the surgeon I did not want my ovaries removed unless they showed signs of disease. At one point I remember the doctor holding my giant tumor up on a plate for me to see! I was beginning to feel nauseous as the spinal was wearing off. I asked him about my ovaries and he came to my ear and said "They look like roses!"(which meant they would remain). I could feel the doctor replace part of my intestines before the procedure was completed.

I was picked up from the hospital by my brother Dick and his wife Dorothy, who took me to their beautiful home in Friendly Hills, an elegant part of Whittier, east of Los Angeles(the early home town of Richard Nixon). Pampered there daily, I took walks with Dick and Dorothy's little doxie named Maude. Maude led me down vine and luxuriant flower-covered hills with lush trees. It was a beautiful, peaceful walk and made me feel like I'd been reborn. Caged behind a tall iron fence was a giant black rottweiler dog. The huge dog almost jumped the fence when Maudie and I passed by each day! However, petite Maudie would just walk proudly ahead, protecting me!

Before the heart arrest experience I had **moved** to write an important screen play. Entering into a contract with the Zane Grey Corporation via Zane's son Dr. Loren Grey (with whom I already had a good relationship based on my magazine article he lauded) I wrote about the relationship between Zane and his wife Dolly. Zane Grey *made the mold for the American Western*. He preceded John Wayne in influencing the lives of every American to the present day, to project an image of America and the American West to the far corners of the earth! My screenplay would focus on the *untold story of Zane's affair with his secretary* (Grey actually had several affairs which sorely tested his relationship with his brilliant wife Dolly). Dolly was the sole support of his early career via her trust fund. She eventually became editor of everything he ever wrote and business manager for all his deals with publishers and film makers. My "Zane" project was written up in many of the Hollywood trade press publications. Dr. Grey allowed me full access to the couple's correspondence, took me to see Zane Grey's writing studio in Altadena, California (full of Native American memorabilia, some of which featured the swastika, a Native American icon, not just a Nazi symbol). Dr. Grey also took me to Catalina Island to see Zane Grey's lodge, which is now a hotel. In writing the screenplay, I had a full grasp of the Zane and Dolly locations which included the cabin on the Mongollon Rim in Arizona.

I spent a year off and on writing the screenplay.

Zane Grey loved Arizona to insensibility, then, when Arizona rejected him, he turned his back on his and my "beloved" state for good. His was that kind of passion. Even his brilliant wife Dolly called him a "juggernaut." In my screenplay, Dolly quotes Zane in a bittersweet moment:

"I love wild canyons dry, fragrant, stone-walled, with their green-chocked niches and gold-tipped ramparts. I love to get high on a promontory and gaze for hours out over a vast open desert reach, lonely and grand, with its far-flung distances and its colors. I love the great pine and spruce forests, with their spicy tang and dreamy peach, murmuring streams and wild creatures." (Zane Grey)

After our research year of working together, Dr. Loren Grey wrote the following to me on the first page of collector's item *Zane Grey: the Man and His Work:An Autobiographical Sketch Critical Appreciations & Bibliography* published in 1928 :

> *To Mary, who I believe understands Pa (and perhaps me as*
> *well) as well as anyone I have known as a friend in a long time.*
> *With affection,*
> *Loren*

My dad, meanwhile, by that time was a consultant for a major research corporation in Palo Alto, California. Dad's Garner Valley library (like that of Benjamin Franklin) filled an entire room and reflected his broad literary tastes. My dad wrote below about "Zane"on January 1, 1983:

> *I have just finished your rewrite of Zane. It's GREAT!*
> *This is by far the best you have done, and now the world will*
> *be waiting for more, and more and MORE. As it did for Zane's.*

Just after my hysterectomy I was set on marketing *Zane*. But I had lost many weeks of income and had no immediate income prospects. I had a mountain of debt. It was at this time that my brother Dick and his wife Dorothy offered a grand gesture! They offered to pay off $18,000 of my debt for a 10% interest in my earnings from the Zane Grey screenplay. I gladly accepted their generous offer.

However, the President of the Zane Grey Corporation(final decision maker about the screenplay's destiny) was Loren's neice, Carol Murphy, wife of the Mayor of Tucson, Arizona. She decided the central love affair theme of the screenplay would be damaging to the father-of-the-American-western 's image and might affect not only the Zane Grey book sales (a source of income to the Grey survivors) but also, Mayor Murphy's political career. Mrs. Murphy would not approve the screenplay. By my contract I had to abide by her decision. A year of work was lost as well as my opportunity to repay my brother Dick.

Hollywood modus operendi, like the cacti I collided with climbing the hill to the Hollywood sign, was teaching me many lessons. But, each project I did **moved** me into different worlds, new insights. I was not ready to jump off the top of a four story high Hollywood sign letter yet!

Carpe Diem(Seize the Day)!

I needed to seize the day because death still stalked me.

My dad (unbeknownst to me in one of the most heroic, loving gestures he ever made) had postponed going to Scripps Hospital outside of San Diego for a prostate cancer operation until he knew I would survive my heart arrest and abdominal surgery awake. The third day of my recovery after release from the hospital I was at my brother Dick's house. Dick and Dorothy drove themselves, me and my mother down to San Diego to my dad's bedside. I was shocked to discover indifferent nurses at such a prestigious hospital! For more than an hour post-surgery, Dad was unattended and cold (noone even checked to give him an extra blanket!) and in excruciating pain! *More care had been given me at a Los Angeles county hospital* than he was receiving at a famous icon of medicine! In a rage I stormed the nurses station, demanding that someone come to my anguishing father!

Dad had lived with heart disease for many years, so now he lived with duel great killers—heart disease and cancer. At home in Garner Valley after his two prostate surgeries, Dad took long walks with his beloved collie Mike. He also resumed as much work as his strength allowed. Then one day in North Hollywood I received a phone call from my mom. She had awakened to find my dad in the twin bed next to her–dead. I hastily got in the car and drove from North Hollywood through Palm Desert then up 5000 feet to Garner Valley. Entering—my brother Dick and his wife had already arrived and were attending to practical details—I burst into tears as I held my mom in my arms. I had the curious feeling *I was being watched.* Dad, during his life, had the habit of lurking just out of sight to overhear what family members were saying. I had the feeling he was doing just that as I arrived just following his death.

I read in the Idlewild Town Crier on January 27, 1983:

> …Bob came to Garner Valley from Rancho Santa Fe…he was a very successful business man. Bob was the Vice President of Westinghouse's Sales Division.
>
> …Bob Oliver had style—he had class! You might not have agreed with Bob all of the time, and I didn't, but there was no doubt that here was a man whose opinions were worthy of consideration and thought. Bob was special because he took time.
>
> …Bob showed me his favorite room—his den. In it I saw this man's life reflected in his books, his handsome desk and in the mementoes of a varied and successful career.
>
> Of course I was drawn to the pictures of the Arabian show horses he had invested in. We talked horses, and Bob noticed my gaze wondering to the spectacular view of our valley.
>
> Bob's eyes followed mine, and he told me how much he loved this valley….Bob Oliver was a gentleman and a scholar…
>
> (Sherri Huard, Garner Valley Views)

In rare synergy, Dad's collie Mike died just two days after Dad died.

Dad's memorial service was held January 22, 1983, and in the notes given the family was a poem he'd written in 1975 as a homemade Valentine to my mom (which amazed me, since Dad had confessed at the time of my divorce the love of his life had been the editor of the *Ladies Home Journal*, with whom he'd had the affair when I was still in high school).

The road we've traveled seems to wind like a twisted ribbon...

Up and down-with hairpin turns and rocky cliffs, dangerous slides
and chasms deep with Jagged rocks and foaming torrents racing
down, down, down
only God knows where.
But with it all, we've climbed and climbed past timberline, past
Scrub, and shale-onward and upward. Faltered? Yes, a hundred
Times, and perhaps a hundred times more
But overhead is a clear blue sky with fleecy clouds floating
Gently by, and a golden sun rims the snow-clad peaks and right
At the top, if we make the grade, is a Welcoming Inn and a
Universe spread out below promising much we'll never know...
'Till we reach the top and search our souls for a worthiness
Of what's below.

I never realized my dad was a poet. I refused to offer to view his remains.
Dad was gone.

Moving back and forth in time, deep within my psyche, then out to
American places in and beyond as far as Einstein's relativity and quintessence,
I continued to develop a very special script that would ultimately became
Ordinary Jenny White(OJW). OJW began as *Female From Crash To
Cable* (produced at Alan Miller's Back Alley Theatre in Van Nuys). Set at the
time of the depression, OJW travels deep within the psyche of an American
female who has eight alter egos, four men and four women (perhaps the play
is the precursor of this book), ranging from a pubescent dreamer to a killer:
Lollypop(a little girl living in the dust bowl is Jenny as *dreamer*); Junior
Congressman (a young politician fighting for justice is Jenny the politician);
Shopgirl (a little Jewish girl is Jenny, hormones raging, who wants only to get
married); Speakeasy (an European immigrant guy, buying when everyone else
is selling, is Jenny the opportunist); Fan Dancer (based on famed Sally Rand,
is *eros* Jenny); Bonus Army Vet (an African American character based on
the historic WWI veterans who camped on the Mall in Washington, D.C., to
seek their "just due" during the Depression and were shot at by their own army
is Jenny's betrayal); Al Capone's Henchman (is Jenny as killer); and Humane
(based on the Irish woman who started America's first bread lines is Jenny as
saver and healer).
Jenny is introduced to the audience as her alter-egos phenomologically

dance around her. Rear- screen- projected award-winning photography is projected as totems of each ego as it appears. The egos dress Jenny in icon wardrobe items of themselves. Out of quintessence (in a spotlight on stage) Jenny sees her betrayal—Bonus Army Vet-self, being shot at by his own United States army. This scene is followed by Jenny meeting the same character as a food stamp official who tells her *she is not entitled to food stamps* to feed her children because she hasn't the money to pay the rent. Jenny becomes that ego, feeling intense betrayal. Jenny's saga continues alternating from vivid cognition scenes to Jenny's present until the audience has experienced all eight characters. Jenny in the end realizes all eight are one, all eight are Jenny. She must love all eight parts of herself, find a way to make each part serve the whole and the life force. The egos redress her in her icon wardrobe items as she sings "So goodbye death, now life's come shinin' through! Those people, dreams an' rainbows risin' new. Gonna spread my wings now. Gonna fly, gonna go! Gonna catcha a brass ring, gonna reach, gonna grow!"

The initial production of *Ordinary Jenny White* was at the 99 seat Los Angeles Equity Waiver Night Flight Theatre in Burbank venue (union actors need not be paid scale since the house is a good showcase, i.e. Dan Mason in *Chicago Conspiracy Trial* at the Odyssey above). *Drama Logue* published a casting announcement that I needed eight actors. The so-deep Los Angeles professional talent pool resulted in a turn out of two hundred actors who auditioned for me in a week (all of whom had either Broadway, theatrical motion picture, series, soap, movies of the week, League of Resident Theatres [LORT]credits, plus had studied with major USA coaches, and had either bachelor's degrees or master's degrees in theater). I could cast only eight. I had decided to play Jenny myself, thus *creating a spot for a star to take Jenny if the play went to LORT* and beyond (Actors Equity Association has a rule that the union member who creates a role in a play's development has the right of first refusal as the play moves forward). An African American member of the Mark Taper Ensemble, David McKnight, Vivian Brown (credited with many television dramas) were among the actors I cast, as was Actors Studio member Tony Patellis, who auditioned for the role of Al Capone's Henchman. Tony had great courage! He auditioned with a gun (which he used very creatively as a prop) as the killer character! Handsome singer-actor Dennis Parlotto, already a veteran as the Stage Manager in *A Chorus Line* on Broadway, was cast as the opportunist Speakeasy (after OJW Dennis would go back to Broadway in *Woman of the Year* with Lauren

Bacall). Dan Mason agreed to consult as a director as did Marcia Rodd.

Reviews, (in self-consolation, *Fiddler on the Roof* had terrible reviews the first time out!) except the Hollywood Reporter were mostly bad (though *Variety* wrote "Mizell dominates the stage with able assist from [a listing of all cast members…"]) and the San Fernando press wrote "the real star of the show is Mary Daisy"). One letter I cherished came from Paul Huminek, president of the San Fernando Valley Chapter of Parents Without Partners. He wrote: *"Your play moved us* (Paul's Board of Directors) *to speechlessness. I think you've written a classic. It's about men as well as women."*

Ordinary Jenny White's re-writes went on after the Equity Waiver run. I continued to re-write and re-write the script, interweaving the themes within the mind, the music, the symbolic use of props, in addition to working for the Los Angeles Theatre Center. LATC management gave me the opportunity to do a performance holding book of OJW with Mano Topou (one of the stars of *Indians* on Broadway) directing in one of LATC's new theatres!

The date was January 26, 1986 when OJW **moved** to eclipse reality (life imitates art) The words of my script predicted the horror of what happened! OJW character Lollypop(the *dreamer*) flings herself on the ground, stares up at the heavens and exclaims, "Sometimes at night I look up at the stars and I think I'm going to explode a millions stars high!" That day (a booster leak ignited the fuel, causing the explosion) the Challenger space shuttle blew up seventy-three seconds after lift off, killing all seven crew members—Francis R. Scobee, Michael J. Smith, Judith A. Resnick, Ronald E. McNair, Ellison S. Onizuka, Gregory B. Jarvis, and school teacher Christa McAuliffe—as OJW was being performed on stage.

Dan Mason would write of OJW:

> I attended the staged reading of …*Ordinary Jenny White* at the Los Angeles Theatre Center. What an accomplishment! Congratulations!
>
> During my three years as Artistic Director of the Shelter West Co. in New York City we used the reading format to confirm initial interest in a play. Plays such as yours would definitely have caused excitement.…
>
> When Michael MacLiammor of the State Theatre, Dublin, Ireland, saw my production of *Spoon River Anthology* he exclaimed 'Ah! The first American mystical play.' Your play can

join that company. It is earthy and spiritual and speaks to us all.

Holly Knox, a scholar on Sally Rand, wrote:

> …I am an author concerned with the now historical data part of Mary's subject matter.
>
> "Jenny" identifies with the contemporary woman. It might be she herself or a mother, aunt or other female relative trying to tie up the ends of her spiritual identity.
>
> To me, it plays effortlessly and not without wit and humor, which I found injected subtly by some superb performances. The playwright's efforts to raise a certain psychic awareness are now more than ever, on target.…

Joan Kaluche, working with "Who's Who International"(along with founding international governors John Astor, Warren Avis, Allen Chase and Conrad Hilton)wrote: "[(OJW's egos are]…truly extraordinary and touch the very heart and soul of woman and in so doing are extremely important for men to experience as well."

I traveled to New York City via a referral to leave the script on the doorstep of Jean Campbell, wife of famed anthropologist Joseph Campbell (Joseph Campbell wrote *The Power Of Myth* featured on PBS by Bill Moyers; Jean is a much admired choreographer, plus founder of an Off-Broadway theater, the Open Eye). I waited three days after leaving the script at her home. The phone didn't ring. However, it's 2000 miles between Los Angeles and New York City, so before I left New York I tried reaching her on the phone. She had just returned from Hawaii and insisted she had no time to read a play by an unknown playwright. I continued packing. Much to my surprise, my phone rang two hours later! It was Mrs. Campbell exclaiming "I started your play and couldn't put it down! You write like James Joyce."

Drama critic of the Los Angeles Times Sylvia Drake wrote:"…was fascinated by the content of your letter" when I wrote to Ms. Drake sharing Jean Campbell's remarks. Amie Brockway of The Open Eye New Stagings in New York after reading the play (which I sent at Mrs. Campbell's suggestion) wrote: "I am impressed with the work, and agree with those who have told you that it is not a play which is commercial, but that it has a definite charm, and could work very well in the right theater and with the right artists."

OJW was produced again many years later at the Performing Arts Center in Tempe. By the time of the Tempe, Arizona, production, OJW had theme music composed by Ron Bacon in Los Angeles arranged and performed by extraordinary musician Joe Bousard. Therefore each alter ego had a music variation of the main theme. My friend Betty Lee Herbert (NYC buddy with whom I sought coaching via Stella Adler's sister Francis) was now a painter and Betty Lee (who had had a fine art exhibition in the United States capitol) had a different painting projected for each of the alter egos! The show started with the actors emerging from their separate animal totums behind a scrim for the opening dance around Jenny.

Moving in Hollywood to Have Three Agents

These were a voice over agent, William Morris, who told me plainly that though my talent was super, he would always hire a star if possible since a star's voice is recognizable; a theatrical motion pictures agent; a commercials agent, and a literary manager. I was pleased when my literary manager called to offer me a contract to do a book-for-hire (forsaking all rights for the up-front fee of $10,000). The book would be for the Vice President of the Los Angeles Dodgers, Al Campanis. I went up to the big blue Dodger stadium at 1000 Elysian Park Avenue in Los Angeles to meet Mr. Campanis in his huge office lined with cases of World Series trophies.

Awed by Mr. Campanis' elegant surroundings, I listened to a large, tall, Greek-Italian tell of being multi-lingual in four languages, graduating from New York University and having an early career in teaching. Then the awesome gentleman sitting at the desk facing me described joining the Dodger organization when he became the double-play partner of African American Jackie Robinson, (who was born in the Deep South near Cairo, Georgia, the latter-day home of my Mizell in-laws). Robinson excelled in four sports at the University of California, Los Angeles, and was signed in 1946 by Branch Rickey for the Dodgers' Montreal farm team. In 1947, the fierce competitor/ daring base runner/solid hitter Robinson shattered a major-league precedent when he broke the color barrier by being brought up to Brooklyn. Al Campanis was a close witness to Robinson's triumph as the great athlete led the Dodgers to six World Series appearances in ten years (1947-1956). In 1962, Robinson was the first black to enter the Baseball Hall of Fame.

Al, meanwhile, went from being a player to being a Brooklyn Dodgers/Los

Angeles Dodgers scout before being promoted to management. He signed Sandy Kofax and Tommy LaSorta. In his luxurious office, Al spoke of making speeches using Spanish in Mexico and South America and described going to back lot games where he would watch the pitching arms of young boys to know in less than a minute that they would be great stars.

I sat there pop eyed listening until Al pulled a very old cherished box out of his desk. It was full of memorabilia about his mother, Tulla. Al wanted me to write Tulla's story: Tulla, an unlikely feminist, was a brilliant but uneducated young Greek girl, whose courage, strength, beauty and charm overcame great difficulties to give Al the life he currently enjoyed.

I took the little box home and studied its contents. It had a primitive-English autobiographical diary written by Tulla herself, legal documents from an Italian court, photographs of Tulla as a young woman and of Al's father, Master Sergeant Guiseppe Campani, a member of the elite Italian Bersagliere. I also took home a gift—new baseball signed by both Dodgers players and Al Campanis!

To write Tulla's book was an irresistible challenge (and, of course, I needed the money). I knew I would **move** to a new place and a different time if I took the assignment. But, I could not know how far into history and to a different part of the earth I would go! In three months, aided by the superb research librarians at the downtown central branch of the Los Angeles public library, I— a professional writer—was supplied with eighty articles and forty books to research. One thing that perplexed me at the onset was Tulla's description of riding her horse to the ruins of Hippocrates' hospital (Hippocrates was recognized as the father of medicine, c 460-370 BC). Yet, when I studied current travel guides of Cos (the Greek island that is the site of Tulla's story) no such ruins existed. It would take much additional research to uncover the fact that the *site of Hippocrates' hospital had been covered by an earthquake* decades earlier! In the process I realized Hippocrates' medical focus—that of building strength through diet and hygiene and resorting to more drastic treatment only when necessary, was a Tulla credo, because Tulla herself was healthy and ageless.

I would also do fifty hours of taped interviews with Tulla. The interview part of the research was a great joy, a party! Traditional Greek hostess Tulla would create mouth-watering Greek vegetarian dishes made from cheese, pasta, olives, olive oil, leeks, onions, garlic and green vegetables served with freshly baked breads and desserts. One day, when I was at her house, Tommy LaSorta came to call on "Mama Tulla"!

I had only three months to research and write 100,000 words without the opportunity for on-location research! I worked around the clock (like Edison was reputed to do), night and day, writing some three to four hours, sleeping a couple of hours, then going back to writing for another six. *I began to live inside the heads of my characters* to the extent that when I finally went to the market on my bike I was shocked to discover the modern world around me! One night, about midway in the writing, I was invited by Al to come to Dodger Stadium for dinner. His box was beside the press box and was attended by a valet who brought dinners right to our seats as we watched the game. Danny Kaye, famous UNICEF dancer, actor, and world's children-charmer, stuck his head in the door at one point to say "hello"!

I took one other break from writing at the invitation of a member of my *Ordinary Jenny White* company, Tony Patellis (the actor who audaciously came to my audition with a gun to cop the role of Al Capone's Henchman). Tony's family owned a Greek island near Cos, so he was eager to share his Greek heritage with me. Reminiscent of Anthony Quinn in *Zorba the Greek*, Tony played Greek music for me, narrated slides photographed on his family's island, and cooked me another Greek dinner. (I would later watch Tony marry a beautiful girl who already had *three sets of twins*! Fortunately for Tony, the children were helping to support the family as they were "principals" in Mattel Toys commercials! Tony's wedding took place on the beach at Santa Monica. The Pacific Ocean crashed gloriously at sunset as all the twins plus the bride and groom [looking like black and white stairs going up and down] wore alternating white and black tuxedos).

Another night during my intense living in Cos and Italy in my mind, I was invited to Al's home in Fullerton, California, to meet his large family. While there, Al shared a photo album with me. It was an album of pictures shot of a trip he made to Athens with his wife. The angle of the camera was directed at the throne chairs of the Theatre of Dionysus! I *moved* back to my reincarnation experience!

Having forsaken my rights as a "writer-for-hire," I never had the pleasure of seeing "Tulla" published. It was Al's plan to place *Tulla* in his mother's coffin.

A couple of years after I finished the book, a post-game Al Campanis interview on network television caused a scandal. Al declared "African Americans are not qualified to be managers in major league baseball." Network evening news highlighted the sports shocker that Al had been fired by the Dodgers! The press were in support of Dodger management's decision to fire Al. They made Al appear an uneducated dolt.(which was an untruth based on my knowledge of his background and his family). I believe Mr. Campanis made the comment he did because he used the same razor-thin analysis (of current traditions in major league baseball) employed to find a star baseball player in less than a minute of watching a kid on a dirt lot in Mexico! Decades dedicated to professional baseball caused Al's unfortunate (for him) exposure of the "pecking order" of underling jobs before a baseball candidate is qualified for management. What he said was *not* a racist remark. He was just telling the truth of his time! Since the tragic end of Al's baseball career, African Americans have risen to management.

In *Tulla*, Al's mother, a virgin Greek girl, falls in love and is seduced by a handsome Italian officer occupier of her Greek island of Cos. After impregnating Tulla, her lover is transferred back to the Italian mainland. But, following the birth of Al, Tulla heroically pursues her military lover to Italy. There she finds him involved with another woman. Not defeated, she takes Master Sargeant Campani to court and succeeds in a lawsuit to give Al his father's name. Finally, Tulla must find the resources to escape Mussolini's Italy. She decides to bring young Al to the promise of America. In the final defining moment of the book, Al, a pre-pubescent boy, tugs at his mother's skirts, saying, "Mama, Mama! Who is that lady with the fire in her hand?" "Mama Tulla" and Al, penniless immigrants—speaking no English—are about to enter New York Harbor.

When I finished *Tulla* I collected my final $2500 check but I had not been actively soliciting other work for four months and on-going cost of living ate up my small nest egg quickly. Like all artists (artists require patrons; even Shakespeare required the patronage of the Queen) I re-joined the "working poor." I still had no health insurance. I had a wonderful Datsun now pushing 200,000 miles which had been beautifully maintained by a cherished Israeli mechanic, Shaul, who would find reconditioned parts and personally tend to my car repairs (I found him after the Old World Restaurant post-heart arrest incident) but, by now, repairs were frequent. Nine to five employers are reluctant to hire actors and writers because they fear the next role, the next script will cause actors and writers to quit. We "working poor" of the show biz unions (over 95% are always unemployed) are on roller coaster of economic highs and lows all the time.

A modest mishap to someone who can land on a cushion of nominal security can land a poor person on the pavement, often literally…beyond appraising poverty's causes and effects, so often inventoried for swift, harsh judgement,(all should come) to the deeper understanding that the working poor are really us…Then the questions tend to be about the "hows"—how, we as a country might now act…To appraise a society, [we need to] examine its ability to be self-correcting. (*The New York Times*, Book section, Sunday, February 19, 2004)

I did two things to confront my poverty *again*. First I **moved** to a middle-of-the-night job as a taxi driver—which had its humorous aspects! I was required to check fluids under the hood of the taxi at 5 a.m. with only a flashlight (I really didn't know which hole was for what!). I was required that I get a chauffeur's license so my fingerprints are on record with the city of Los Angeles. I also had to pay a daily up front lease of $100 to Valley Cab. Veteran taxi drivers get the best jobs from the dispatchers—those to LAX round trip from the San Fernando Valley. I had to look for my customers sometimes sitting in front of hotels for hours. I was lucky to pay my lease every day! The good that came from the job was learning to drive streets through canyons instead of taking freeways (which were already bumper to bumper during the week). One day in Studio City, I was driving along Ventura Blvd. toward Sepulveda and was flagged by an Asian couple. They wanted to go back to Universal Studios to catch a carry bus to LAX. To get them there I needed to be heading the opposite direction! I could not turn left anywhere. I attempted to turn right on little side streets over and over again to discover a street that would not allow me to turn left at a traffic light (*I continued to make bright conversation*)but no luck! Meanwhile, the *meter was running!* Keystone Cops again! Finally I headed in the right direction, drove past Lankershim Blvd. to the east gates of Universal only to learn they were locked! I had to turn around, *meter still running,* to speed to the Lankershim entrance of Universal (luckily I was not stopped by a cop), spiraling into the hotel entrance with not a second to lose! The Japanese couple's carry bus was completely boarded and ready to disembark! I couldn't believe it when they paid what the meter read and gave me a $20 tip (they could have gone all the way to LAX for what they paid)! However, that experience convinced me to quit taxi driving!

Secondly I decided to do another book—a book that would be published! A good book idea would be to exonerate Neal Roberts (never indicted) of

Don Bolles' murder! *How naïve I was!* To think I could succeed where ten years of investigative reporters and law enforcement officials had failed! I had not seen, spoken with or even read about Neal since leaving Arizona. It was now the ten-year anniversary since the shocking murder of journalist colleague Don Bolles, whom I met on the trip to Peru. I called Paul Dean, a former investigative reporter with the *Arizona Republic* and now with the *Los Angeles Times*. "Where is Neal Roberts?" I asked.

Paul knew me from his *Arizona Republic* days so he gave me Neal's address. I learned Neal worked as office manager for a law firm located in the historic Luhrs Tower on Jefferson in downtown Phoenix (Luhrs Tower was the one time basement site of all Arizona's microfilmed real estate transactions harvested by our former mentor Fred Eldean). Paul Dean believed: "Neal knows the answer to the as yet unsolved Don Bolles murder. He will someday say 'I've been living with this son-of-a-bitch all these years and this is what happened.'" (*Paul Dean, The Mysterious Man In the Middle, When Neal Roberts got immunity, did he also get away with murder? A New Times Special Report*, June 1986)

Playing heroine(O! How I love the role!) I followed up my phone conversation with Paul by writing a letter to Neal, asking him to meet me to discuss a book. I included my literary resume and tear sheets of published articles.

Phoenix friends Olivia and Buster Quist (she is a one million dollar saleswoman for Russ Lyon realty, her husband Buster is the owner of a successful insurance company and a former Olympic track star) agreed to have me as a houseguest for a couple of days. Their beautiful home is on stilts over a wash on MacDonald Drive in Phoenix. The house is perched not far from the Barry Goldwater house and has spectacular views.

Neal came to pick me up there for our meeting (he was obviously feeling no pain from early-in-the-day alcohol!)

What was I thinking? Why didn't that cause me to STOP immediately?

Neal drove us to the Pink Pony Bar and Restaurant (home of celebrity caricatures created by Disney actor/artist Don Barclay) on Scottsdale Road in Scottsdale.

While we had lunch Neal told me he planned to assume the care of his oldest daughter, Debbie, a schizophrenic. Neal was optimistic about his daughter's improvement while in his care. Debbie Robert's siblings, Blair (a lawyer in Orange County, California) and Kimberly (a housewife in Phoenix) have described her as being a sunny, lovely, honor student and cheerleader at

Sunnyslope High School in North Phoenix, prior to attending the University of Arizona in Tucson for a year. Debbie's schizophrenia had its onset at the time of Don Bolles' murder.

How could I not admire Neal for taking on such an awesome responsibility in addition to his own troubles? His decision magnified my belief in him. Neal's story, I thought, would be not only a fascinating mystery-solving book *if I could uncover new information* but, also a heartrending story of his humanity. Neal, however, appeared circumspect, fearful and tight lipped—not the man I had known from earlier years. At our lunch meeting after I had made the trip from Los Angeles, Neal gave me only permission to do taped interviews with who was his then current attorney, Harry Stewart, and his secretary. I taped the interviews before returning to Los Angeles. I still believed Neal had been misrepresented and abused. I viewed him to be an underdog—a role I could identify with. *I was an underdog too, a single parent without child support.* My Titanic had hit an iceberg (Woody's alcoholism) and I was lucky to be ***moving*** in a lifeboat. *I* was the Bonus Army Vet of my play *Ordinary Jenny White*—Jenny's betrayed self.

During the next ten years of my life, Neal would prove to be an unsolved mystery, my book—the one that would absolve Neal of the crime he is identified with—remained unwritten. "Let all men know thee but no man(or woman) know thee thoroughly" (Benjamin Franklin) could easily be said of Neal. In earlier years, when married to each of his two wives (Lois and Antje) Neal had been the friend of both my husband Woody and me. With his handsome and sexy looks, brilliant mind, charismatic personality, and humanity toward those less fortunate, he had it all!

I ***moved*** into temptation.

Meanwhile, two-thirds of my parents' income had disappeared at the time of Dad's death—Dad's consultant and Social Security income. Therefore, Mom's principal asset, a Garner Valley house, (so remote and so high priced) was listed for three years. Few perspective buyers climbed the 5000 feet from I-10 toward Idylewild to look at the lovely Garner Valley home on twenty-five acres! One person who did come and fell in love with it was Frank Sinatra, Jr.! However, his business manager would not let him buy Mom's house, saying Frank Jr. could not afford both a Beverly Hills house and a mountain getaway. When Mom's house finally sold and commissions and mortgages were paid, proceeds were split between my brothers Dick and Tom (who had financially sustained Mom after Dad died). Beth Claudine Reynolds Oliver for the first time in her adult life ("Betty" to my dad) had to move to a home not owned by her, albeit a beautiful one with a pool. The house was owned by my brother Dick (who now had assets amounting to over $1M) and was only one mile from him in the Friendly Hills area of Whittier, California. Mom invited me to move to her house to save rent. I took her up on it and soon found a job close by at the Universal Publishing Company(publisher of legal and medical directories in the west).

At Mom's house I swam laps every day and continued to do what research I could from a distance on the Neal Roberts book.

For Christmas I drove to Phoenix to see my son Gary and his wife, Lynn. On Christmas eve, in a gesture of good will, I took Neal Roberts and his daughter Debbie the gift of a sand painting (the Native American icon for healing). Neal returned the gesture by inviting me to visit Phoenix over Valentine's Day. I was entertained by the one-time "handsomest man in Phoenix" for dinner at lovely Carefree Inn resort. By the end of that weekend I had succumbed to unmarried Neal's rhetoric (his deep baritone wove wonderful, colorful tales about his parents, his schools, his early years with the Arizona Attorney General's office, Supreme Court Justice Sandra Day O'Connor, Robert Kennedy, Barry Goldwater, anecdote after anecdote), his intellect, and his charm (in 1986 Neal seemed to me to be a "Big" in "Sex and the City"). I learned Neal had to overcome incredible tragedy as a young man to succeed as he had. I found him irresistible. Not only did a book proposal intrigue me (Neal's favorite quote about his proximity to the Don Bolles murder was "I was the invited guest at a gang bang"), but so did Neal himself.

Months later, back in Whittier at about 6:45 a.m., I was typing a letter in Mom's glassed in office overlooking the swimming pool. Mother was out by the pool, watering trees and plants which was her early morning routine. All of a sudden I heard a sound so massive it seemed to explode overhead! I believed for a moment we were victims of another passenger jet crash (one had recently crashed on rooftops in Fullerton)! I was living a perverse nightmare, such was the sheer volume of the sound at that moment! A moment later the floor and walls of mom's house began to *move* and I knew I might die yet again. My mom and I were in the middle of an earthquake! (*The "Big One" earthquake will be a hundred times worse than the Whittier quake I was experiencing because each tenth of a point up on the Richter Scale multiplies times ten*).

I swung my head around to look at my mother. The earth she was standing on was propelling her up and down almost four feet! I had the terrified thought that the earthquake would erupt in the swimming pool sucking her in (Mom couldn't swim!). I ran from my typewriter, grabbed her and pulled her in under the roof. I hugged my mother to me as the air surrounding us filled with flying antique glass from floor to ceiling display shelves.

"I love you, Mom! I love you, Mom! I love you, Mom!" I kept repeating. I was certain we would die.

After an eternity (actually a little over a minute) the movement stopped. Mom and I were standing in a foot of rubble. Seismologists say I ran over the energy of a small atomic bomb to get my mother. The rubble at our feet contained the remains of a 100-year-old-antique china figurine of Mozart playing a piano. The lovely piece of china had been a special and cherished relic to Mother. I watched horrified while she began searching the ground for the hundred pieces of the Mozart china relic all smashed to smithereens. She was trying fruitlessly to place the tiny bits of china together. I thought surely Mother had lost her mind in the trauma. After a few minutes of surveying wreckage inside the house I went into the garage to view cars smothered in everything not secure there. Finally I got one car unburied and drove up to my brother Dick's house to discover he'd had a twenty foot wall of plate glass blown into his large family room. He and his wife were O.K., however.

Back at Mom's house, both Dick and I comforted Mom and learned the next door neighbor's dining room had been destroyed. We went down to the main switch on the street to turn off the gas line. We could get no television! We did not know whether the earthquake's epicenter had been in downtown L.A., resulting in California floating into the Pacific, or was local! Eventually I learned Mom and I had been *only ¾ mile from the epicenter of a 6.9 earthquake*! The earthquake had leveled all the historical buildings in downtown Whittier and left huge gaping holes in the streets! News anchors predicted we had experienced the *"precursor of the 'Big One'"*(which will be along the San Andreas fault).

Hastening to create survival food, water and shelter within the house (our little island of safety), I risked getting on the freeway to drive to work the following day. It was a surreal day of sweltering heat and stillness. That night I went to bed (about 36 hours after the original quake)and at about 3 a.m. the largest aftershock hit! I was awakened to a bed heaving to and fro like a boat in an angry sea. Paintings and lamps crashed on top of me! I screamed to my mom, "Meet me at our survival stash!"

However, by the time she got there it was over. The aftershock caused rafters in the living room to come down, fire place rocks to come loose, water pipes to break, causing a flood and me to grovel on the floor. *God to tell me what I should do!* went through my mind over and over. The answer came quickly and clear. It was vital that I get inland to see my first grandchild (Gary and Lynn were expecting a baby in March). It was urgent that I do important yet unfinished work (I'd been kept alive for a reason after my heart arrest). I urged Mom to drive inland to Arizona with me but she replied, *"Dad is gone. If it is my time I will join him."* She did not want to leave California. She did not want to move again.

So I spent what hours remained before midnight putting everything I could into my Datsun hatchback, slept a couple of hours and began driving in pitch black night. As I drove out of Whittier I was convinced *the Big One would happen,* perhaps even that night! It would crack open the San Andreas fault in Riverside to create a gulch so large my car would fall in! I drove like a maniac all night. Even after I crossed the state line into Arizona I imagined I could feel the earth moving at a rest area. I was by that time a *seismophobic* (a fear of earthquakes)!

"We are made of elements forged in the stars and scattered through space. We are recycled stardust with the gift of consciousness" says John Noble Wilford, *New York Times*, February 13, 2000.

In leaving L.A. in 1986 I turned my back on twenty years of contacts and success in my career (I hadn't "made it," but I had done significant work). I would start all over again from scratch in a punishing market, at least regarding jobs and cultural maturity.

I wasn't the only one who left! Friends soon left too. Dan Mason moved to New York. Big Bill Whitehead(6'5" former football player at SMU), who was in Hollywood when the Whittier earthquake hit, moved back to Texas within a month!

In Phoenix I was fortunate to have the welcome of a series of wonderful friends. I lived at Buster and Olivia Quist's home, Judy and Jerry Chruma's home(see above), and architect Kamal Amin's home. Kamal had designed an energy-saving underground studio and living quarters on a hill lot in Fountain Hills, then built a house on top. A newly arrived immigrant from Egypt in he teens, Kamal had been not only a Taliesin architect but the right hand man to Frank Lloyd Wright before FLW's death (Kamal supervised Wright's funeral both in Wisconsin and in Arizona, and designed the new wing at Taliesin for Mrs. Wright following the funeral). As an independent architect, Kamal had earned an award for the cardiovascular building in Scottsdale on Earl Drive.

His studio was filled with Frank Lloyd Wright memorabilia, his home with beautiful works of art, both gifts from friends, and from his homeland in Egypt. Kamal, who designed the furniture in the dining area at Taliesin, also designed the furniture in his home. His paintings and seragraphs filled the walls.

Meanwhile, my son Gary's wife, Lynn (a 4.0 business graduate from Arizona State University who would earn a 4.0 MBA)left a NCR executive position to start a very successful small business. Lynn employed a dozen women to work part-time cleaning homes in Scottsdale and Moon Valley. I was fortunate to start earning *some income* by doing contract assignments for Lynn.

Time passed quickly to the time of Lynn's confinement. I was still living at the Chruma home and was summoned by Gary to Good Samaritan Hospital. Lynn had gone into labor! Her dad, a former Naval officer and graduate from Annapolis, now a consultant for Salt River Project, drove Gary and Lynn to the hospital. Lynn's mom was sick with the flu so it was Lynn's sister Leigh Cassidy King (a former professional dancer in Las Vegas) and I who sat on the floor outside Good Samaritan's delivery rooms. We waited for what seemed hours to hear the new baby had been born. Occasionally Gary would give us a progress report. Finally he emerged to announce a baby girl had been born! I asked him, "Aren't you exhausted?" (Gary'd had no sleep for thirty-six hours).

He quickly answered "Tired? I'm not tired, Mom! I just had a baby girl!"

Leigh and I were allowed to say "hello" to Lynn and to peek in the window of the nursery as new babies were given eye drops and post delivery care. Gina Marie Mizell (my granddaughter) was the only baby not crying! Instead she reached her little arms toward light sources (new babies cannot see—*did she feel the heat?*). "She's the prettiest baby there!" I exclaimed much to my son's embarrassment (fathers, grandparents, and siblings of all the other babies were also pressing their noses to the window!) I'd only said what was true! Gina was a gorgeous baby!

After Lynn got home I went by to help with baby Gina on Lynn's payroll days. Her employees came to the door all day to collect their checks. One day I was changing my baby granddaughter on her bassinette and singing "Over the Rainbow" softly. All of a sudden, Gina began moving her tiny mouth as I sang! Gina was singing! It was a magic moment! Gina would subsequently belt "This Is the Night" from *Lady and the Tramp* on the top of cocktail tables at age two, rush up on the stage during a senior company rehearsal for her Aunt Leigh's dance recital at age three, become "Miss Petite America for all the

USA Western States" at age 8, and train as a dancer in eleven dance classes a week to the current age of almost 16 years!

More income was needed. I realized I could also take a "janitor's" job, so I cleaned Scottsdale law offices in the middle of the night, which allowed me anonymity plus daylight hours to seek legitimate work and continue my book research.

By then I had moved to an elegant two-story Scottsdale condo owned by Meredith Harless, former Ziegfield girl and widow of Congressman Richard Harless. Moyca Manoil, my *Arizona Living* magazine editor, had graciously referred me to Mrs. Harless.

Kyle Lawson(*Phoenix Gazette* entertainment editor introduced above) would write:

> Introducing a new flat? Give a party!
>
> Mary Mizell, the actress and playwright, hosted a weekend party to "introduce"the condominium she's renting from Meredith Harless. It's a beaut, with Dalis on the wall and a bedroom that's literally in the tree tops, "a perfect place to write," Mary says.
>
> Meredith, a former Ziegfield girl, is the widow of Congressman Richard Harless. We all were oohing over a photo Mary found of Meredith and MGM star Wallace Beery, taken on the set of one of Wallace's films in the 1930s. Meredith looked like a younger, prettier Norma Shearer, and in fact, the resemblance isn't fancied. Her sister worked as Norma's stand-in during Hollywood's Golden era.
>
> Mary's other guests included educator Loretta McCurnin, who couldn't pry her husband, Leo, away from the Pistons-Celtics game; writer Carol Osman Brown, fresh from compiling a history of Greater Phoenix Jewish News, and her husband, Bing, who's with Salt River project; and dancer-choreographer Judy Chruma and her husband, Jerry, an executive with Motorola. Now that Ballet West is no longer bringing its "Nutcracker" to town, Judy is "semi-retired," but the family's still involved with show biz. Their son, Jeff, a keyboardist of promise, is weighing offers from several local bands.
>
> Patricia Myers, columnist for *Phoenix Metro Magazine*, kept

everyone in stitches with her dating adventures. Her latest swain is six-foot-six. "I have a wonderful relationship with his tie rack,"Patricia quipped.

Many months after Gina was born, while on Lynn's payroll I was outside an elegant home in Moon Valley when I saw a garden hose in the driveway. Knowing the home was without occupants I decided to quickly squirt my badly-needing-a-wash car. It was blistering hot, at least 110 degrees. I was wearing "zoris"—slip-on shoes, and as I rounded the corner, I moved too fast. My feet slipped in water which drained from the hose onto the pavement. I went up in the air! Maybe I pointed my toes (the result of early Martha Graham dance training) because I came down squarely on the cement on my left shoulder! The moment of impact was the first and last time I've consciously realized *I have a skeleton*! I could feel every bone in my body vibrate.

Waves of pain stunned and paralyzed me. I could not move for at least a half hour. I simply laid in the pooling water. Finally, moving an inch at a time in excruciating pain, I dragged myself into the strange house I had come to clean. I telephoned Lynn, canceling the morning's assignment. Then (miraculously the blow was taken on the left shoulder since I am right handed), I somehow drove myself home. By evening my entire arm was so swollen, so black and blue I drove to Maricopa County Medical Center in south Phoenix (I had no health insurance), where I sat most of the night waiting to be seen. Eventually some very kind, competent physicians plus x-ray technicians examined me. I had broken my shoulder. It was as if a knife had sliced my shoulder cleanly across the top. Doctors could do nothing except give me a sparkling white sling to hold the arm up, allowing two sides of the bone to mend, plus a prescription for pain.

Recovering at the Harless condo (still wearing a sling for my shoulder while cleaning law offices in the middle of the night with only one arm) Lon Carli, the Arizona President of Screen Actors Guild (1987-1990),who had been a pre-Los Angeles student of mine, knocked on my door. When Lon saw my white sling and learned of my broken shoulder he urged me to swim every day in spite of the pain. "If you don't," he said "your arm could freeze in that position and you'll never be able to get it over your head." I took his advice immediately and six weeks later, when my physical therapy was to start the therapist found I did not need it! I'd been getting my arm over my head for a couple of weeks!

Ron believed me to be a great acting coach. "You should begin teaching actors again!" he urged and promised to refer some SAG actors to me. I took his advice. Starting all over again in a punishing market for the entertainment industry, I went back to square one, but I was grateful for any work! Gary's sister- in-law's dance studio—Leigh Cassidy King's Dance Center—had begun operations a year earlier. I paid Leigh a small percentage of my fees to use her space for an acting workshop. I began making presentations in schools about the workshop. Leigh had a great professional dancer's background, having worked with choreographer Bob Fosse and danced professionally in Vegas for twelve years. She married entertainer-producer Sammy King. The couple had their own private plane and did shows in Paris, France, until their daughter Christy reached school age. That's when Leigh decided to become a homeowner in Phoenix and start her dance studio. Over the ensuing years, Leigh Cassidy King's Dance Centre dancers would be featured on *Star Search*, employed on cruise ships and in Vegas shows (her own daughter, Christy King, a genius dancer with a perfect dancer's body, worked in Vegas immediately upon graduating from high school). One of Leigh's studio dancers was admitted to the American Ballet Theatre in New York City. Today Leigh's recitals are *shows* (for which students purchase up to $1000 in costumes), produced with $10,000 rented lighting equipment, special effects and headliners from Las Vegas. Leigh's husband Sammy King (currently producing in Palm Beach) acts as technical director. Eventually Gary's wife Lynn would become Leigh's marketing director.

For me, classes at Leigh's studio would be a *quiet beginning* to what would grow to be 501©(3) tax-exempt Actors Workout Inc., an Arizona theater corporation, now almost twelve years old.

Meanwhile, I continued to do research to enable a Neal Roberts book.

The playwright Tennessee Williams said: "Life is an unanswered question, but, let's still believe in the dignity and importance of the question." In spite of Tennessee's actual life, which had many sordid episodes, much loneliness and grief, Marie St. Just (Tennesee's great friend and author of *Five O'Clock Angel* about her experiences [including their exchanged correspondence] with him) created a truer profile of his many works and friendships than his own autobiography. Yet, I realize now I did *not* love many parts of Neal Roberts! The Bible says you cannot love God and Mammon (the Devil) at the same time, so I was in an agony of conflict much of the time I was with him. I realize I hated, was repulsed, and horrified by some of what he was and told me, yet I loved his rhetoric, his "thirst for righteousness," his essential generosity, his overcoming terrible tragedy as a youth, his huge intellect when he was sober, and of course (until he completely destroyed them with alcohol) his handsome looks.

So I *move* to tell the skeleton story of Neal Roberts according to the Bible: "Judge not that you be not judged" (Matthew 7:1).

"[Love] does not rejoice at *wrong* but rejoices in the *right*" (I Cor 13:6).

Wrongs:1)Neal's maternal grandmother—married four times, once to a Native American—had no time to rear Neal's beautiful, brilliant mother Vernetta Sweet (who was reared in Montana by her grandmother).

Rights:1)United States President Zachary Taylor (12th USA President 1849-1850),"old rough and ready"(Mexican War hero), was Neal's paternal ancestor. Samuel Mitchell Taylor, a lawyer, was his great-grandfather.

Wrongs:2) Vernetta graduated cum laude from the University of Southern California at age 17 (as a brilliant mathematician she interfaced with Einstein)but may have fathered Neal with John Wayne (a USC football star) while John did a film in Montana. Neal's resemblance to John Wayne in looks and movement was striking.

Rights: 2) Nathaniel Taylor Roberts of Pine Bluff, Arkansas, graduated from Annapolis, hastily married Vernetta, eloping. Wedding revealed in Pine Bluff tea. "Taylor"(from Zachery) was a "perfect gentleman but hard as nails"(Yearbook~2 years rowing) at the Naval Academy.

Wrongs: 3) Neal, a "fat military brat," at five years old came downstairs to the living room following one of his parents' parties and drank all the alcohol remaining in about twenty glasses—thus very possibly becoming a child alcoholic.

Rights: 3) Neal (b. 7-23-1931) grew up under the care of grandmother in Pine Bluff and his great- grandmother in Montana (Vernetta's grandmother) while his dad served in the Navy during WWII, reputedly shooting down four Japanese planes from the deck of his ship under attack (the Navy had no record of Taylor's heroism when I attempted research). Vernetta taught math away from Neal.

Wrongs: 4) After the war, Taylor and Vernetta moved into the beautiful Encanto area of Phoenix. Neal attended Kenilworth School. When in third grade at Kenilworth School he was told by his mother the reason a certain teacher abused him verbally was because Taylor was having an affair with Neal's teacher. When another teacher criticized the South, Neal dumped a can of red paint on her from a balcony, but Neal's mother arranged that he be excused without punishment.

Rights: 4) Vernetta and a good friend created the rose garden adjacent to Encanto Park on Palm Lane and 15th Avenue. The beautiful rose garden is now a city park.

Wrongs: 5) Neal began drinking alcohol and having sexual relations secretly in Encanto Park at age 12.

Rights: 5) Vernetta began breeding dogs for show, keeping pups in cellar.

Wrongs: 6) Taylor attacked a man who complimented Vernetta when the family was out to dinner, throwing the man through a plate glass window. Taylor was acquitted in resulting lawsuit and bragged to Neal that he could "kill the President of the United States and get away."

Rights: 6) Neal grew tall and thin as a teen, overachieving in math via his mother's tutoring and began his amazing life as an athlete.

Wrongs: 7) At North High, Neal graduated in the same 1948 class with Max Dunlap (convicted and in prison for the Don Bolles murder). Vernetta revealed to Neal the identity of Neal's illegitimate sister (fathered by Taylor), who also attended North High.

Rights:7) Neal was a basketball star. Neal took a "big brother" protective role over his half sister.

Wrongs: 8) While visiting his "Aunt" Beverly (who was actually his father's cousin)in Pine Bluff, Arkansa, Neal accidently ignited a vacant lot grass fire and burned his entire body, resulting in months of hospitalization.

Rights: 8) Beverly and her husband Howard became surrogate parents and confidants to Neal.

Wrongs: 9) As Neal began his freshman year at Phoenix College (PC) Taylor knocked Neal twenty feet when he was in a hurry to get to basketball practice instead of helping Vernetta in the garden. Vernetta had a stroke.

Rights: 9) Neal was a basketball and tennis star, a journalist for the PC campus newspaper, and won the Golden Gloves.

Wrongs: 10) According to a 1948 *Arizona Republic* news story, Neal, "then 18, had wanted to give his invalid mother a goodbye kiss. Instead he met violent death face to face. Taylor Roberts, 41-year-old operator of Roberts Sales Company plasticraft store at 3242 N. Third St., and his wife Vernetta, 37, were dead. Mrs. Roberts, who according to yellowed news paper clippings, had suffered a stroke the previous December, lay on her bed. She had been shot once in the head. Taylor Roberts reportedly died of a gunshot wound to the mouth. The apparent death weapon was found beneath his body on the bedroom floor."
"I saw my parents' brains smeared on the walls"(Neal testimony).

Rights:10) Neal would be "adopted" by nearby Willo district family, the Blairs, parents of one of his best friends. He would subsequently name his only son Blair. His friends at PC rallied around him, electing him President of the Men's Club. He was also a Beta Phi Gamma national journalistic honorary fraternity and Club 13 member.

Wrongs: 11) "Secretary of State Wesley Bolin—who was coroner at the time—labeled the deaths murder and suicide and did not call for an inquest." (1948 *Arizona Republic* news story)

Rights: 11) Taylor left a suicide note saying family was "broke"and he could not continue paying Vernetta's medical expenses. He left $5,500 and Vernetta's insurance benefits to Neal.

Wrongs: 12) After being offered several basketball college scholarships and choosing the University of Arkansas because he was guaranteed a car, a job on the college paper, and all tuition and board expense paid, Neal went with his team to New Orleans where the team was "entertained" after the game at a whore house.

Rights: 12) Neal accelerated to a degree at Arkansas and was accepted at University of Arizona Law School, Tucson, where he was a Member of Phi Delta Phi, the National Law Fraternity. He graduated 2nd in his class.

Wrongs: 13) Neal was a notorious womanizer throughout college and law school.

Rights: 13) Neal was already a father upon graduation (Debbie) having married Lois while still a student.

Wrongs:14) Neal learned to "torture" suspects by handcuffing them to a pipe and banging on it to get confessions on his first job in the Arizona Attorney General's office.

Rights: 14) Neal did all the trial work in the Attorney general's office to create the I-17 freeway. He bought a home in Sunny Slope, fathered Kimberly(girl) and Blair (boy). Horse owners and summer beach house goers, the Roberts were among the "in"crowd of Phoenix. Lois and Neal came to the Mizells home on Jack Rabbit Lane for silk-screened Christmas cards and wall hanging making. Neal visited Barry Goldwater at Young Phoenix's Men meeting. He joined Harry Stewart and John Flinn in a law partnership in the Luhrs Tower. John Flinn argued successfully the Miranda case before the Supreme Court. Neal also argued cases before the Supreme Court and was a friend of now Supreme Court Justice Sandra Day O'Conner. Neal was a Naval Reserve Attorney, serving trials on board ships in San Diego.

Wrongs: 15) Neal's clients included Harold Friend and the Baptist Foundation(later involved in fraud and misuse of investor funds (*New Times*, July 2-8, 1998). Neal's expensive El Dorado automobiles and stays at a Lake Havasu hotel were in lieu of cash payments to avoid taxes.

Rights: 15) Neal raised a large percentage of the funds to build Orangewood Presbyterian Church in Phoenix.

Wrongs: 16) Lois Roberts divorces Neal based on his adultery with secretary Arlene Lyons. He is visited often by old school chum Max Dunlap and Ivanhoe Bar drinking chum John Adamson.

Rights: 16) Neal buys guest ranch north of Phoenix to entertain his children while a bachelor. He meets and weds German model Antje, gains luxurious cabin in White Mountains with a "wrap around pool" and office in Spanish complex at 90 W. Virginia in Phoenix. I become close friends with the beautiful (inside and out) Antje and swim there often. Neal is a private pilot. Antje almost dies in hospital from a blood clot.

Wrongs: Neal again commits adultery with Arlene Lyons.

Moving through an Explosion(from Chapter One)

*The sun gets very hot in Arizona in the summer. Hot enough to fry an egg on the pavement they say though I've never tried it. That's because our small part of the earth in Arizona is tilted more toward the sun and closer to the sun in its orbit on the days of 115 degrees. It was on a frying-egg-on-the-pavement day that a bomb exploded under a car killing Phoenix, Arizona investigative reporter Don Bolles who'd been reporting on the mob, shattering his body so badly he died in days. I was at Surgi Center undergoing a diagnostic and therapeudic D & C for a troublesome fibroid tumor and as I was coming into consciousness from the anesthesia I heard an announcer on the radio say "Investigative reporter....has been rushed to the hospital in a critical condition after a bomb exploded under his car!" "I know him!" I cried out. Like a circle psychic energy I not only knew him, but was **moved** after the fact, into the vortex of one of the darkest dramas that ever occurred in Phoenix.*

There was a Big Bang 13 million years ago when all matter burst into superclusters of galaxies and billions of sun-stars!

Wrongs: 17) The day Don Bolles is murdered (June 2, 1976) both Max Dunlap and John Adamson are at Neal's offices shortly before the murder. Neal flies Adamson to Lake Havasu that night(documented in Phoenix and national press)

Rights: 17) Neal's former law partner John Flinn is hired by Neal. Flinn gets

Neal immunity for his testimony which protects him "if he didn't lie." Antje loans Neal $10,000 to hire Flinn and sues for divorce based on Neal's adultery with Arlene Lyons.

Wrongs:18) Neal was indicted and convicted with James Robeson of (co-defendant of Don Bolles murder)bombing a building owned by Native Americans so he could collect the insurance.

Rights: 18) Neal was acquitted of the bombing in appeal to higher San Diego circuit court. Neal was represented by Harry Stewart.

Fast forward to Christmas1985, Valentine's Day 1986, the Whittier earthquake when I returned to Phoenix to live, the hospitality of good friends who welcomed me to their homes, survival jobs, cleaning offices in the middle of the night with a broken shoulder, teaching actors again, learning to know Neal as a confidant, paying $98 for Neal's FBI file (my right as per the Freedom of Information Act, received August 20, 1996) but uncovering no new facts about the Don Bolles murder(Neal's file was threaded with black overlinings—information I could not read).

Ted Schwartz (author of *The Hillside Strangler*) created a meeting between Neal and me at the Five 'N Diner on 16th Street in Phoenix because he wanted to do Neal's version of the Don Bolles' murder but, there was no new information to uncover.

Over the years, in addition to being the beneficiary of Neal's love of cooking (he always wanted to "get me fed") and his love of animals (Neal was the one who brought Halloween, a tiny, stray black kitty with a tubal pregnancy, into my life, paying the vet bill for her operation), I watched while the Bar Association attempt to save Neal by sending him to alcohol rehab in Sedona. I watched while he lost the use of his legs from supposed multiple sclerosis (later diagnosed by doctors while I was present as alcohol poisoning). I watched while he was arrested and imprisoned for a year for failure to appear for a lenient "hotel" sentence for DUIs (a legal perk arranged by a friendly lawyer which would have meant Neal would spend the night in jail for a month instead of prison for a year). I watched while he continued to drink until he drank himself to death (1999). His beloved daughter Debbie, who helped care for him when he was a complete invalid, died a year later. His daughter

Kimberly (like her maternal grandmother Vernetta) had a debilitating stroke as a young woman, but continues to have a productive life, active in the Orangewood Presbyterian church, mother to her teenage son Dylan, who is a student and actor at Sunnyslope High School. Neal's son Blair, a tennis pro in Orange County for many years, graduated from law school, married and is the father of a son by his wife Ginger's first marriage, plus a daughter and son of his own. Blair continues to adore his dad. Neal's multiple sclerosis diagnosis secured a large insurance policy's proceeds be paid to Debbie. Upon Debbie's death the large proceeds of Neal's only asset went to Lois (Debbie's legal guardian while she was alive). Lois can be credited with keeping Blair enriched with goals!

Neal was a Damon Runyon character who loved ovations. He created his own Damon Runyan cast of characters day in and day out. Handsome as he was, with his beautiful baritone voice and rich imagination, Neal would have made a great actor! Triumphing as he did early in his life over horrific events, his enormous gifts were eventually wasted. I believe his proclivity for dark bars at the end of his life must have been a return to the womb. Having lost his good name, his body, his useful work, he ultimately had nothing to live for and knowingly killed himself with alcohol. The power to make a life had to come from Neal reaching for and connecting with the Higher Power. Of course, *I* was powerless to help him! I couldn't even write his story!

In a dream I had after his death, I was in the midst of a room that was cluttered with mess and dirt. I worked and worked to clean it but I felt sad and lost. I left, but when I returned I entered a room where I saw Neal's clothes with money and wallet strewn casually over a surface (as was his custom). It was clear Neal had been there looking *for me*. Maybe Neal (with the heritage he had from Vernetta and Taylor) never had a chance! Maybe, now that he is gone he has a chance. *Is* there anything new under the sun? What goes around comes around!

My inheritance from Neal in addition to his wonderful phrase used frequently, "Truth will rise above fiction like oil above water," is the following letter (written during one of the few times Neal was totally sober—in prison):

> *Dear Mary,*
> *I have read and reread Frankel's* The Meaning of Love *and* The Meaning of Suffering [I had recommended Frankel's book knowing he was imprisoned in a Nazi concentration camp during WWII]. *It is difficult to not agree with his reasoning and his*

theories. Logotherapy is a practice that deserves much credit and is probably being greatly accepted.

Frankly I am sorry I did not become more acquainted with his words before now. Your personal potentials are beyond belief and no one could brag on them more than this one particular guy.

It is a shame my life went so asunder, but at least I gave it (with the exception of you) a good shot. It obviously wasn't the best and usually not the most pleasant, but if nothing else interesting. I have regrets for some of my behavior and no platitudes for myself. On the other hand, I have no regrets with one notable exception. You. I never expressed to you my appreciation for your efforts, compassion and most of all love. Please forgive me and accept them now and may [it] last with you forever.

As you know I want your project [Actors Workout, Inc.] to succeed and give you the fulfillment you so richly deserve. Noone has worked harder and is more entitled.

Wish the kitten [Halloween] and your family Happy Valentine's Day for me.

All my love. Happy Valentine's Day.
Neal

Why am *I* so lucky to still ***move*** up and down, back and forth, round and round, in and out of life on this planet?

Part Six
Sunset

*2001-2004 – 9-11, Afghanistan War,
Actors Workout,Inc.*

While I was watching Neal's refusal of alcoholism-recovery(denial) speed him toward death, I (having been in Al Anon for seven years prior to divorce from Woody) worked on my the "project" Neal mentions in his letter (Actors Workout, Inc.).

Ever since homo sapiens achieved consciousness, it has been said the sun rises in the east and sets in the west, but you and I know that's not what happens! *We are riding on a giant spaceship, going round and round in circles all the time, right side up then upside down*! We know when our part of earth faces away from the sun we don't fall off because a giant magnet holds us to terra firma (except when there's an earthquake!). Our talents are like that miraculous gravity magnet, *moving* us all the time, keeping us from falling off into oblivion. Throughout my adult life I have needed my miraculous gravity talents to keep me from falling into oblivion over and over again!

I have been reading the autobiography of Vanessa Redgrave. Ms. Redgrave, frustrated after three years of disciplined study and graduation from traditional British-drama-focused Central School of Drama in London, searched for new ways to practice her craft, exciting ways to become a better artist. From age 14 she had had the opportunity to bike ride country roads to experience Shakespeare's plays at prestigious Stratford-upon-Avon as the daughter of British star Michael Redgrave. Yet, she came to new insights about acting when she read *An Actor Prepares* by Stanislavski. She then learned of New York City's Group Theatre using Stanislavski's way of working. Later, as the guest of her father, who was performing on Broadway, she attended classes at the Actors Studio.

Acting is not just getting a new life. It's getting a new self. Acting for me began in my grandmother's back yard in Omaha. I was allowed to wear grandmother's wedding dress and create "shows" using her sheets drying on the back clothes line as curtains. I had all the open space of her back yard to play my drama! (from the beginning of Mary Daisy's *Moving*)

I learned to love audiences and audience ovations when I danced with my brother Bob at Lincoln, Nebraska hotels when I was five years old. Love of acting, actors and audiences is my gravity.

Directing began in the same back yard when I plucked the blossom off a hollyhock, pealed the green cap away from the stem to expose the holes, plucked a hollyhock bud with a bit of stem and inserted it in the hole making a lovely lady with a long colorful skirt! With several of these homemade hollyhock dolls moved about I created stories. As I grew older I also created hours long dramas with paper dolls. (from the beginning of Mary Daisy's *Moving*)

I had directed many shows before 1992—all the youth shows I script-doctored and did with music and dance as a Young Players sole proprietor with Judy Chruma as choreographer and Dianne Kay (later a principal in the "Eight Is Enough"television series) performing over six years progressively larger roles; *Weep Twice*, the play at the Scottsdale Players; *Weep Twice*, the 3-camera television shoot at CH 5 (now CBS in Phoenix) with Nick Nolte; all the shows I directed for the Orme School Fine Arts Festival final night in the Horsecollar Theatre (later named the Buck Hart Horsecollar Theatre for the former headmaster there who joined AW after he retired), plus125 actors in the industrial film *Orme School Revisited*, narrated by James Stewart; *The Pied Piper* at the Phoenix Little Theatre (now the Phoenix Theatre) with Sarah Rice (later on Broadway with Angela Lansbury in*Sweeney Todd*); *Flea In Her Ear* at the Performing Arts Center in Phoenix, produced by the pros who took Nick Nolte to Equity Waiver in Los Angeles; *Female From Crash To Cable* at the Back Alley Theatre in Van Nuys, CA.; a performance holding book of my screenplay *Reaching*, moderated by Robert Reylea, producer of *Sophie's Choice*, at the American Film Institute in Hollywood; and a performance holding book of *Reaching* at Leigh Cassidy King's DanceCentre in Phoenix, December 19, 1988.

In 1989, Tony Shepherd came over to Phoenix's Hotel Biltmore for another jointly produced Tony Shepherd Actors Seminar which included a performance holding book of *Ordinary Jenny White*. In Phoenix (counseled by the President of Screen Actor Guild Lon Carli to begin coaching actors again) I named the Phoenix talent in my workshops—Actors Workout(AW).

Then (remembering the $1 a year arrangement the Los Angeles Actors Theatre had with Bank of America for space at Santa Monica and Western in Hollywood) I made a deal with management at el Pedregal, north of Phoenix at the Boulders near Carefree and Cave Creek (bedroom communities created by our mentor Fred Eldean). El Pedregal is an open adobe arena, festooned with flags of many colors, surrounded by two stories of elegant shops, art galleries and restaurants. According to the AW–el Pedregal agreement, AW had the use of an open air arena plus one of the leasable stores(until it rented) for theatres!

In 1991 I staged *The Itchy Feet Run*, (IFR), which was a repertory of short plays highlighted by Los Angeles "Best Actor" Dan Mason's award winning *LIT 305*. Dan, my cherished friend and colleague, agreed to teach a seminar of acting classes and do his award-winning show for $1000! So at el Pedregal in the open store space he shared techniques gleaned from the prima donna of acting coaches—Uta Hagen plus Michael Chekhov (Russian playwright and Anton Chekhov's nephew).

Below is the review of Dan's *LIT 305* which was directed (as in the Los Angeles production)by his close friend and colleague Guy Giarrizzo:

> Written by Ralph Hunt(professor at the University of Ohio in Mansfield), *LIT 305* features the bravura performance of Dan Mason as a literature professor frustrated by many things: an educational system that does not educate; his wife's affair; the world's rejection of his poetry; and his denial of tenure by the university…Mason's acting ability and range of emotions is amazing. His moods turn on a dime, and his uncanny performance of a man about to step over the edge eerily unnerving. (Christopher McPherson, *The Phoenix Gazette*, May 29, 1991)

The beginnings of Actors Workout are inseparable from my theatre/film beginnings. Great theater, the weaving together of optical, aural and emotional threads, is joined at the hip to spirituality.

Itchy Feet Run 1991 would also feature under my direction my play *Football Baby* (from taped interviews with twenty professional and college football players in Los Angeles). I created a truly controversial play about abortion. *Football Baby* would receive both glowing praise (from Planned Parenthood pro-choice advocates who urged me to get the play to all middle and high school age youth) and damnation(from pro-life people). Tennessee Williams' *Mooney's Kid Don't Cry*, *The Lady Of Larkspur Lotion*, and *This Property Is Condemned*; plus Susan Kander's *Millie* and a new play, *Where Nightingales Used To Sing* from the playwrights group at the Back Alley Theatre in Van Nuys, California, completed the list of works. Quite an ambitious offering for a start up organization!

For IFR–el Pedregal–June, 1992 Actors Workout, Inc.(now incorporated as an Arizona non-profit theater) produced Sam Shepard's *Fool For Love* (Buck Hart, now retired as the Headmaster of the Orme School, played the father). Under my direction, Actors Equity Association (AEA) actor Fred Sugerman performed *Christ Sermon On the Mount* in the outdoor courtyard, utilizing lush trees, flowers, shrubbery and sky as set pieces (Fred's toddler daughter Kaya and my 4-and-a-half- year-old granddaughter Gina did bit parts in the show). The show enjoyed a half page picture story in the *Arizona Republic* religious section. Later, AW and Fred would team up on *Christ Sermon On The Mount* via an Actors Equity Association contract in Phoenix during *Sunday On Central* and in North Scottsdale. Still later Fred would take his interpretation of Matthew 5 and 6—centered on Jesus' teachings—to Central Park in New York City (Mel Gibson's awesome 2004 The Passion of Christ lacks of Jesus' teachings). Fred Sugerman (a Jew) had long hair (in 1992) and a swarthy complexion. Without makeup or additional head or facial hair, Fred amazingly resembled centuries of religious art!

My Aunt Gladys (a poet published in the *Ladies Home Journal*) *told me one day I'd written a poem when I declared in Grandma Daisy's backyard "The sky has taken off its old grey dress and put on its beautiful blue one!"* (from the beginning of Mary Daisy's "Moving")

Writing plays was a natural outgrowth of my need to make words. I had written a youth environmental play—*Pipe Dreams*—while still in Los Angeles. The play elicited the support of the Los Angeles Unified School District but I left in the wake of the earthquake before I could gain funding to produce it. However, in the IFR's June 1992 period, a first workshop production of *Pipe Dreams* took place on the Saturday morning of the first weekend. Fred Sugerman played the bad guy-boss of polluted earth in *Pipe Dreams* (genuine actor that he is)!

Mayor Herb Drinkwater of Scottsdale wrote after the morning performance of *Pipe Dreams*: "On Saturday, June 13, I truly wish I could be two places at the same time. 'Pipe Dreams' sounds like a terrific show and noone is more supportive of getting our youth together and cleaning up the environment than I am…"

My new granddaughter Gina, at 4 and a half, came to *Pipe Dreams* with her dad (her mother Lynn would give birth to my grandson Dan in a few months and did not attend). After the show, Gina exclaimed:*"Pipe Dreams* is the best show I've ever seen!" She then went home and drew all the characters (evidence of the impact the show had on her young mind)!

Moving AW into tax-exempt status via *Pipe Dreams*

In February, I filed for Actors Workout, Inc.'s tax-exempt status. Believing *Pipe Dreams* needed as much funding as I could raise (though I had no lawyer or CPA) I spent over $800 in two weeks publishing AW's articles of incorporation three times, making long distance calls, packaging big mailings, and faxing answers to the regional IRS office. *In March 1993, I convinced the IRS AW deserved to be tax exempt~501©(3)!*

"Fools rush in where angels dare to tread." I had total naivete about non profit arts funding! Though the Arizona Department of Education/Health Services had already pledged to give AW $3000 for a production of *Pipe Dreams*, the city of Tempe $1000 (via my daughter Melanie's environmental colleague Mayor Harry Mitchell), and St. Joseph's Hospital environmental department $1000, the total *Pipe Dreams* budget with grants and grants in kind came to $31,000.

The cutting edge achievements of the Hubble telescope confirm *Pipe Dreams* plot line, i.e. we humans are part of an unimaginable whole, miraculously alive on earth! (Proof: a)Orion Nebula images that confirm the births of planets around newborn stars; b) Eagle Nebula images showing where stars are born; c) "Deep Field" images in which Hubble peered back in time more than 10 billion years to reveal at least 1,500 galaxies at various stages of development.) But we earthlings will not only find it *possible* but *may be forced to move to outer space due to earth's pollution*! However, *Pipe Dreams* StarPiper returns to earth with love and hope at the end of my play!

In *Pipe Dreams*, ideographs of earth and space roll out as AW bridges the gap between earth and space, between rich and poor, between races, between entertainment and education (AW's mission). Animals dance through the audience. A Scrooge-like "I Hate Life" character, whose nickname is "Boss," is Mayor of Last Tree Falls, Earthlack, Cosmos. He steals the people's gold, pollutes the water with toxic wastes, the air with fossil fuels, stacks the landfills to overflowing, despoils the forests, and so junks up Last Tree Falls *all the animals, birds and wildlife have left*! A homeless cripple, Handi, (with a surprise father) witnesses when a leader's mind "is full of junk his town is full of junk." Book lover Teacher files a class action lawsuit because toxic waste from airplanes has been sprayed on Last Tree Falls! Boss continues to rule Last Tree Falls like a rat. One soul only, "Speak To The Grass," can magically get "diamonds bright" water, plant and grow in a metaphysical place. Teacher declares (speaking to Speak To The Grass)"You are 70% water!" And her response "And there is no place to drink!" Speak to the Grass *sees* an educational opportunity in a virtual habitat, a heaven- on-earth, profit-making vacation place—Ecosphere Trip—with Xeriscape gardens. Kids will want to visit Ecosphere Trip as much as Disneyland! She attempts to sell Boss on her idea as a way to capitalize on the multi-billion dollar kid market, but Boss won't buy it.

Eventually Teacher (who has fallen in love with Speak To The Grass) decides the only way to save life on earth is to leave it! It is 2007 and time for the first space flight to Mars where water is suspected to have existed! "I'll lead you to a promise land. Light years away, a dream at hand. Where we can live, love, work and play in freedom and order every day." When all life is gone and Boss has only the gold he has stolen, Boss realizes earth is empty as death. Teacher-StarPiper sees Boss' remorse on his space ship computer. He decides to bring life back to earth in a do or die last chance: The company and audience sing and dance throughout the open space in the finale! "I've led you to a promised land, light years away, a dream at hand, where we can live, love, work and pray to save our planet every day."

Pipe Dreams started on its long journey beginning with a first tour in metro-Phoenix—where it played Scottsdale Civic Center Amphitheatre, Margaret Hance Hance Park in Phoenix, Kawanis Park in Tempe, the Glendale Amphitheatre and the Arizona State Fair. The show, authored and directed by me, was performed by professional actors, dancers, and technicians and was a triumph of producer-director-company-crew-sponsors-venues teamwork, manifested in setting up and striking in the five different venues, playing to 4000 school children in five days! *Pipe Dreams* was covered by three television stations featured on nightly news and videotaped by a full crew and remote truck cable television organization.

The following was among the plaudits for *Pipe Dreams* from city councilwoman (later Mayor of Scottsdale) Sam Campana:"I so enjoyed the performance on Sunday. ....Continued success on the road and on TV! Hugs-Sam(Sam is a lady!)

Don Dustin, director, Performing Arts, Los Angeles Unified School District wrote:"….Should you secure funding, our school district would be interested in acting as a host city for this project."

The following year AW won Mayor Rimsza's environmental award Honorable Mention, competing against such giants as the Salt River Project. The award was presented by now Mayor Phil Gordon. Receiving the award at the San Carlos Hotel in Phoenix were me and Mayor of Tempe Harry Mitchell(who arranged a loan of Tempe's PA system and staff to the city of Scottsdale for Scottsdale's *Pipe Dreams* performance when AW's budget could not cover outdoor PA).

A grant from the Harris Foundation allowed AW to implement a 2000 *Pipe Dreams* tour to 80% African & Hispanic students. The second *Pipe Dreams* tour starred Tarah Paige dancing the Bird of Life and choreographing the animals who dance in the audience. Tarah auditioned for me in the middle of a summer doing dangerous flips and turns plus Irish dance on the cement driveway in front of my office studio in the Willo district! Tarah Paige (who had moments in her solo that made my spine tingle) is the #1 gymnast in Arizona, #18 elite gymnast out of 200,000 USA featured in Sidney during the Olympics. Tarah played a 5000-seat Texas house during the summer of 2002 and L.A.'s Crystal Cathedral for the Christmas show December 2002. She was in the top ten finalists among a field of 1000 for ABC's *All American Girl*, and the #1 dancer for MGM Grand, Las Vegas, in 2003. She is currently in production as an actress performing a lead role in a direct-to-video independent film, *The Clintons* (not the presidential couple).

For *Pipe Dreams'* second tour I sought the opinion of an environmental scientist regarding the script— Wayne Roth Nelson, PhD (from the University of London). Below is what he wrote:

Dear Mary,

I thank you for sending a review copy of your script for "Pipe Dreams." As an environmental health scientist and sometime poet I was excited to find the play blends voices that speak to both science and poetry. And of course to the cruel politics of using and abusing our little blue planet called home.

Your script of passionate dialogue and vivid metaphors reveals many hot-button issues of science and politics touching on our whole ecosphere. I am referring to issues of survival that are not the special domain of scientists and politicians—killing off rain forests, exhausting ocean fisheries. The play uses character stereotypes—Boss and Speak to the Grass and others—to enliven these issues.

Your play also hammers the misconception that humanity can engineer its survival by means of so-called enlightened self-interest, lusting for personal and corporate wealth. Instead, what the ecosphere needs NOW is a swelling public soul to overwhelm private greed. "Pipe Dreams" seems to me an instrument for helping to grow that public soul.

Such a transformation may begin with audiences experiencing how our natural home as animals in the cosmos is so battered by dehumanizing corporations, by the mentality embodied in the character of Boss. You make this conflict accessible in what I view as a modern morality tale like a Punch and Judy show that engages the minds of everyone.

So much of science that starts out unflinchingly honest is deformed by politics, even by scientists themselves whose work may be crippled by their addiction to research grants that twist their findings under the thumb of Boss. The ideas of science need the acid test of public exposure, as in the theater, to keep science honest and truly useful.

My best regards and hope for your efforts to help grow the public soul.

Sincerely,

Wayne Roth-Nelson

Moving AW to Historic Heritage Square, Pioneer Living History Museum, Cave Creek

After *Pipe Dreams*'s first tour in October of 1993, AW was invited to be the honored troupe to perform at the Centennial celebration at Historic Heritage Square located at Monroe and 7th Streets in downtown Phoenix. *Women Pioneers* (a five-character, one female actor show based on the diaries of the women who came West on the covered wagon) was performed by actress/lawyer/judge Lauren Eiler. *Western Heroes* andd *Abraham Lincoln* were performed by Emmy-winner Richard Blake. Richard had performed *Abraham Lincoln* 4000 times across America, including at the

Ford's Theatre in Washington, D.C. I sought and gained the use of over a thousand dollars-valued turn-of-the-century props that were utilized by the actors as they changed character, layering on and off wardrobe items, changing positions of cubes, and selecting scene props in full view of the audience (Lauren went from being a pubescent bride to the "Pathfinder" on her way across America in a covered wagon, to being a woman watching family members die from cholera then in the midst of an Indian attack, to portraying a prostitute in Jerome, Arizona, to evolving to the mature young wife of the "Pathfinder," hanging her lawyer husband's sign on the shack of her western home!) The actors performed body miked at noon out of doors for four months. *Women Pioneers* was booked for a special performance to a group of visiting Japanese in Cave Creek and both *Women Pioneers* and *Western Heroes* played the Pioneer Living History Museum north of Phoenix.

I continued to create a superb senior company—ome I trained in my acting workshops, some were already union members or had theater degrees and paid credits. I found grant-in-kind venues so all funds would not be used for rent). Debt-free AW played not only Carefree's el Pedregal, Scottsdale's Civic Center Mall Amphitheatre, Glendale's Amphitheatre, Tempe's Kwanis Park, Margaret Hance Park in Phoenix, the Arizona State Fair, Phoenix Heritage Square, NW Phoenix's Pioneer Living History Museum, Cave Creek's town center, but also Phoenix Stetter Gallery, Tempe's Performing Arts Center, the Phoenix site of the Arizona School for the Arts, Phoenix's Burton Barr Library, Phoenix College, a church to benefit the Sun Lakes Association, Scottsdale Center for the Arts (as part of the GET OUT EXPO for three times), Scottsdale's Kerr Cultural Center(owned by Arizona State University), the Authors Café on Goldwater Blvd. in Scottsdale; and City of Mesa Library. I marketed only via publicity (not paid advertising because there were never funds available to buy broadcast and print ads). I wrote grant after grant, winning only a few. Without a big bank balance or a fund-raising board, AW continued to do new, indigenous work!

AW's long range goal is to change Phoenix from being a buyer of product to being a seller of *product.*

Moving Aw to Downtown Gallery and Mary Daisy to a Bike

The Stetter Gallery at 1115 N. Second Street, just south of the present Burton Barr Library was the next stop for AW. In April and May of 1994, AW produced Lauren Eiler's *Women Pioneers*, the IFR's *Mooney's Kid Don't Cry* with Tom Janssen and Kim Roberts plus *Where Nightingale's Used To Sing* with Elizabeth Sheffer, *Scenes From 'Taming of the Shrew'* with beautiful actor-dancer Tamara Jonasn, and *Lassiter* (inspired by Zane Grey's *Riders of the Purple Sage*) with Don Logan.

During that season I made the front page of the Central Phoenix Community section of the *Arizona Republic* in pictures and story *moving* in an old fashioned way!

"Daisy, Daisy, give your answer do!…You'll look sweet upon the seat of a bicycle…":

No Auto, No Problem: with Bike and Bus,
Busy Woman Doesn't Miss Her Car
By Alfredo Azula

Mary Daisy became a bicycle commuter by default.

When her car was wrecked by an uninsured motorist last fall, she looked around for alternatives to buying another automobile. [It was the final straw after having to put three transmissions in a "gently used" Nissan in three years, I found I was $8000 poorer with no asset to show for it!]

"I was kind of sad about it for a few days and then I got on my bike and the bus, and I've been there ever since," she said.

Daisy rides her bicycle to her job as a director of a lunchtime series of plays at a downtown art gallery and runs errands.

"It's like I've gone back in time to when I lived in New York, working as an actress, walking, riding the bus, subwaying everywhere," she said. "Or when I was studying at ASU [Arizona State University] I left my car at the stadium and I would bike all around campus. I've really enjoyed it."

Daisy is one of thousands of Phoenix who are using two-wheelers as transportation.

Surveys conducted by Maricopa county officials indicate that 3 to 4 percent of Phoenicians use a bicycle to commute at least once a week.

Riding the bicycle as part of a daily routine has many benefits, Daisy said. She's got an automatic exercise routine. Riding, Daisy says, gives her time to relax her mind. She doesn't have to fight traffic [on a recent trip to Tucson in a rented car, I found I missed being on the bus where I could take a midday nap during the trip!]. And she's saving money that would have been spent on car payments, insurance and repairs.

"I also feel very, very good I'm not polluting the environment with a massive polluting object," she said.

Phoenix is one of the few cities in America with 2 bike racks on all the buses. When light rail arrives (underground utilities are already being laid under Central Avenue) by 2006, each car will carry 16 bicycles! I do about ten miles a week on my bike. That's 520 miles a year or 5200 miles in ten years (one and a half times across America!)

Moving into Tempe Performing Arts Center and Prestigious Rehearsal Space

AW gained the top floor of the Wells Fargo Bank tower downtown as a grant in kind training and rehearsal space, but AW's venue after the Stetter Gallery was the rented Tempe Performing Arts Center for a production of *Ordinary Jenny White*. It was Albert Einstein who said, "Imagination is more important than knowledge." I believe my *Ordinary Jenny White* is an *awake dream which continues to imagine itself!* Every one of Jenny's eight alter-egos in the Tempe Performing Arts production had its own a painting rear screen projected, created by my New York City chum Betty Lee Herbert who had a show in the Washington, D. C. Capitol rotunda and has a painting designated for the Louvre. Each ego had a variation of the theme music arranged by talented musician-arranger Joe Bousard!

After seeing the show a letter came from then President of the American Association of University Women, Cindy Holmes, dated June 18, 1996:

"…Seeing…. your youthful troupe gave me an insight into your ability to bring out the talent of up and comers…."

Moving to Free Performances for the Underserved at Church of the White Spire

Max McQueen, the entertainment editor of the *Tribune* papers, knowing AW paid steep rent at the Tempe Performing Arts Center suggested AW seek grant-in-kind space from the Congregational Church of the White Spire (CWS), home of the successful Arizona School For the Arts charter school, near the Phoenix Burton Barr Library. Pastor Steve Wayles agreed that no admission in exchange for use of space would be fair. Many performances-holding-book plus occasional full costume productions were staged so church members, students, underserved and the surrounding community could see a show free. A season of staged readings patterned on the series I participated in at the American Film Institute in Los Angeles set the pace for years of shows. Tarah Paige (who had performed in *Pipe Dreams*)came to AW at that time. Tarah starred in *The Naked Eye*, a screenplay-holding-book, which rehearsed at CWS then performed at Phoenix College sponsored by PC's screenplay writing department. Sean Boone, a youthful Sammy Davis, Jr. clone-hyphenate actor-dancer-singer(what an astonishing voice!), performed the title role in a black staged reading of my screenplay *Reaching* (*Reaching* had had an all white cast at the American Film Institute in Los Angeles and at Leigh Cassidy King's DanceCentre in Phoenix).

Also seen in a performance holding book was *An' If That Mockingbird Don't Sing* by my Los Angeles friend Bill Whitehead, "Best Playwright In Texas." *An' If That Mockingbird Don't Sing* had had a very successful production in Los Angeles Equity Waiver in addition to the Alley in Houston. It is the poignant story of a country western singer during the time of the Civil Rights movement in the South. AW's production starred Ann Margaret look-alike Margie Ghigo (who is on the national board of AFTRA and has performed as a singer and dancer on the same bill with Rosemary Clooney). Again, the production was rehearsed at CWS then performed in open space adjacent to Arconsanti handcrafted bells on the second level of the Burton Barr Public Library. Playwright Bill Whitehead sent a beautiful large bouquet of flowers to the company for the production. The show deserves a full production!

All the world is AW's stage, which is AW's slogan, declares all living souls on earth are one!

"We are made of elements forged in the stars and scattered through space. We are recycled stardust with the gift of consciousness," says John Noble Wilford, (*New York Times*, February 13, 2000).

Having created the slogan and believing what it implies, I sought rights from successful Hollywood writer Jeb Rosebrook (*Junior Bonner, Gambler III, A Hobo's Christmas*, segments of *The Waltons*, and the CBS *Miracle On 34th Street*) and Wolper Productions in Hollywood to do a performance-holding-book of *I Will Fight No More Forever* (the story of Nez Perce Chief Joseph's heroic flight to freedom). Doing the show meant recruiting Native American actors via Arizona State University, the Heard Museum and leader in the Native community, Robert Tree Cody (concert floutist who performed to standing ovation audiences at the Scottsdale Center For The Arts, plus at the command of the Queen of England, then later did AW's performance holding book of *Floaters* at Phoenix College). The recruiting took a long time because Native Americans in the Phoenix market are professional artists, dancers, and floutists, but have had no training as actors. More than twenty Natives were called for in Jeb Rosebrook's script. Randy Kemp(Choctaw-Yuchi-Creek actor-fine artist [with works in museums and galleries across America] and floutist), Petur Redbird(Creek-Seminole actor-dancer [pictured on a giant mural at the Oklahoma state capital, part of Discover Native America dancers at the Atlanta 1996 Olympics, featured in the Don Contreres hard cover, full color *We Dance Because We Can* book]), and Shannon Rivers (Pima-Yaque Sundancer/manager of Gila River displays [controlling 41 billboards entering Phoenix]) trained to take the major roles and to double up on bit parts. They also brought family members to do extras and contributed authentic costumes valued at thousands of dollars for the Native dance in the show, i.e. Petur Redbird's costume of brown feathers that spectacularly went from his forehead to his ankles.

I Will Fight No More Forever was staged in March of 1998. Buck Hart also starred as the American General Howard, Chief Joseph's adversary. Jeb Rosebrook wrote after the performance:

A note of congratulations to you and Actors Workout for the marvelous performance of I Will Fight No More Forever on Monday night.

Considering the actors had but three rehearsals and the job you had to do to combine parts, the end result was superb.

I agree with you...the screenplay, adapted for the stage environment, would make a powerful play; one in which Native Americans could take great pride, and one from which the rest of our country can learn from, as a lesson of today, as much or more so than it was just over a century ago.

The stage presentation...would utilize mixed media of photographs from the actual event, and a musical score, Native American in origin and spirit which would give the play the tone it so deserves.

Again, my congratulations to you and a wonderful cast. I do hope we will get a chance to work again.

Randy Kemp, coupled with Delphine Tsinajinnie,(Navajo performance artist with past performances in California, Utah, Martin Luthur King events, the Arizona State Senate, on CD and on cruise ships) would later star at CWS in *Grandfather/Grandmother*, from authentic documents and AW developmental improvisations. The show, which featured the remarkable vocal talent of Delphine, whose big singing voice fills huge spaces, also revealed the trauma of young Indians being taken from their homes on the reservation to attend schools hundreds of miles away. Natives move into an integrated society with difficulty and continue to find their spiritual roots on the reservation.

When AW was sought for the first September 7, 2000, Tribune Newspapers sponsored GET OUT EXPO, it was AW's Native American company that took center stage at the Scottsdale Center For The Arts to much acclaim.

Actor-fine artist-floutist Randy Kemp would use segments from both *I Will Fight No More Forever* (he starred as Chief Joseph) and *Grandfather-Grandmother* to perform a one-man show in November 2003 at the Mesa, Arizona central library. This time AW would utilize Randy's fine art as rear screen scenery for his monologues. AW Board member Laraine Correll, Arts Librarian for the City of Mesa wrote: "Randy's performance was flawless as he drew the audience into a special place with his artwork, acting and music."

Randy has also contributed art for AW special events.

Moving to Create AW's Vision for the Future via Board Members and Prestigious Volunteers

Sports are very prioritized in Phoenix! One of the persons who pioneered sports venues via broadcast journalism was one time professional baseball player-turned-sports-announcer Bill Denney. His winning personality, personal appearances in metro-Phoenix over two decades plus his on-air coverage of the Fiesta Bowl, America West Arena, and Bank One Ballpark caused me to visualize conjoining sport and theater (think the Olympics and the Theatre of Dionysus in Athens where I had my reincarnation experience) by seeking Bill Denney as AW's President. I knew Bill from earlier PR days, when I worked for the Arizona Association of Industries. Bill accepted my offer and served as AW's president for three years until his untimely death. Philip Carpenter, vice president of the First Interstate Bank (merged now with Wells Fargo Bank), gifted AW $1000 to pay for liability insurance and was AW's treasurer. Philip arranged AW grant-in-kind training and rehearsal space on the entire top floor of the Wells Fargo Tower in downtown Phoenix! Philip also arranged use of Wells Fargo copy machines to print programs, flyers, etc., saving AW thousands of dollars annually. Bill Denney and I went to my friend Kamal Amin (the architect who had been a right hand man to Frank Lloyd Wright), asking him if he would design a theatre-sound stage cultural center for the twenty-first century.

This was the first step in a long journey toward AW's now goal to create tax-exempt Actors Workout Community Land Trust that will lease land to profit investors of Theatre For The New Millennium, began at AW's Original 80 Dinner catered by Nick Ligadakis' in Scottsdale. An unveiling of Kamal's design, which would wind like a sea shell underground, was unveiled to the guests. Max McQueen of the Tribune Newspapers gave Theatre For The New Millennium its first major feature story—"A THEATRE FOR THE 21ST CENTURY: Actors Workout founder Daisy plans a solar facility for the new millennium" followed by Kyle Lawson's full page picture feature entitled:

"THE DREAM THAT'S DRIVING MISS DAISY:

Actress aims to raise funds for theater, arts center."

The caption under Kyle's picture of Kamal's plans reads: "The site of the theater for the New Millennium in the Valley has not been chosen, but plans for the facility are on the drawing board."

A quote from Goethe appeared near my photo: "Whatever you can do or dream you can do, begin it. Boldness has genius, power, and magic in it."

The Original 80 Dinner program bore the following by T. S. Eliot: "We must not cease from exploration and the end of all our exploring will be to arrive where we began and to know the place for the first time."

Tax attorney Bob Ciancola, who attended the Original 80 dinner with his wife, wrote:

> *I wanted to write to tell you how much my wife Vera and I enjoyed the "Origial 80" dinner on June 14. It was stimulating to have an entertainer seated at each table and quite a surprise to see what appeared to be ordinary "guests" suddenly spring into action during the evening, breaking out into song, dance comedy and dramatic readings. They are truly some of the most talented people we have ever witnessed and it was a unique opportunity to mingle and converse with them.*
>
> *One of the truly inspiring things was to observe the diversity of the entertainers, ranging from a practicing physician to an Olympic athlete. Especially memorable to me was a talented Native American actor who played traditional wood flute and gave a dramatic reading as Chief Joseph in I Will Fight No More Forever (Randy Kemp), and one of the most beautiful "Irish" tenor voices I have ever heard, coming from a young man who only moments before was simply enjoying his meal with the rest of us (Sean Kersh). If Actors Workout can showcase people such as these and provide venues, experience and coaching for the as-yet undiscovered talent in our community, it will surely be fulfilling an important mission.*

Bob Ciancola would later nominate me as Arts Advocate of the Year at the Business Volunteers For The Arts Awards breakfast.

Shortly after the Original 80 Dinner, I traveled to Washington, D.C., where I was the house guest of my Goucher College friend who introduced me to classical music—Aida Schoenfeld. "Curly" (the daughter of an ambassador who served in five different foreign countries) knew Washington, D.C. well so she was a great hostess! She directed me to the Russell Senate office building where I visited the office of my own senator, John McCain(who was not present) but, it was fascinating to eat in the cafeteria where United States lawmakers ate. The next day we visited the National Cathedral, where Curly served as a docent. As we were leaving we saw a bridal couple entering the sanctuary against the wind—a sign for never-before-wed Curly, enamored with her not-yet-affianced beau! She would soon marry her "Reddy"! The wedding took place in the National Cathedral! During my visit Curly me drove by the Vietnam Memorial and treated me to a sumptuous lunch in Georgetown.

Before I made the D.C. trip I had corresponded with Librarian of Congress, James Billington. "Jim"invited me to join a school chum of my brother Bob, Clarke Nash, for an elegant luncheon served on the deck of the Library of Congress overlooking the United States Capitol! In the course of the luncheon, when I mentioned my work with Native American actors, Jim volunteered information that the Library of Congress has an entire floor of original Native photographs and documents (that opportunely could be utilized as rear screen projections in a staged production about Chief Joseph or the Navajo *Long Walk*–a play I am interested in authoring). Jim also had one of his assistants take me to the Library of Congress internet center and the chance to examine up close(I wearing provided white gloves) original letters written by *my sixth cousin Abraham Lincoln* while a guard stood by!

I also traveled to the Big Apple for a Circle in the Square Seminar with Jose Quintero, *Long Day's Journey Into Night* Broadway director, via a grant and the housing hospitality of Dan Mason.

That Thanksgiving of 1998, during rehearsals of the second production of *A Christmas Carol With Music & Dance*, which also starred Buck Hart, I was invited to my son Gary and Joanne's split level home for dinner. Gary's home had white carpeting throughout, so visitors were asked to go Oriental by taking their shoes off at the door! In my stocking feet I started running to the lower level, calling "Happy Thanksgiving!" to my grandchildren Gina and Dan! But life spun out of control on the first landing! I began to *move*, sliding down the flight of stairs on the carpet faster and faster. A wall loomed ahead. I was going to crash into it with my whole body. To break the impact I must have instinctively stuck my left foot out! When I picked it up, through the skin, my fingers realized *the foot was no longer on the leg*! My grandchildren screamed for their dad as unbearable pain exploded where the foot should have been connected to the leg. Not knowing what had happened, Gary suggested I move to the couch. Finally he realized he'd better contact my primary care physician. While I lay on the couch my little grandson Dan came to me and asked so very sweetly "Would you like a glass of water, Mar?" (I'll never forget his charming offer of help).Gary had to almost carry me up the stairs and to his car for a trip to the emergency room of the closest hospital.

When x-rays were finally developed I learned I had the worst possible break! Ortho surgery would be required to put my foot back on my leg with pins and screws! No Thanksgiving dinner that day!

In a cast sitting in a wheelchair with a walker close by, packed in ice (I was unable to put weight on my left leg for six weeks) I directed an eight-hour rehearsal of *A Christmas Carol With Music & Dance*! The show was performed four times. Nick Ligadakis(from the Original 80 Dinner) provided sack lunches for about two hundred homeless children who were bused to the performances by AW volunteers.

Since my office studio was the leased top of a house in the Willo District of Phoenix, any coming and going was by moving one step at a time on my rear end! When I had been in physical therapy for several weeks I was finally given an ortho boot. It came time to get back on my bike but the ortho boot extended way beyond the bicycle pedal! I was truly scared when I first tried it and scared again when I hoisted my bike onto a bike rack on the metro bus still wearing my big ortho boot. Finally I was max terrified at the intersection of Central Avenue and Osborn in Phoenix when a fifty mile cross wind blew me (in my ortho boot) and my bicycle into the right lane of south moving traffic! Fortunately there was no car coming because I had *moved* again toward death.

That winter, in addition to *Grandfather/Grandmother*, AW produced *Freedom* (nominated for Drama Beat Choice "Best Actor" award), a one-man show which starred Chinese-American Ty Ng, whom I trained as an actor for a year. The brilliant Ty had won the USA Entrepreneur of the year award for his computer business and would go from *Freedom* to get an Off Broadway show and to join SAG. I wrote *Freedom* with scene after scene in which Ty performed alone, using Chinese traditional movement, props and costumes, tracing his own grandfather being imprisoned by the Communists on the mainland, to the first Chinese mayor of Phoenix, to a freedom fighter in Tiananmen Square being murdered on top of a tank, and finally to Ty himself accepting the Entrepreneur of the Year award in Washington, D.C.!

Meanwhile, I had written another full length play inspired by a brilliant investigative reporter working as a contributer to *Phoenix New Times*. One thing that constantly *moves* on the planet is water!

My play *Water*, (in a developmental performance-holding-book January 24, 1999) starred Dan Mason (who flew in from New York City for the booking), Margie Ghigo, Petur Redbird, Faith Hibbs-Clark (beautiful hyphenate actor-coach-writer-publisher-now talent agent, who had performed with a Chicago Equity company prior to her work in Phoenix) and David Richardson (whom I trained as an actor-an international motivational speaker/climber of Mt. Everest) and John Collins, Ph.D. in Theatre, veteran of six years of AW shows, whose big baritone voice narrated *Water*.

For the *Water* program I wrote:

Water, the odorless, colorless, transparent liquid is the most abundant substance on earth! In solid form(ice)and liquid form it covers about 70% of the earth's surface! Why must we care so deeply about preserving it in pure form? Isn't it everywhere? Under us, over us? Could the disappearance of water be the reason the Hohokam(pre-historic native American people, for which the Phoenix bird is an icon, and modern Phoenix a metaphor)-who lived here long before our New Millennium Information Age- vanished? Water is not only the most abundant nutrient found in the body(accounting for roughly 2/3 of body weight, it also by far is the most important nutrient. Responsible for and involved in nearly every body process including digestion, absorption, circulation, and execretion, water is the primary transporter of nutrients throughout the body, is necessary for all building functions of the body, helps maintain a normal body temperature and is essential for carrying water material out of the body. The average adult body contains approximately 45 quarts of water and loses about 3 quarts of water daily. In desert climates (such as Phoenix) it can lose as much as 10 quarts daily. "The famed Ray Bradbury (*Arizona Republic*, January 1, 1999) declared "Arizona will keep improving and making space for all of America, which is going to come…the continent is sliding toward (Arizona)." And the archeologist Bostwick countered "It all revolves around water in the desert."

I had long been attracted to Ibsen's *An Enemy Of the People*. An environmental play about the struggle between polluted water and the profit motive in a small European town(whose tourist income depended upon a falsely advertised 'healing spring'). Terry Greene Sterling's award-winning *New Times* articles about Phoenix groundwater pollution, plus her courage in researching the theme for 10 months and going public with the facts (that Arizona's largest employer, Motorola, allowed by the state of Arizona to police itself regarding cleanup, has polluted the ground water table under Phoenix for the next hundred years) motivated me to write this fiction based on investigative reporting play about one Phoenix couple's lives and conflicting goals against the big picture of the moral and spiritual evolution of homo sapiens….

My fictional play was also based on the true story of my husband Woody's work as a contract graphics designer for Motorola at the same time our Jack Rabbit house used water from a well in the plume of Motorola contaminated water and the subsequent death of our baby Ricky from neuroblastoma cancer.

Dan Mason had just returned from Edinburgh where he performed a triumphant *LIT 305* and would go on to a Broadway production of *Amadeus* directed by Sir Peter Hall, Director National Theatre of Great Britain.

Water audience member Millicent Duffy wrote: "I was fortunate enough to be an audience member on January 25th at the Church of the White Spire when your play *Water* was performed. It was a truly memorable evening of theater. The play was so crisply paced in it's direction that I felt I had not enough time to savor some of your lines, and wonder if the script is available for sale? If it has not yet been published, could I perhaps arrange to buy a copy from you?"

Water deserves a full production.

The entire nation was in front of television sets through election midnight in November of 2000. I awoke in the middle of the night the morning after the election, turned on the television and learned George W. Bush had won the election despite losing the popular vote by over a million votes. Then, weeks later, when Florida's decision was made by only 527 votes, I learned partisan Supreme Court Justice Sandra Day O'Conner (from my own state of Arizona) had cast 1 vote that elected a United States President! It was like death. It seemed the entire meaning of our American democracy had been mocked.

Moving to Create AW Salons

In spite of that pervasive feeling of death, I was ever eager to experiment with new ideas. I remembered the thrill I had experienced as a young acting student in New York City's Greenwich to an unusual-talk-of-the-town restaurant. The restaurant was famous for its gourmet food and was owned by former opera singers. In the middle of our entrée I was surprised to see one of the owners clamber up on top of the table next to us and sing an aria!

That moment inspired me to *move* Actors Workout out to Goldwater Blvd. in Scottsdale for a series of eleven once-a -month salons at renowned chef-humanitarian Nick Ligadakis' tiny (only 26 seats) bakery-café. Nick had attained his reputation for superb Greek dishes and pastries via piloting a series of ever bigger restaurants including the downtown San Carlos Hotel (where AW received its environmental award from now Phoenix Mayor Phil Gordon). Every pre-Thanksgiving Nick made news in all the metro Phoenix broadcast and press by closing his restaurant (with an ever increasing group of volunteers and turkey donors) to prepare up to 2000 Thanksgiving dinners for the homeless!

Now Nick, who had authored several self-published books which he retailed in creative ways, had elected to have a small venue, the Authors Café (which displayed his and other self-published authors' books) in the midst of Scottsdale art galleries, where patrons could have soups, salads, simple entrees, or a mouth watering dessert (from a hundred choices in his display case!). Using the Greenwich Village restaurant as a model I envisioned Actors Workout professional artists performing short shows right in the midst of the diners! After the show I would pass the hat (a custom observed by entertainers on London street corners) collecting enough to give the talent (guaranteed by pre-show contract) $50 as an honorarium, plus an equal or larger donation for AW. These salons would require no overhead expense with advance costs being only publicity, programs and my time to direct the talent. Thus AW's superb multi-cultural talent base would be served and develop.

AW had done 1998 and 1999 *showcases* at CWS (which included once a champion skateboard artist employed by "Got Milk" in California who, as StarPiper from *Pipe Dreams*, did turns in the air when the character StarPiper leads all life off earth!) so AW's first salon featured March 6, 2001 used a showcase format (see the Original 80 Dinner Bob Ciancola letter).

The star talent in publicity and in the event was Ray Anderson, arguably America's #1 interpreter of Teddy Roosevelt (also AW's talent offering in the GET OUT EXPO September, 2001, complimented by soprano singer Merrill Leffmann, who interpreted Anna Roosevelt in her *Alice Blue Gown*). Ray, a spitting image in face and body of the President who urged us to save Grand Canyon "for our children and our children's children" plays Teddy to a 5000 seat Medora, North Dakato house every summer during tourist season, plus does a one-actor show *Bully* in a smaller house there. Recently Ray performed Teddy at Mt. Rushmore! Ray, therefore, has acquired his own turn-of-the-century Rough Riders wardrobe as well a Presidential top coat and striped pants for performances. When Ray did "Bully" for the AW's first Salon audience they were dumbstruck by the quality AW offered for a small donation in addition to enjoying superb food!

Month after month, the salons continued, interlaced with the April tour of *Pipe Dreams*, which was performed first on Earth Day at the Kerr Cultural Center in Scottsdale then to 2000 80% Hispanic and African American middle school students at Palo Verde Middle School in Phoenix.

Moving AW to 9-11

It was to be an exciting return salon September 11, 2001 when Native American Randy Kemp(Choctaw-Yuchi-Creek) would perform a scene with his daughter Rykelle (talented young actress-fine artist studying at Glendale College) from a show they had performed in the lobby of the Frank Lloyd Wright Grady Gammage auditorium at Arizona State University coupled with drums and an additional monologue performed by Shannon Rivers. Shannon was Keith's actor colleague from *I Will Fight No More Forever*. In the interim Shannon had gone on to be cast in Hallmark Hall of Fame's *Lost Child* and to perform a theater role in Scottsdale for playwright Dale Westerman (*One Flew Over the Cockoo's Nest* playwright).

That morning I got an unbelievable phone call from Shannon Rivers. "Turn on your television, Mary Daisy! America's being invaded!"

I couldn't comprehend what he was saying at first but did as he asked. And there, before my eyes, were the World Trade Towers, one already in smoke and flames from the first airplane. I saw live the second airplane crash and called my dear friend and colleague Dan who was in New York! He was terrified but, for the moment safe, because he had been warned before he took the subway to ground zero for an innocent audition appointment. I watched horrified as the twin towers fell one by one, then as another plane crashed into the Pentagon and into remote Pennsylvania. Via e-mails I learned my son Gary was in Las Vegas and cut off from driving home to Scottsdale since Hoover Dam had been closed and that (by the grace of God) my brother Tom (now CEO of Holiday Inns Worldwide~Six Continent Hotels), who normally circled the globe, was mercifully in Atlanta and safe. I learned Shannon's mother was grounded somewhere in America. As the day wore on I had to make a decision about whether to hold the salon at Nick's Authors Café that night.

The New York Times, Sunday, September 23, 2001, published the following which is how I felt about continuing with the show for whatever audience might come to the Authors Café: "The most noticeable change to which dramatists have awakened is the possibility that theater matters. In times of crisis, our instinct is to gather in circles around the fire, to witness and share common stories. The theater, with its immediacy of flesh talking to flesh, of actors sharing space, time and breath with a living audience, has an emotional imperative in the aftermath. Of and for the ephermeral, theater calls forth in us a communal quickening to feel the loss of the living and the presence of the dead. More important, playwrights have an ethical legacy to follow the charge to ask questions" (Paula Vogel).

The tiny Authors Café venue had a full house. As we were waiting to begin, Shannon, so worried about his mother grounded somewhere in America and other relatives in New York, didn't feel right about performing. Randy felt as I did. Shannon stayed alone in his car until the final minute but agreed ultimately to "go on with the show." At the end Randy, Rykelle, Shannon and I joined hands and asked the audience to stand and pray with us. It was a moving moment when the Native American artists prayed in their Native tongues and the rest of us prayed in English for our loved ones, for New York, for America, and for the world.

9-11 forced Actors Workout to *move* toward its own death. First, AW lost a possible "seed" funding source for the Theatre For The New Millennium (a Northeast Phoenix Troon resident who lost big in the stock market had became leery of risk). Then student actors could no longer afford fees to train. AW received only small donations at salons. I personally suffered emotionally because two of my adult children were laid off and remained unemployed long enough to cause financial duress for years (since I had scant funds to help them financially). One of my board members was also laid off. Kamal Amin, who had pro bono designed the spectacular Theatre For The New Millennium, pulled his design from AW's website, because AW had not raised enough money to proceed and he might be able to sell the design elsewhere. Pre-Christmas 2002, I was forced to move AW's office due to my landlady's stroke. *Now the feeling of death had become overwhelming.* Yet I knew I was one of the lucky ones. I had not lost a family member or beloved friend during that horrific day. I was safe and *still here*, more than 2000 miles away.

Of all the things that have been said about AW, the following stick in my mind:

"I know you will succeed," Matthew Earl Jones, brother of icon actor James Earl Jones;

"…They [AW actors] are truly some of the most talented people I have ever witnessed," Bob Ciancola, Tax Attorney.

"AW has provided for me a community of dedicated artists developing their craft," John Collins, PhD Theatre, former theater director Phoenix Country Day School/AW Senior Company in shows since '92 at el Pedregal at the Boulders.

"A note of congratulations on *I Will Fight No More Forever*…the end result was superb," Jeb Rosebrook, Emmy nominee, writer *Junior Bonner, Miracle On 34th Street, The Waltons*.

"It was the best show [*A Christmas Carol With Music & Dance*] I have ever seen," Bill Denney, former AW President/professional baseball player/ CBS & NBC affiliates Phoenix sports anchor.

"*Pipe Dreams* is magical," Ted King Phoenix actor/developer.

"*Ordinary Jenny White* [Tempe Performing Arts Center] is an extraordinary show," Elizabeth Scheffer, minister.

"AW…presents timely and important issues…."Harry Mitchell, State of Arizona Legislature, former Mayor City of Tempe.

"I can unequivocally state that this [AW] is a quality company that produces educational but, also… artistic productions of exemplary status, " (regarding *Pipe Dreams* at 80% diverse population middle school) Lyn Bailey, Ed.D., Principal Palo Verde Middle School, Washington District/Phoenix.

"You [Mary Daisy] are the consumate pro," Diann Peart, Ph.D./Eco Professor, Arizona State University/Director of the Institute of Urban Gardening.

Moving AW Post 9-11 Back to Life: But Should AW, Could AW Continue?

AW salons did continue. The extraordinary African American Sule Greg Wilson(who has performed at the Smithsonian and Yale Universitry) did a triumphant salon playing ancient African drums. Actors Equity Association actor Mark De Michele worked with me for six weeks to develop a one-actor,

14 character performance of Sam Shepard's *Savage Love*. Lauren Eiler revived her *Women Pioneers* one actor, five character show. AW did a dinner show of *Don Juan In Hell* by George Bernard Shaw then scenes from Dickens' *A Christmas Carol* at the Authors Café. One of the most successful shows (it enjoyed two standing-room-only audiences back to back) was my authored *Zane & Dolly* performed by Buck Hart as Zane Grey and me as his wife Dolly. The show received a booking as an entertainment for $1000 donors to the Sun Lakes Association fund to build a new library."*Zane & Dolly* was outstanding"[Authors Café, Goldwater Blvd.,Scottsdale] Frank Roberts, President Orme School Board of Trustres, Mayer, Arizona.

Finally, for three months I did monologues of all eight characters of *Ordinary Jenny White*! The great British actress Ellen Terry taught Lynn Fontaine in 1938 ""one invaluable thing…always think the thought behind the words. Pay no attention to the diction or the reading,' she told me, "but fill your mind with the thought and let the words pour out of your mouth."

As an actor in *Ordinary Jenny White* monologues, I had the difficult task of *changing character, hair, wardrobe, movement, dialect and thought for eight different characters!* My good friends and colleagues Faith Hibbs Clark and Margie Ghigo critiqued the show each in a solo audience and gave me notes. So I had only two rehearsals with two different directors.

Below are soundbites about AW Salons!

"Great show! Great food!," "Inspiring!," "Intimate!," "Passionate!," "Purely delightful," "So many emotions!" "We loved the show!" "Fantastic idea! Brings intimacy in an isolated world!" "Yes! Great idea!" "Yes-I thought it was a great show. The especially nice part was the size/intimacy of the venue." "Yes,the intimacy is incredible!" "Yes. Encouraging people to live in passionate expression as AW Salons allow is a concept to support!."

AW also did one Open House Theatre, the creation of AW X-President Helen Pugh, at a multi-million dollar home in Troon featuring AW's David Richardson's slides of his Everest climb.

Moving to Actors Workout Community Land Trust of 100 Jobs

Think regarding jobs—the variety of creative personnel required to produce the highest quality work—producers, playwright/screenplay writers, directors, actors, designers, choreographers, composers, musicians, dancers, singers, theatre/film marketers and administrators. Where better to place a National Repertory Theatre (which will both provide programming and create new work) than at the gateway to the world's leading tourist attraction—the Grand Canyon! I see that my goal of creating Actors Workout Community Land Trust (a pedestal of 100 creative jobs under a tax-exempt umbrella leasing to profit investors of Theatre For The New Millennium) has its roots in a dream of the Lunts. The reason Lunt and Fontanne did not realize their dream of a *National Repertory Theatre* was economic. Sets and costumes for several shows would have been excessively expensive, as far as storage and access in a conventional proscenium theater, whereas AW's visualized Theatre For The New Millennium, which will utilize computerized visuals, sound and light at lightening speed, will be able to offer five shows in the same live performance space in one day for maximum cost efficiency and maximum earnings! In addition, fine art, film, video and the internet can be combined with live performance in innovative and exciting ways!

As early as 1930, Alfred Lunt wrote an article for the *New York Times*:

> The present efforts in the theater to create permanent and repertory companies are, it seems to me, splendid ….the opportunity to play continuously with the same group in a permanent company brings much harmony into a performance. A fine ensemble can be developed which will heighten the play's values and the author's intentions. It also eliminates, I think, the necessity which so many actors feel- that they must act their parts not for the good of the play but for the good of themselves. Under the system by which actors cast about for engagement after engagement they may instinctively work with the idea of making themselves conspicuous in order to obtain another part at the termination of the present play. Under the permanent company plan, with its attendant economic security, an actor can afford to act his part for the good of the play. Best of all,

however, is the point that playing a variety of roles an actor must, of necessity, broaden, mature and purify whatever talent he may possess…

True repertory nurtures and encourages budding talent. It offers opportunities and a perpetual freshness which your young player will never find under the long-run system. It keeps a freshness in its performances, for although it isn't really necessary that a good performance should go stale, it often does. You can't say a rosary every night for seventy weeks and have it sound the same as it did the first time. Another great point in favor of a repertory company is that it acquaints players with many major items of dramatic literature. It brings them into a dazzling succession of new contacts and new roles, and if they are able and receptive, it is superb development.

Applications for the "seed"funding of Actors Workout Community Land Trust(AWCLT)–Theatre For The New Millennium(TFTNM) and to many leading philanthropic organizations.

When TFTNM is operational, income opportunities for non-profit tax-exempt AWCLT in addition to leasing land to TFTNM investors will include grants, ticket sales for AW plays & other shows, tours off-campus of AW created shows, videos of AW created shows, concessions, publications, educational programs, advertising, endowment.

Programming possibilities in live performance space:

AM Kids Show; PM Dance Company;

COCKTAIL HOUR, with a Classical floutist, string quartet, or world class choir;

8 PM MAINSTAGE Actors Equity Production, i.e.=AW's *I Will Fight No More Forever* by Emmy-writer Jeb Rosebrook's play about Chief Joseph'heroic flight to freedom. Use of Library of Congress photos rear screen,"Indians"by Arthur Kope (surreal play about the life of Buffolo Bill), newly created work by the 100 creative artists;

BAND AT 10:30PM i.e.Clandestine, the Native American and electronic sound with World's Champion Hopi hoop dancer booked already in Berlin, Australia, Ireland.

Meanwhile, income possibilities for TFTNM profit investors include: TFTNM Leases to synergistic businesses, film multiplex, cafe, restaurants for the gourmet, film producers for sound stages, film post-shoot support services—i.e.editing and developing, talent agencies, art galleries, gift and special clothing shops, beauty products and shops, food court. Fleet of emissions-free buses.

Tourist packages would include: on-site TFTNM attractions, airlines tickets, resort reservations, restaurant reservations, child care, golf t-time, casino visit, sports venues tickets, transportation from Sky Harbor Airport to TFTNM and from TFTNM to Historic RR to Grand Canyon, reservations at Grand Canyon, tours of complex, tours of film sound stages, family-hands-on areas/classes (think the offerings of Wickenburg Inn), guest companies i.e. "seed" funding stars in plays of their choice; the Oregon Shakespeare Festival; Baryshnikov quality dance companies; reknowned Western one-man shows like James Whitmore's *Will Rogers*, Hall Holbrook's *Mark Twain*; Best Plays from Edinburgh Festival; World Premieres of films (on largest film screen in the world!); Arizona Film Festival; National Theatre Great Britain; Moscow Art Theatre; Kubuki.

Creation and sale of products, i.e. books, toys, games from AW created new product. Attractions at TFTNM in addition to live theater = :21 tribes of AZ., tribe lectures, dances, art work, crafts. Childrens' Circus, Wyatt Earp shoot out, Authors Café shows free to diners.

AWCLT~TFTNM feedback from community leaders includes:

"The project [Theatre For The New Millennium] is a very exciting one and unquestionably would fill the requirements for a badly needed facility to accommodate the various uses you have outlined....our company is very interested in becoming involved in the overall planning and construction...."Herman Chanen,CEO Chanen Construction Company, built Phoenix Sky Harbor Airport's Terminal 4.

"Thank you for your interest in Harkins Theatres and for sharing your ideas and vision of the Theatre For the New Millennium with us. We applaud your commitment and enthusiasm for this project," Dan Harkins, independent owner major chain of multiplex film theatres in Phoenix.

"I applaud your work in this [environmental] area..."Arizona. Senator John McCain.

Moving Toward a New One World

Scots-Irish, Euro, Polynesian, Asian, African, Native American, Jewish board in 2004, *AW's mission is to bridge the gap between the rich and poor, between the races, between earth and space, between God and humans, between entertainment and education via its literary projects, its company, board members and audiences.*

Gifted Scots-Irish-Brit Tom Oliver, now retired as CEO of Holiday Inns Worldwide, is AW's honorary chairman and a monthly financial supporter of office overhead. (My brother Dick supported office overhead following 9-11 for 13 months and my son Gary and his wife Joanne gifted AW, matched by Aetna/USHealthcare, for a total of over $1000. Six-foot-six, handsome Euro-American Dieter Bollmann, CFM, is now AW's President. Randy Kemp(Native American triple threat artist above) has joined the board as Vice President. IBM Administrative Assistant former Hawaiian Jaci Estes is AW Secretary. Scots-Irish Laraine Correll, Arts Librarian of the city of Mesa, with Washington, D.C. credits on her c.v., is a member of the board. Keith Ritchie, AW VP and producer-director at Channel 12, selflessly worked for a year to create a five minute dynamite TFTNM infomercial pro bono. Keith also shot professional talent monologues at Urbana Studios during the inception of the Iraq war (which will be used on AW's website). Asian-American Iris Song, dba iSong design, has joined the organization as an "advisor." African-American Sapphire King, actress-poet, with a MA in engineering, is also an "advisor." Jewish-American Rae Anne Marsh, former editor of a Scottsdale magazine and now a free lance writer, dba Glamour & Glitz, edited grants for AW.

AW co-incorporator Fred Sugerman volunteered his services to bring his Santa Monica dance workshop to Phoenix pro bono for the Evolving Artists Seminar(April 2003), held partially at the Flinn Foundation in Phoenix. Maria Wroz(guest artist from Poland), brought tapes of her work with Grotowski to share at the event which began with a cocktail party at famed Wrigley Mansion now owned by Geordie Hormel (heir to the Hormel fortune). In the summer of 2003, organizer extraordinaire Brandon Ladd Burkey, former Director of the Phoenix Film Project (who had attended AW's Open House Theatre at Troon) honored AW at a private party in Paradise Valley, where AW benefitted from a percentage of bar receipts. I was honored among film dignitaries at a party for 225 (February 22, 2004) then invited to Brandon's Oscars Party at the Wrigley Mansion Club.

A year ago, on June 28, 2003, I visited Dan Mason who, post 9-11 sought work in Hollywood. Dan escorted me to the Malibu, California, wedding of Fred Sugerman, who married his lovely Colleen in a combination Jewish and Protestant ceremony. Fred wrote the following on the back of a Christmas card in 2002:

> *There are three people alive I would call heroes of mine. Nelson Mandella, Julia Butterfly (the young woman who spent three years living in a giant sequoia tree) and you. Your child-like faith, enthusiasm, and exuberant artistry inspires me. Witnessing you feeds my soul. I am your witness. I am your fan. I am your friend.*
> *Lovingly,*
> *Fred*

AW's story ***moves*** like the rapids of the Colorado River faster and faster toward *"a great moment in live theater is like a grain of sand in the Grand Canyon at sunrise"* (Mary Daisy).

Part Seven

Evening

2001-2004 – 9-11, Iraq War and Post
War, Family, USA, God, Moving

Why Do We *Move*?

We ride Earth around the sun through the seasons—winter, spring, summer, fall—through night (our nightmares and visions) and day (our dreams and goals) as our earth spins on itself! Earth trembles in earthquakes, changes in erosions, floods, tornadoes, and hurricanes when entire populations live or die! The sun, either a lot of it or none at all (as in the five months of darkness at the poles) impels us to immigrate or emigrate. The oxygen in the air *propels* us (as in Peru's Machu Pichu, where peasants have large chests to compensate for the oxygen-poor air at 10,000 feet) or not via air pollution (if we will not deploy alternate forms of energy).

Global warming's dire results are shown in Alexis Rockman's 2004 painting at the Brooklyn Museum in which New York City—shown from the Brooklyn waterfront circa 5000 A.D. is soaking in 82 feet of water! Yet drought has caused Arizona's Lake Powell, "…the vast blue diamond of deep water that government engineers created in one of the driest and most remote areas of the country beginning in the 1950s," to lose nearly 60% of its water (*New York Times*, 5-02-04)! Glen Canyon Dam may possibly be unable to generate electricity by 2007!

All the parts of my body have been *moving,* cells dividing, reproducing, organs functioning hour after hour, day after day, year after year, so my body is entirely different every seven years!

In love I conjoined, carried, labored, bore, reared and educated *my* offspring while I traveled through not only body after body in this life, but also the generations in my genes. (Each chromosome of each species with its definite number and arrangement of genes governs both the structure and metabolic functions of the cells and thus of the entire organism). I interact with my *family,* my own and other species, flora and fauna, either with awe and respect, or in fear, greed and the urge to kill (via avoidance or indifference).

I am all of homo sapiens' history, from the first found remains in Africa to the Information Age and cyberspace, from the beast to the angel(and back and forth), ever striving to overcome the beast while discovering, entrepreneuring, warring, governing, worshipping. I've found a mission in work.

I *moved* through life and death. Ricky taught me early on the difference and the miracle of being here now.

Lynn gave birth to a healthy baby boy September 7, 1992! Gary and Lynn named my grandson Daniel Joseph Mizell. From earliest babyhood, Dan showed keen interest in how things work. When he began to crawl it was toward electrical plugs! Dan has always favored toys he could take apart and put together again and today Dan, a straight A student, is destined to design new programs for computers (according to his father, my son Gary)!

In the years since my dad died, my mother and I became more than just mother and daughter. We became good friends. We joked but sincerely believed we should "…give each other flowers before we die!" One-on-one celebrations were arranged whenever possible. Mom came to Phoenix after my return (following the 1986 Whittier earthquake) when Neal treated the two of us to world famous Biltmore Hotel's brunch (the décor of the Biltmore was created by Frank Lloyd Wright). Neal charmed Mom, but prophetically she advised me against a relationship with him, warning, "There's too much trouble on the track!" It was clear to her Neal carried too much baggage from the past.

As was my custom regarding family at Christmas, I traveled if necessary to spend time with each family member according to our schedules. So post-Christmas 1993, a sharing was planned with my mom in the Whittier, California, home of my brother Dick. I had overcome my *seismophobia* (fear of earthquakes) enough to go to L.A. again, so reservations had been made and tickets bought for a December 26 round trip. However, before I could leave, I got a call from Dick saying Mom was too ill to see me! Soon I learned my brother Tom had flown to L.A. and my brothers had taken mother to the hospital. Tests revealed Mom had inoperable ovarian cancer! When I received the next call from Dick, I was urged to fly to California as soon as possible because Mom might not live more than a few days! I was in shock! This was so quick, so unexpected! Mom was 87 years old, but she had been out with the power mower every week!

I took the next available flight to California to see Mom. She appeared just a tiny waif of her former self lying in her hospital bed. *I could not believe the change in her in so short a time.* It was after the New Year but Dick's house was filled with Christmas decorations, plus a beautifully decorated tree! Mom had arranged to keep everything up to delight me post Christmas. I had taken her Christmas gifts which she opened, then I shared just received news that the Arizona Department of Education/Health Services would gift a production of *Pipe Dreams* $3000 if the budget could be raised. *She threw up her little fist and moved her mouth "Great!"* though no sound came out (a tube went down her throat).

It became *my* duty to tell my mother about her hopeless condition because my brothers, including brother Bob now among us, could not face her with such candor. Out in the hallway adjacent to her room we siblings (Bob, Dick and I—Tom had to return to corporate business) had to make the decision to pull the tubes on Mom (denial of food and water to a patient so life would not be prolonged). There would be only time at the hospital for a quick visit from my niece Cheryl and her husband Jim, who flew in from Phoenix. Medicare rules decreed that since the hospital could no longer treat her, Mom would have to be moved to a hospice. The move proved to be very traumatic for her and therefore to us.

On my way to the airport to return to work in Phoenix, on January 18, 1993, Dick parked and waited outside the hospice. I saw my mother alive for the last time. She had become as a little baby, speechless, small, with morphine to keep her as comfortable as possible. Yet her little hands and eyes reached up to me. I was alone with her. "Mom" I said, "I must go back to work, but I'll never be far away! I'm like E.T.'s finger!" (the radiant love finger of Steven Spielberg's outer space creature). Raked with sobs I cried, "O Mom! I love you so much! Fly away, Mom! Fly away!"

That night when my plane took off it hit me—*I'll never see my mother again!* What a bleak, empty realization! But, like precious Ricky, how could I want my mom to suffer more? "Fly away mom! Fly away! Be with Our Father in Heaven now," went through my mind over and over again as I entered the clouds. Mom *moved* to join my dad, January 23, 1993.

In a generous gesture, my brother Tom(at that time Senior Vice President of Federal Express) arranged to bring a small Federal Express jet to Phoenix with his wife Jane and my nephews Ryan and Brett on board. He picked up Phoenix-based family members for Mom's funeral (me, James, Gary, my niece Cheryl and her husband) for the flight to Ontario. My niece Wendy Beth (Tom's daughter by his first marriage, at the time an attorney in Portland) and mom's niece, Sandy Reynolds Purcy, joined us at the Riverside cemetery by Mom's open grave. I put roses I'd brought from Phoenix on the urn containing her ashes because Mom was cremated and buried beside my dad. I wrote and read a short eulogy. Family members went to a nearby restaurant for lunch following the burial, then the Phoenix and Memphis based family members flew home in the Federal Express small jet. It helped to be together. We could comfort each other.

Mom, in addition to being an artist at remodeling homes and landscaping grounds, was an incredible worker, taking care of so many for so many years. It was Mom who held the family together. She was also a poet! She wrote the following for a 1976 Christmas card. It describes how she discovered there is no Santa Claus.

CHRISTMAS 1919
That's How I Knew!
The sleigh bells rang as Old Dobbin and Bill
Quickened their hoofbeats on soft fallen snow
As the sleigh neared the farmhouse over the hill
With its promise of warmth and food they would know.
The rosy-cheeked girl turned to the window
For the first glimpse of Santa's gift of a tree.
But-Grandma was lighting each bough with its candle-
There WAS no Santa—T'was easy to see!
An unhappy child in the midst of great joy,
She stubbornly yanked at the string on a box,
"This could not be too unusual a toy
Perhaps no more than a pair of new socks."
But buried in tissue, unbelieving, her eyes
Saw a gold cross strung on a gold chain
It took a few years to know Christmas lies
In the heart of each loved one, to always remain.
B.R.O. '76

In July of 1994 I received word my mom's brother, Dr. Verne Reynolds, MD, 87, of Boise, Idaho, had died. Vigorous and successful, Uncle Verne died at exactly the same age as did my mom. Below is from the Boise Statesman, July 22, 1994:

Dr. Reynolds was born January 14, 1907, in Elwood, Neb., to William Lewis and Daisy Reynolds. He grew up there, and really enjoyed Western life, especially riding horses and herding cattle.

The family moved to Omaha, Nebraska [my mom kept pet chickens in Elwood, which she gave to her grandmother when the family moved. Imagine Mom's distress when her grandmother arrived to see the family off on the train with a picnic of fried chicken!] where he [Verne] graduated from Omaha Central High School, and was on the National Scholastic Honor Society, National Athletic Scholarship Society, and the National Scholastic Society for Writers....

After attending University of Illinois for a Bachelor of Science degree in 1930, then the University of Nebraska for his MD in 1933, Uncle Verne interned at St. Frances Hospital in Jersey City, New Jersey. His three years' residencies were at Bellevue Hospital in New York City, and Margaret Hague Maternity Hospital in Jersey City. Verne married my Aunt Agnes (a nurse) in St. Mary's, Pennsylvania, then began practicing in Lincoln, Nebraska, with my great uncle J.J. Loomis (the doctor who delivered me when my mom had an unexpected visit from an intern former fiancée). It must have been during those years at a Reynolds family outing (all present sought to move a picnic table) that I put my hand in a wasp nest and Uncle Verne, the doctor, came to my rescue!

In 1942, Uncle Verne passed the exams of the American Board of Obstetrics and Gynecology, then served in the U.S. Medical Army Air Corps during WWII. He left the service (as a much decorated officer) with the rank of Major in 1946 and moved to Boise where he was the first to be certified and limit his practice to Obstetrics and Gynecology. In Boise he had an outstanding career! He founded the Woman's Clinic, served as President of the Pacific Northwest Obstetric and Gynecology Association in 1957, and was a member of all prestigious medical associations and hospitals in the Boise area. It was to my own Uncle Verne that I went for long distance counseling about my fibroid tumor. Uncle Verne believed that if it did not bother me I could carry it. I did carry it for seven years.

Uncle Verne and Aunt Agnes had retired and purchased an Arabian horse ranch by the time of Gary and Lynn's wedding. At the pre-wedding night cocktail party, Uncle Verne told me an charming story! I asked "Since you've delivered so many babies, do you now deliver baby Arabian horses?"

Without batting eye he replied "Of course!" as if delivering baby horses was the thing he'd always done! Years later, after Verne's death, Aunt Agnes told me that she slept in the barn next to the pregnant mares 'till they went into labor then ran up to the house to fetch her peacefully sleeping spouse when it came time deliver!

While struggling to gain rights to do *I Will Fight No More Forever* (the action of the Nez Perce tribe is near Boise, Idaho) in Phoenix I ***moved*** to witness again divorce up close and personal. There were *no divorces among my grandparents.* There was no *divorce for my parents*(who lived *un*happily together the last twenty years of their lives, though they remained devoted to each other's welfare). There have been no divorces on the Reynolds side of the family, even though my Aunt Gladys married a Ph.D. organist fifteen years her junior for the first time at age fifty!

But, there have been four divorces among me and my siblings (I always believed death did part Woody and me when his heart stopped beating from the combination of alcohol and tranquilizers). Is this symptomatic of the era in which we live in America?

I was shocked one day to pick up the phone to hear my superstar son Gary's troubled voice. "Mom, I'm leaving Lynn." Gary is very circumspect, tough and self-reliant, so its not surprising I'd heard nothing of his pain. But *pain indeed* he was suffering. I was deeply alarmed! Something, I could not imagine what, was deeply *wrong* in my son's storybook marriage to his high school sweetheart! I urged Gary to go someplace quiet, to pray, to ask God what to do, to just be alone for awhile. He did that at a motel for a few days, then rented a room at the home of one of his Aetna/USHealthcare colleagues. Soon I learned he'd rented a two bedroom apartment near the Paradise Valley Mall. I was called on several times to come there to be with my grandchildren when he had plans and they were visiting.

The suffering my own divorce must have caused my children became clearer as the months passed. I witnessed poignantly that separation and planned for divorce is a terrible thing, not only for the principals to go through, but also their children and extended families.

I learned Gary's salary was the primary income for his family, that pro bono he had written the business plan for the initial loan to start Leigh Cassidy King's Dance Centre (though he was never compensated and his wife Lynn owned no part of Dance Centre) yet the entire Cassidy family, not only went to work part-time for Leigh (Leigh's husband Sammy became the tech director for Dance Centre's superb summer recital shows, Lynn and Leigh's dad Earl was Dance Centre's financial consultant, their mother Colleen ,[an experienced school district secretary] became secretary, sister Jan [a former Las Vegas dancer who injured herself then studied to a university degree as a nurse], after marriage in Seattle, moved back to Scottsdale to work for Leigh, *as would Gary's wife* Lynn, who became DanceCentre's's marketing director!).1

Lynn's expertise increased the enrollment of the successful Cassidy family enterprise to 500 youthful clients! Everything she and Gary did had to be coordinated with the master schedule of Dance Centre (even my grandson Dan's birthdays resulted in meetings for the studio)! What was it like for Gary to be fifth wheel in a group to which he no longer belonged and from which his family gained no appreciable benefit? My son found himself increasingly *lonely in his own home*, unloved, and definitely second fiddle to Dance Centre, while he continued to be the hardworking bread winner in an increasingly competitive marketplace.

On Thanksgiving day 1997, Lynn brought Gina and Dan to my office-studio for a short time to visit with Gary. After Lynn left, Gary asked me to pick a rose from the garden because he planned to have dinner with his friend Joanne Marie Milazzo, VP National Sales, Aetna/USHealthcare. I mourned for Lynn (because, ever since she and Gary were sweethearts as juniors at Chapparrel High School in Scottsdale, I've genuinely admired and cared about Lynn). But, who (except the persons involved) can truly know what happens between a man and a woman? What I could not know was that Gary was about to experience joy and luminescence in the true love of his life—Joanne Marie!

Gary brought Gina, Dan and Joanne to a fully costumed and performed production at CWS of AW's *A Christmas Carol With Music & Dance* in early December. The standing room only show had a company of thirty actors, dancers and singers working in open space throughout the audience! It starred in two successive years Buck Hart (former headmaster of the Orme School) as Scrooge with Tarah dancing the Ghost of the Future. Elizabeth Sheffer would tell me she could hear a pin drop (a sure sign a show has an audience in the palm of its hand) in an audience ranging from toddlers sitting on the floor through seniors carrying walking sticks!

Pre-Christmas day 1997, Gary decided to drive to California(where Joanne owned a condo near the beach) with Gina and Dan. I was invited to drive with my son to play auto games with my grandchildren between Phoenix and Whittier (Gina and Dan hated long car trips almost as much as Gary had when he was little!). The plan was to spend the night with my brother Dick. My son James was already encamped at Dick's doing extra work and catering for films. James shot a video of Dick, Joanne (who had driven in from her beach home to join us), Gary, Gina, Dan and me opening gifts. I had given Dan a set of paints. Within fifteen minutes Dan had gone out on Dick's deck (which overlooks a kaleidoscopic view of downtown Los Angeles) and returned with a Van Gogh-inspired painting of nothing but the sun in bright yellow!

Gary returned to Phoenix and an apartment empty of Christmas decorations (Lynn had kept those assets of the marriage) but I was touched when Joanne unselfishly flew over to Phoenix with many of her cherished Christmas decorations to festoon Gary's apartment! Joanne is instinctively giving and empathetic.

Soon Gary informed me Joanne brought more joy into his life than he'd ever known! What Gary and Joanne must have discovered in each other was unusual maturity based on inordinate trauma and suffering at a very young age, plus triumph over odds to succeed in a highly competitive marketplace, and a longing for true companionship and romance. In addition, Joanne (who desired to remain childless) committed to help Gary and Lynn (who would receive joint custody) rear Gary's children to maturity. They fell deeply in love. A new soul *moved* permanently into my life!

Gary and Joanne's wedding (my grandson Dan was ring bearer) was held May 30, 1998, at a small church close to the ocean. The simple ceremony was followed by a close friends and family reception dinner in an elegant restaurant. Each guest was gifted a bottle of superb wine with a golden wrapping labeled with the wedding date(a keepsake of mine to this day). Little Dan returned to Dick's Whittier house with me for the night. The next day Dick took Dan on a tour of his shutter factory where Dan saw machines as big as the average house! Dick took Dan with him on a big fork lift while he moved huge stacks of lumber from one place to another, then cut with a big machine little pieces of wood as building blocks for Dan to play with until the bridal couple collected him for a flight back to Phoenix!

9-11 put a new and sacred meaning on the word family. How lucky I am to have three living children bearing genes that will *move* through generations long after I am gone! I sent the following to them in e-mails Christmas 2003.

To James Robert Mizell, my New York City-born son (the sun broke through the rain to illuminate his face through a stained glass window on Mother's Day when at six months he was baptized), who bore the brunt of his father's alcoholism (the divide between a WWII member of Patton's Third Army and the Vietnam War), toughed it out as a free lance itinerant musician after taking conscientious objector status and fleeing his home; worked four part-time jobs (when student loans delayed being paid for a year) to attain his Cum

Laude 3.7 GPA, Dean's List AA degree in television, interned at FOX in Los Angeles, survived to proactivity a major colon surgery, then was downsized in layoffs after 9-11 and finally, after three years of contract labor work and mounting debt is working camera assignments for the stage hands union, I wrote:

> *It's important at this Christmas season you know how grateful I am for the acts of kindness and understanding you have given me over the years. Thank you for:*
>
> *Urging me to come to North Hollywood to share for awhile your rent, thus ushering in 11 quite amazing career years for me;*
>
> *Being the one to solicit blood donations when I had to go to the hospital in a hurry for abdominal surgery;*
>
> *Being the one to drive me to the hospital and home after my heart arrest and after my eventual surgery awake;*
>
> *Being the one to transport my set pieces when I had AW salons;*
>
> *Being the one to take me when I had to have my beloved Halloween (girl kitty of 13 years) put down and for Nite's(my new black kitty, Mother's Day gift 2003) first vet exam;*
>
> *Taking me to several Christmas eve services;*
>
> *Being a fun and helpful roommate, wiring me for communications, transporting me during emergency health times since 9-11.*

Today James is a camera-operator/videotape-operator doing conventions for clients like Lexis-Nexis, Weston Resorts, etc; in addition to being an AV Technician/audio-engineer/stagehand/electrician for *Oklahoma* at Grady Gammage Auditorium~Arizona State University, Riverdance; David Bowie, Kenny Rogers, and Sarah Brightman concerts via Rhino Productions & Staging; and for I.A.T.S.E. (Stage-hands union) serving clients like the Cattleman's convention, Oasis Gift Show with Jackie Chan, and "Independence Day"working for Mr. Brown, LLC Productions, and RYP Filmworks in Phoenix, plus Emerald Light Pictures and 20th Century Fox in Los Angeles. James has credits as a production assistant on a major League Baseball commercial, Montgomery Ward commercial, with Sammy Sosa, and a "Rush Hour" teaser. In addition he's been a news-van operator/ENG-technician for both broadcast television's KTVK CH 3 and KPNX CH 12 in Phoenix.

He's worked for a film lab, performed background talent work in around twenty feature films and movies of the week, and Capital Records in Los Angeles. A talented guitarist-composer-arranger, "JR" has many fans among his friends after doing free lance "gigs" for a decade in Arizona and California. James also graduated with honors from a course in computer graphics and enjoys tech challenges of all kinds, including working on his truck and serving as tech director for AW shows.

To my daughter Melanie Anne Mizell (whom I welcomed joyfully as "Melanie!"Blessed baby girl, healer of my grief after Ricky's death, as I saw her born), bilingual in French and English, a young woman who, at age sixteen entered the University of Arizona in Tucson without books (because I struggled as a single parent without child support) to eventually earn a Bachelor of Arts, with Honors, Political Science degree in 1990 (winner of the first O'Mara Fellowship Award writing a project on solar energy)! She did that while working as an intern in government relations for the United Way of Southern Arizona, as an intern in the Office of Energy and Environment, for the City Manager's Office for the City of Tucson, as a Supervisor and Recreation Specialist for the City of Tucson, Parks and Recreation, and as a Teaching Assistant in Special Education for the Tucson Unified School District, I wrote:

> *It's important during this Christmas season that you know how grateful I am for your many gifts and innumerable understanding kindnesses!*
>
> *Having me as your guest of honor when you received the O'Mara Fellow award;*
>
> *The many times you've been the delightful hostess, offering your heart and intelligence, sumptuous meals, outings for coffee and a muffin or bagel, walks, prayers, fresh flowers, your fairy garden and little books;*
>
> *The countless Melanie-created beautiful cards with oftentimes $5 or most recently $30 tucked inside;*
>
> *The phone calls when my health was threatened, i.e. when I was at Scottsdale Healthcare Hospital prior to ortho surgery*

having broken my foot off my leg;
   Your loving concern, counseling, and small money gifts for your brother James;
   Your inspiring careers and how they have instructed me.

Today my daughter Melanie is a creative thinker, excellent writer, skilled manager, relationship builder, strategic planner, facilitator, analyst, and designer with a multicultural perspective. Her career highlights have included not only the exciting challenge of her new job as Project Manager of Tucson's 501©(3) The Diaper Bank, but also the Southern Arizona Association for the Visually Impaired(SAAVI), where she coordinated production of marketing materials and media relations, redesigned a stunning agency brochure and newsletter, served as community relations liaison, gave presentations to the public, other agencies and community groups, coordinated special projects, i.e. an art show at Tucson's Tohono Chul Park ("You were such a great person to work with on the project and you made it easy for me. You were helpful, made suggestions, met deadlines, and took full responsibility for collecting SAAVI's contributions to the exhibit," wrote Peggy Hazard, Tohono Chul Park, Tucson ,Arizona to Melanie), and redesigned SAAVI's volunteer program to reflect best practices for volunteer management.

One of her most outstanding contract assignments was that of project manager for the City of Tucson, when she worked with an appointed task force that included community leaders, Air Force officials and government representatives who were challenged to develop recommendations for Air Base reuse. All of Melanie's recommendations presented in a beautifully designed report were unanimously adopted by the Mayor and City Council! For a Regional Environmental Organization, my "Mellie" coordinated special events such as regional conferences and directors' meetings, including one in Scottsdale. As program coordinator for University of Arizona, Mellie developed and coordinated an environmental program for the Student Union. For the City of Tucson and Pima County she's been a waste reduction planner. For the Commission on Arizona Environment a graphic designer. For the Pima Council on Aging a grant writer. Mellie's also been a public policy analyst on solar legislation, a teacher (substitute) with the Tucson Unified School District, a visual/performing arts specialist, and a garden designer for various private clients. My daughter has enlarged my view of my spaceship-earth beyond measure. Her career has touched the lives of thousands in southern Arizona.

To my son, Gary Michael Mizell, who may be my answer to prayer—the reincarnation of my lost Ricky—victor over lifetime odds (between age 6 months and nine months triumphing over spinal meningitis and head surgery [finally starving himself in the hospital, forcing doctors to allow me to take him home, then never crying for 48 hours], who at age nine called 9-1-1 when his father was "dead" on the floor from alcohol and tranquilizers and still pitched a no-hit game in Little League; was a four-letterman member of the king's court in high school then had to quit sports to work all night at a gas station to help support the family; worked every vacation and summer as head of a department of K-Mart while carrying a full load at the university graduating with honors; lived in my Mummy Mountain "garrett" with the mice while at Arizona State University; graduated from that university with high honors and five job offers; then went on to a 4.0 MBA as a married man-father-executive, and who, since 1996, has been Vice President of Key/Select Sales and Service, Arizona, Nevada, Utah, the top listed representative of his company in the Phoenix Business Journal's Book of Lists, with a life mate who is *beautiful inside and out*, I wrote:

> *GARY & JOANNE!*
> *It's important during this Christmas season that you know how grateful I am for your innumerable monetary and other gifts and for your kindnesses and understanding:*
> *The dear and gracious way you cared for me when I broke my foot off my leg, both at the hospital and bringing me home with supplies;*
> *The beautiful Thanksgiving and Christmas dinner parties making those occasions festive and elegant;*
> *The gifts of money to me personally;*
> *The membership at the art museum during the Monet exhibit allowing me to take many guests;*
> *The gifts of money to Actors Workout and the "match" from Aetna/USHealthcare;*
> *The exciting Mother's Day and birthday meals at a restaurant;*
> *The gift of my bed last year when I was forced to move into a space with no furniture;*
> *The gift of the white couch and chair for the living room;*
> *The gift of Nite (the replacement sleek black boy kittie that*

was rescued by Joanne from a two and a half months stay in a cage in the Humane Society), and many supplies assuring his nutrition and healthcare.

Arizona State University(ASU), Gary's alma mater, is now in the top twenty business schools in the *nation*. Gary took the most challenging of five offers when he attained his business degree from ASU—account executive of Dataplace (working directly with a former President of ITT to open personal computer centers in the metro-Phoenix area). Dataplace became the second largest small computer business in Arizona before it merged with Businessland when Gary moved on to Director of Marketing Analysis for the HMO Cigna for five years. He was hired then by HMO F.H.P.(now Pacific Healthcare) followed by Blue Cross and Blue Shield, where he was Director of Sales in Arizona (a position he held for five years).

Finally Gary was sought by Aetna/USHealthcare just as it was being established as a division of Aetna Life Insurance Company.

Gary's wife Joanne is elegant, svelte, beautiful (her face and smile resemble the British actress Emma Thompson), a successful business woman, an animal lover—especially cats(today Joanne does volunteer work finding homes for animals at the Humane Society), a devout Christian, and a vegetarian as am I. Joanne radiates love. The daughter of a career Anaheim, California, teacher, Joe Milazzo, and a Girl Scouts career woman mother (Joe married his current wife Ana Marie, a teacher, a few years ago), Joanne, like Gary, suffered great loss and had great responsibility at a very young age. Her beloved younger sister Cathy went through the throes of chemotherapy to an agonizing death from cancer before Joanne was nine years old. During her sister's suffering, Joanne helped Cathy with her school work. Following Cathy's death, Joanne's mother collapsed and left the family, so Joanne's home became a single parent home with her father in charge. To earn spending money, Joanne describes summers spent in daylong babysitting of young clients at the beach. An honor student in high school, Joanne attended Cal State University at Fullerton after graduation. By that time, however, Joanne was highly motivated to make money and make money she did quite successfully! She worked sixty hours a week in addition to carrying a full load, but did not continue to a university degree. Rather she abandoned the academic life for an upwardly mobile career. By the time Gary met divorcee Joanne Milazzo at a Hartford, Connecticut, Aetna gathering, she had owned four different homes, held her esteemed seniority position with Aetna for several years, and earned enough to acquire a $250,000 condo! Joanne's office is now in Phoenix, though she continues to serve big clients in Los Angeles and elsewhere.

Moving to Celebrate Life at a Big Family Reunion (BFR)was My Brother Tom's Idea!

Tom startled me one day not long after 9-11 when we found all family members were safe! I had sent on-line the first edition of the Reynolds-Oliver-Mizell family directory(ROMDIR). Tom asked poignantly "Why don't we all get together? I'd love to see all those people!" Tom, based at Grovenor Square in London with his wife Jane, was still circling the globe for Holiday Inns Worldwide–Six Continents Hotels as CEO. Tom and Jane maintained two homes, the second in Atlanta, Georgia. To assemble everyone on the ROMDIR at a BFR would entail coordinating all the complex, busy schedules of people from London, Atlanta, Portland, Los Angeles, CA., Boise, Idaho, Tucson, Scottsdale, and Phoenix! To complicate matters further, everyone was money downsizing or flat broke (after being laid off) after 9-11! However, Tom made "a godfather deal" at the Holiday Inn Sunspree Resort in Scottsdale, Arizona. My brother Dick offered to pick up the tab for my hotel.

My niece Wendy Beth Oliver, and my brother Bob in Scottsdale helped me communicate and make arrangements between 9-11-2001 to May 5, 2002. Some of us had never seen each other, i.e. Tom Reynolds (son of my Uncle Verne and his wife Agnes), a thriving dentist in Boise, and his wife, the warm, lovely Karla (a retired nurse, mother of three and grandmother of three), had never met any member of the Mizell family. For others it had been a decade since they'd seen one another.

Agnes Reynolds, wonderfully healthy and vibrant at age 94, flew in with her son and daughter-in-law from Boise! Tom and Jane made the trip from Atlanta back to London and were joined by their handsome graduate of the University of Georgia-sports agent son Ryan, who flew in from Atlanta. Wendy Beth came from Portland. My brother Dick, president and owner of Steiner & Mateer & Aqua Coatings (one of southern California's largest shutter manufacturing companies coupled with an industrial paint manufacturing company) drove over with his dog Renegade from Los Angeles. Renegade stayed with my niece Cheryl Zenor (Bob's daughter, a cardiac nurse), her husband Jim (a high tech wizard) and her winsome son Brett (age 11) in

Scottsdale's low range mountains suburb of D.C. Ranch. My brother Bob came from Scottsdale. My daughter Melanie drove up from Tucson. My son Gary, his wife Joanne, daughter Gina and son Dan came from Scottsdale. My son James and I came from Phoenix.

BFR events began when I gave everyone a rose with an enlargement of an old photo of our mutual family (Grandmother Daisy and Grandfather William Reynolds, mom's sister Aunt Gladys, my mother and father Robert and Beth Oliver, and Verne and Agnes Reynolds). We gathered for Mexican food at Phoenix's El Charro restaurant on Camelback Road (restaurant-research and reservations for dining had been meticulously made by my brother Bob). My son James (today a video cameraman for Phoenix conventions) began shooting close-ups of star-player-family-members and cut away shots of the Mexican stained glass window and table settings for what would become the BFR edited video. The next morning all assembled first at the Sunspree's special hospitality room with coffee, juices, beer, wine, cheeses, crackers, pasteries, fruits, candy and nuts provided by my brother Tom (every Sunspree room also had fresh flowers, a cowboy hat with red, green and brown corn chips in the rim, guacamole dip, fruit, cheese and crackers and a bottle of wine).

Mid-morning, we all drove to the split-level poolside home of my son Gary and his wife Joanne for an elegant brunch. My daughter Melanie, who drive up from Tucson that morning, gave each person an elegant hand-crafted self-created card. More Sunspree hospitality room, rest and a change of clothes led to driving to Rawhide north of Scottsdale for dinner. James shot not only family members but the stampeding of bulls as the group re-lived the Old West! I was surprised to see a former actor student of mine decked out in a can can costume as the country western band singer! Buxom Wendy Crawford (a fine young actress) flirted with the BFR men while Ryan Oliver (who found time to play golf with a friend earlier in the day) endeared himself to parents and grandparents alike (Gary and Joanne, Cheryl and Jim, my brother Bob and me) because he played games with hungry grandkids while we waited for tardy food to arrive. Full of the Old West we drove up to my niece Cheryl and Jim's home by their pool overlooking a spectacular view of surrounding Scottsdale, and had rich desserts, coffee and wine.

The next morning (Sunday, May 5) the BFR had a Sunspree elegant champagne buffet (accompanied by mariachi live music) to celebrate Tom Reynolds' (the spitting image of his dad—my Uncle Verne) birthday! Joanne had ordered a beautiful specially made sheet birthday cake which we all enjoyed after first singing "Happy Birthday"to a surprised Tom Reynolds! Before everyone headed for airports and cars to make the trip home, James took a group shot at the front of the hotel. By the time the resulting video record of our time together had been edited and sent to all, it was clear the BFR had been a smashing *discovery of each other's* experience!

Moving to really know our family, I discovered we are a group of individually high achievers, fun loving, interesting, warm and lovable! How exciting to claim our family as kin and to know them as friends!   M   y brother Tom's wife, Jane Mooney Oliver, a natural beauty, was born and raised in New York (Queens), then joined American Airlines right after high school(that means Jane was living in one of New York's boroughs all the while I lived on Manhattan Island and in Jackson Heights! *Wonder if we ever crossed paths?)* Jane's parents were Irish on her father's side and German on her mother's side.

At American Airlines, my sister-in-law started on the ramp handling flights at La Guardia, then sales in New York City. Ultimately, from sales she was recruited into a Stewardess Supervision program, a small part of which involved doing the flight attendant training program in Ft. Worth, and then flew for a couple of months as part of the mangement training program. She then spent a couple of years managing different sets of flight attendants before she "retired" to have my splendid nephew Ryan Oliver. Jane has been an extraordinary wife and mother, making lovely homes to follow Tom's career and accompanying him on adventures around the world!

Conversant in Spanish and Swedish, Wendy Beth Oliver Garcia-Ramirez (my brother Tom's daughter by his first wife Tony), graduated with honors from the University of Chicago, with an B.A. in English Language and Literature. She then attained the J.D from Duke University School of Law, followed by solo travel through Asia and Latin America. Wendy Beth, the former general counsel of public NYSE, has distinguished herself as an attorney by creating a legal department that reduced legal fees, improved the quality of legal services provided by outside vendors, enhanced a corporation's ability to negotiate favorable terms in transactions and developed policies to reduce risk and liability to her company. She has also negotiated a multi-million dollar license and services agreement to enable operation of division servicing more than $1 billion in mortgage loans; successfully directed the legal affairs of a corporation; planned and implemented the company's insolvency strategy resulting in two promotions from vice president to executive vice president within one year. In addition, she's negotiated terms of $40 million bridge financing to provide working capital to company with limited liquidity; developed a plan for the wind down of business to create significant cost savings and preserve the value of corporate assets; plus negotiated and structured the sale of a UK subsidiary to management resulting in increased return to the seller from £5 million to more than £12 million.

However, Wendy Beth would probably agree that even in her over-achieving life as an attorney, it was her July 10, 2004, in Portland, Oregon, the repeat in the USA of her July26, 2003 marriage in Mexico City to Ph.D. and author Jose Carlos Garcia-Ramirez, that's been the most exciting event of her life! Paint from a palette of purple, pale rose, and white first the wedding invitation of blue-purple iris on white. Imagine a bride's bouquet of white roses, a bride the vision of white in chiffon with a long train, a matron of honor (attorney Emily Karr) in pale blue satin and lace, corsages for family members in pale pink and white roses with deep blue California Bluebells, wedding programs in purple and white, a minister's sermon, vows of bride and groom, and marriage program in English *and* Spanish, a cascade of white bubbles awash over a groom's black tuxedo and you have the picture of Wendy Beth and Jose's second wedding!

My brother Tom, with his first wife Tony Oliver, sandwiched the bride down the aisle to the ornate wood carved nave of the Mt. Tabor Presbyterian Church in Portland. The Lake Oswego *flor jardin a casa Tony Oliver* set in lush Douglas fir, ponderosa pine, and red cedar, with dozens of white covered tables centered with floral displays of pink and white carnations and bluebells framed the reception. Wendy Beth and Jose danced the *salsa solo* after cutting separate bride's and groom's cakes! Then a funny—moving not very well—row of mostly WASP men faced a row of WASP women to gamely attempt to follow very talented Hispanic dancers! My movie-star handsome nephew Ryan Oliver did very well learning the *salsa*! He danced it with his mom, Jane Oliver, who obviously had the time of her life! My great-nephew, 13-year-old Brett Zenor (Cheryl and Jim Zenor's son) floored the best man to catch the wedding garter! Members of the Oliver, Reynolds and Mizell families (plus Tom's friends from Sun Valley and Memphis) traveled from Boca Grande, Florida, Atlanta, Georgia, Los Angeles, California, Boise, Idaho, Scottsdale and Phoenix, Arizona, to support Wendy and Jose! (Members of Wendy's maternal-Merrill family came from as far away as Pittsburg). *And so my family has moved to unite two countries!*

I remember the day Ryan was born because my brother Tom, who, at that time, seldom telephoned me, called long distance to announce excitedly "I saw my son born!" (Tom also telephoned the day he was on the front page of the business section of *USA TODAY* after accepting the CEO of Holiday Inns Worldwide job). Ryan holds a 1999 University of Georgia, Pre-Law/History BA degree, having achieved a 3.47 GPA (in his Major a 3.8 GPA), achieved Presidential Scholar three times and Dean's List two times. On campus, Ryan was the Campus Representative for Nike, Inc.,planning and promoting campus-wide Nike events. In addition, Ryan was the liaison between Nike headquarters and the University of Georgia, interacting with school officials, athletes, and students about Nike products and issues, implementing P.L.A.Y. CORPS activities and involvement in the Athens community. Adding to his outstanding academic and professional achievements, while an undergraduate Ryan was the University of Georgia's Vice President of the Student Body- elected by its 32,000 members, member of the executive committee and President of the Student Senate. Ryan sat on search committee for the new University President, wrote legislation to include a new student seat on faculty- led governing body, The University Council. As Senator of School of Arts & Sciences (Chairman of Academic Affairs Committee) Ryan wrote and adopted the school's first concrete honor; revised the University's multi- cultural requirement; implemented safety measures on campus through an improved lighting campaign. As Freshman Senator, my nephew assisted an executive committee in restructuring the SGA Constitution; participated in committees focused on increasing voter turnout; created the Freshman Council seeking more input from freshman students. He was President of Sigma Chi Fraternity for three years and Treasurer for 1 year (during which he oversaw a record-breaking fund raiser for Children's Miracle Network). Ryan was also a member of three Honor Societies, the Golden Key Honor Society, Order of Omega Honor Society, and the Omega Delta Kappa Honor Society.

After graduation Ryan spent two years with eSkye Solutions, Inc. of Atlanta as account manager and Georgia market manager. Following six months as an eSkye's sales executive, Ryan had responsibility for daily operations and expansion of eSkye Private Trading Exchange for Georgia's beverage industry. He planned and implemented marketing and sales strategies for potential eSkye customers; managed and supported all current and potential customers.

Today Ryan is the business development manager for career for Sports Management, in Atlanta, where he has created unique and innovative marketing concepts for potential clients; Created measurement systems to evaluate the company's ROI thorough sponsorship investments; key contributor to landing new clients, which resulted in one of Career Sports' most successful years in its 17-year history.

In his *spare* time Ryan does community service with Kate's Club, an organization with the purpose of empowering the lives of children grieving the death of a loved one, through interaction in the local community where he has served on its Board of Directors as a member of the fundraising and program planning committees and Big Buddy, where he mentors and provides assistance to children dealing with the loss of a parent; plus creates monthly group outings taking the children to various events and cultural experiences throughout Atlanta. Ryan is a huge fan of his beloved Chicago Cubs and loves sports of all kinds.

I enjoyed getting to know my nephew Brett and his beautiful statuesque girlfriend Emily at the rehearsal dinner and party in his dad's hotel room the night before Wendy Beth's wedding (unfortunately Emily slipped in the Crowne Plaza Hotel bathtub and had to be rushed to the emergency room for an x-ray, so the handsome couple missed the wedding and reception)! Brett holds a degree in Building Sciences from Auburn University in Auburn, Alabama (its program is one of the five best programs in the country). Currently an engineer with Holder, the second largest builder in Atlanta, Brett knows architecture and construction well enough as a structural supervisor to help build some of the best and biggest buildings in the world! We had a great talk about Frank Lloyd Wright's Taliesin in Arizona and my hope is he'll come to Phoenix to see it up close and personal!

My niece Cheryl Oliver Zenor's story is one of heroic achievement without a college education, or a second paycheck during the time when her first two children Johnny and Chrissy were young children (Cheryl's first husband John was an alcoholic from whom she obtained a divorce and like me received no child support). Cheryl worked an infinite number of jobs to support her young family while *never giving up the dream to attend college and attain a nursing degree*!

Cheryl met Jim Zenor, a fine computer programming wizard. She married a second time and gave birth to her third child Brett when her older children were teenagers! Today, her son Johnny, a successful salesman in Denver, is married to a doctoral candidate, and her married daughter Chrissy just became a mother for the second time. And, most amazingly, Cheryl has attained her nursing degree from Arizona State University and is a superb cardiac nurse with credits that include the Mayo Clinic in Scottsdale and Good Samaritan

Hospital in Scottsdale! Meanwhile, her bright and popular son Brett is a winsome eleven-year-old and one of the most thoughtful pubescents I have ever witnessed. For recreation, Cheryl sings in her church large

My brother Bob continued to triumph over incredible disability odds and tragedy throughout his life, becoming a top salesman for IBM. An undiagnosed kidney stone led to kidney failure and his son Chris (an exceptionally fine student and athlete) became mentally ill during high school and died tragically in Mexico during his twenties. His daughter Cheryl, a triumphant cardiac nurse, was there as the closest living relative (with her husband Jim and son Brett) to monitor my brother Bob's pre-Christmas 2003 seven weeks of hospitalization as he underwent a series of operations (which ultimately totaled over 30) to establish a new shunt for three-times-weekly dialysis. While at Samaritan Healthcare Hospital in Scottsdale, Bob"flatlined" four times yet, miraculously, aided in no small part by Cheryl's oversight, walked out of an aftercare facility to stand for a family photograph in Cheryl's lovely home on Christmas eve of 2003!

Bob took care of himself at his apartment, drove himself to treatments, to his mortgage sales office, and to the home style buffet where first he treated me to brunch then I treated him on his birthday. *Bob told Cheryl he had God in his life the month before he died—June 4, 2004!* His services were held at the Veterans Memorial Cemetery north of Phoenix (where my husband Woody is buried) June 28, 2004. That day my sons James and Gary and I found Woody's grave and plaque after much searching, stood with arms around each other and said, each of us, a prayer before I put a rose on Woody's grave. The service for Bob was very impressive—with taps, gun salute, Cheryl presented with a flag, a chaplain saying a prayer. Brother Dick from California, Cheryl, Jim and I said a few words.

On July 10 (the day of my neice Wendy Beth's wedding) at Crowne Plaza Hotel in Portland, Oregon, at 10 a.m. we held a second memorial for Bob. Tim Allen, Bob's most recent boss, had much admiration for Bob's mind and courage in the face of his medical odds. Surely Bob's loving heart and brilliant mind are free now to *move* in Heaven! Post both services I received this letter from Librarian of Congress James Billington

July 14, '04 Letter From USA Librarian of Congress James Billington:

I was devastated to hear the tragic news about Bob. And I am doubly sorry to have received the news here too late to send something to the memorial service. Only now as well did I get

to see the letter you posted to me alerting me to his declining health on November 18. Government bureaucracy is at its worst. But I feel unusually sad at not knowing sooner and I hope you will share this letter with his family since I do not have their addresses, and, in particular, please tell his brothers, whom I did meet long ago, to get in touch with me if they are ever in Washington. It would be good to see Olivers again!

Bob was-as your fine memorial letter makes clear- a really memorable guy. He was, as you so well put it, a truly Big Man at BC (Bala Cynwyd Junior High School, Bala Cynwyd, P.A.) & LM (Lower Merion Senior High School, Ardmore, P.A.). He was not only bright, he was engaged in everything with a dash of both passion and humor. It was the WWII years, and he expressed the patriotism we all felt and that he later exemplified in the service. He won the American Legion Award and much else, but he was never full of himself or in any way prematurely obnoxious as BMOC's are likely to become. And he was recognized and admired both as a leader and as a friend by a wide variety of his peers for the entire junior and senior high school years.

He and Clarke Nash (retired professor from Georgetown University) were the behind-the-scenes orchestrators and stage managers of a remarkable drama program that really played a wonderful role in both high schools. And Bob was just as much at home working invisibly backstage as he was distinguishing himself on a podium or stage. He was also the envy of all his friends because of his wonderful way with the girls, whom he seemed to charm not just with his good looks and intelligence, but with a magnetism and manner that melted the gals without angering the guys.

I got something of a feeling for the uniqueness of your Oliver family by being more than a few times in your home. I was fascinated by the fact that Bob called your mother by her first name—and by the fact that she seemed to like it that way. Somehow Bob was always an adult in the best sense of the word.

I remember Lon Horsey (my best friend and a close friend and admirer of Bob's as well) describing a visit to Bob when he was recovering from polio. Lon was amazed and delighted by

Bob's courage and humor and said to me, "You know, Ollie just gets better and better." He meant as a human being, not just a patient and he meant moving up from an already high standard.

I miss not having seen him in recent years and I grieve at the realization that I never will again.

Love and deepest sympathy to you all. Jim

My Boise dentist cousin Tom Reynolds (who resembles my Uncle Verne so much!) was advised by my Uncle Verne to become a dentist instead of a doctor because Uncle Verne was strongly opposed to "socialized" medicine. Skipping a generation, however, Tom's son Brian is a surgeon in residence in Spokane, Washington. Brian and his wife Angie (an industrial designer of distinction) have a one-year old baby boy Branden. Medicine is definitely in the Reynolds family as Tom's wife, Karla, whom he met while he was in school in Portland, Oregon, is a retired nurse. She follows in the footsteps of her mother-in-law, my 95-year-old Aunt Agnes, still going strong in a retirement home in Boise! Tom's son Mike, his wife Kelly, and children Matthew and Katie live in Boise, owning and managing an old-fashioned ice cream parlor! According to Tom, his wife Karla gets the opportunity to babysit often and in the spring they both get the opportunity to do a lot of yard work! Tom and Karla's daughter Karin, who worked in a medical office in Boise prior to marriage the summer following the BFR, now lives happily in Kuna, Idaho as Mrs. Cory Van Dam.

I have ***moved*** through my nightmares to dreams.

From my nightmare of Ricky shackled to the rung of the roller coaster, a little yellow skeleton dying, unreachable, unsavable to my nightmare of my husband and Neal, unsavable too—speeding to their self-chosen deaths, to my dream of the universes created in an explosion of molten love and my awake dreams of self-realizing-healthy-family members, shows, talents, AWCLT–TFTNM.

I am not my body! I ***move*** through bodies as my dreams urge me on!.Sleeping, dreaming, rolling over, sitting up, standing, walking, running, dancing, performing, riding in a car in Nebraska; sledding, skating, tobogganing, biking, floating and jumping in pool water in Ohio; riding through tunnels under mountains on the Pennsylvania turnpike en route from Mansfield, Ohio to Philadelphia, Pennsylvania; riding trains, flying in an airplane, acting in plays in Pennsylvania; jumping into the surf of the Atlantic Ocean in New Jersey and Maine; riding a horse, swimming to red Cross instructor status, riding the train to Washington, D.C., New York City, St. Petersburg Fla., Annapolis, Maryland, Princeton, N.J., New York City, N. Y., Dartmouth College in Hanover, New Hampshire, and the University of Pennsylvania in Philadelphia while in Maryland; riding in a jeep, and swimming in lakes while in Connecticut; riding in a car, swimming in a fresh water spring while in Damascotta Mills, Me.; riding the ferry boat to the Statue of Liberty, subways, taxis, carry-buses and buses while in New York City; riding in cars through tunnels under rivers to enter Manhatten Island; flying to Atlanta, Georgia with my fiancé; riding in a jeep station wagon across America to Arizona; climbing ladders and digging ditches to build a house in Scottsdale, Arizona; riding elevators in the hospital while one baby was dying and another was saved; swimming in the Gulf of Mexico while on a cross country family camp trip; swimming in the Pacific ocean near San Diego and Los Angeles; wading in Christopher Creek on the Mongollon Rim in Arizona; riding an inner tube down the Verde River east of Phoenix, swimming, riding in a speed boat, a houseboat and in a single engine airplane on Lake Powell behind Page Dam (with a coast line in and out of canyons as long as the Pacific coast of United States); flying in a balloon with the man who attempted to fly across the Atlantic ocean; flying in a private jet to Baja, California in an air race; on story assignments at the Grand Canyon, hiking half way in and out on the Bright Angel Trail, riding a mule all the way in and out, then at the west end of Grand Canyon hiking all the way in and out to the Havasu Village; riding a pontoon barge on the rapids of the Colorado River through Grand Canyon, then a canoe down the Amazon River in Peru; flying over the Andes in Peru; climbing up to Machu Pichu in Peru; flying over the north pole to London, U.K. and Milan, Italy; riding in a bus across the new London bridge in London and walking over the old London bridge in Lake Havasu, Arizona; walking across the Brooklyn Bridge from Manhatten to Brooklyn in New York; climbing down from the Parthanon in Athens, Greece to the Theatre of Dionysus; over a year's time driving my Datsun twice a month to and from Phoenix, Arizona and Los Angeles, California, then driving all over the 647 square miles of L.A. for eleven years in persuit of a writing, acting and directing career in "Hollywood"; riding a gurney to death and back in Los Angeles, running over the epicenter of the Whittier, Ca. earthquake, and riding a gurney to put my foot back on my leg in a hospital in Scottsdale, Arizona.

I Move to interact with minds! James Billington, Librarian of Congress; Father Divine, Philadelphia African American who claimed to be God; Nancy Clark Reynolds, Special Assistant to Governor Ronald Reagan, Washington lobbyist; Archibald MacLeish, Poet Laurate and Librarian of Congress;

Theron Bamberger, Producer Bucks County Playhouse, #1 "stock" company in America; Mildred Dunnock, star of Broadway's *Death Of A Salesman* with Lee J. Cobb; Sanford Meisner, Group Theatre director/topAmerican "method" coach; Joseph Anthony, Actors Studio director, director *Rainmaker* Broadway and film; Martha Graham, creator of modern dance; Merce Cunningham, choreographer; John Forsythe, Beatrice Straight, Leslie Nielson, stars on CBS live television's *Studio One*; Worthington Miner, director of Alfred Lunt and Lynn Fontaine, director *Studio One*; John Garfield, star of ANTA's *Peer Gynt*; Fred Eldean, former CEO John Page Land Company who created the original land deals for Carefree, Fountain Hills, Laughlin; Jacque Mercer, Miss America 1949; Barry Goldwater, U S Senator Arizona, Republican Presidential candidate; Nick Nolte, Oscar-nominated actor; Sarah Rice, ingénue in Broadway *Sweeney Todd* with Angela Lansbury; Dianne Kay, Nancy in *Eight Is Enough*series; James Stewart, Academy Award-winning actor; Jack Stewart, founder of "In All the World Only One"Camelback Inn; James Edmondson, Oregon Shakespeare Festival leading actor/director; Sir John Gielgud, British star and quintessential Shakespearean actor; Cedrick Messina, British director of BBC's Shakespeare series; Ronald Reagan, Governor of California; Dr.Art Mollen, founder of the Phoenix 10K; Jesse Owens, Olympic gold medalist; Frank Shorter, Olympic gold medalist, Kathy Miller,winner Victoria Sporting Club award for valour in sport; Max Anderson,1st to fly the Atlantic Ocean in a balloon; Sir Peter Hall, director National Theatre of Great Britain; Sandra Day O'Connor, USA Supreme Court Justice; Georgie White, pioneer Colorado River rapids trips; Delbert Mann, Academy Award-winning director *Marty*; Richard Thomas, star actor *The Waltons*; Lyn Stalmaster, casting director *Coming Home*; Tony Shepherd, great grandson L. B. Mayer; Don Bolles, *Arizona Republic* investigative reporter car bomb murdered; Neal Roberts, top Phoenix attorney suspect in Bolles murder who received immunity; Richard Dreyfuss, Academy Award-winning actor; Robert Wise, Academy Award-winning director *Sound of Music*; Shelley Winters, Academy Award winning actress, Valerie Harper, star in *Mary Tyler Moore* series; Loren Grey, PhD, son of father of the American western Zane Grey; Grey Frederickson, producer of Godfather feature films; Bobby Riggs, tennis star; Lee Grant, Actress/Director; Al Campanis, VP Los Angeles Dodgers, Dan Mason, L.A. DramaLogue "Best Actor"; Phil Gordon, Mayor of Phoenix, Arizona Judy Mohraz, CEO Virginia G. Piper Foundation(former President of Goucher College).

Along the way I've had my role models, i.e. my grandpa Will Reynolds, who arrived in Elwood, Nebraska on a covered wagon, to invent there a novel way to teach his kids math! He pounded ten nails on a board, then painted numbers one through ten under each protruding nail. The kids (my Aunt Gladys, my mom, and my Uncle Verne)from a distance had to throw jar rings (the kind used in preserving) at the nails then *add the numbers they "nailed" in their heads*!

Grandpa Will (who had been selling bonds in Omaha, Nebraska, resulting in his customers losing all their money in the Great Depression[$60,000]), went to work for the AAA in Lincoln (which necessitated his moving away from his family in Omaha) so he could make enough money to buy and sell lots! Each time he made a profit he repaid one of his former bond customers so when he died he had re-paid every person who had purchased bonds from him though he had no legal responsibility to do so! "God willing and the creek don't rise" I will be able to do the same repaying of my many debts.

Woody's mentor Fred Eldean sat in his Scottsdale, Arizona, kitchen phoning friends and clients asking them to send $25,000 checks without a contract! Their trust and his faith put together $1M to buy land that became Carefree, Fountain Hills, and Laughlin, so I keep sending proposals for the "seed" funding Actors Workout Community Land Trust (AWCLT) needs to fly!

Although, according to a 2003 study by the Fordham Institute for Innovation in Social Policy, Arizona, Nevada, and New Mexico are "social recession" states because of chronic problems like crime, child poverty, suicide among the elderly and high school dropouts, I (living below the poverty level in freedom) am connected in the Information Age to my family, colleagues, friends, community, country and the world via cable, phone, voice mail, fax, all of cyberspace (having taught myself computer skills), e-mail send and receive, snail mails, the Sunday *New York Times* (with its Week In Review, Arts & Leisure plus Book Review sections). Actors Workout, Inc. (AW) is owner of its own domain, has corporate listings in the Yellow Pages, registration with the Better Business Bureau, Guidestar, the Arizona Community Foundation, and certification by United Way.

Questions I'm Pondering Now Include

Is America to be leader of the world or hated by the world? Wars and prisons or Head Start! and college tuition help? "Faced with soaring tuition and dwindling aid, a record numbers of students who would excel at college are no longer applying"(*The New York Times*, editorial, April 25, 2004). "USA's military and political tactics in Iraq are creating the conditions for civil war there and giving Al Qaeda a powerful rationale to recruit young people to declare jihad on the United States" (former USA Senator Bob Kerrey, in a New York Times letter to the editor). "They serve so that we don't have to. They offer to give up their lives so that we can be free. It is, remarkably, their gift to us. And all they ask for in return is that we never send them into harm's way unless it is absolutely necessary. Will they ever trust us again?"(Michael Moore, *The New York Times*, May 23, 2004)

Arizona Senator John McCain's experience as a POW in Vietnam is so much greater a sacrifice to America's wars than any member of my family has experienced, yet my family members have experienced devastating effects of America's wars and my great-great-grandchildren will be paying for them! I believe *pre-emptive* war puts the USA in the same camp with the world's worst dictators (the war on Iraq has murdered more than 10,000 Iraqi civilians and created monsters of us via the abuse of Iraqi prisoners!)! Parallels between what is happening now and the Vietnam War are appearing daily.

The Vietnam War was the central event of our generation. Like a massive shock wave, it affected, in widening circles, the 58,022 lost in the war [eight of them women]; the 100,000 or more who may have been killed themselves since their return; the 153,329 severely wounded, and the 150,375 more lightly wounded; the estimated 250,000 victims of Agent Orange; the half million or more who still suffer from the nightmares and flashbacks of post-traumatic stress; the 3.78 million who saw duty in the war zone; the 11 million who served in the Armed Forces during that time of doubt, drugs, and rebellion; the 27 million men who were threatened by the draft and had to rearrange their lives around it; and all the lovers, wives, friends, brothers, and sisters, as well as parents, grandparents, and children of those who served, died, vanished, protested, or fled.(*Do You Believe In Magic?* Annie Gottlieb)

Each of us has the choice every day to kill or love. *The only person one ever has to overcome is oneself.*

A report from the Center for American Progress by Christian Weller and Radha Chaurushiya states: "The distribution of economic gains is upside-down in this (2004) recovery, compared to previous ones. Profits received a larger share of national income than wages. Hence, profits soared to new record highs amid the first "job loss" recovery since the Great Depression. Adding to families' woes are rapidly rising costs, housing education and medical care jumped at double-digit rates in recent years. To maintain consumption levels, many families borrowed more. Living on $801 per month Social Security, I am still $20,000 in debt, paying off some credit cards in a consolidation, while paying for small needs via three small credit cards, biking regularly to the 99 cents store and Savers [a recycled super store], using three-month credit options when I buy from catalogs, renting a room in my apartment to my son James, doing reports and fund raising for AWCLT. My brothers Tom and Dick gift Actors Workout, Inc. a small amount each month to cover part of AW's overhead.

However, the debt is taking its toll. Families are being squeezed as they have to repay more and more debt while the labor market is still trying to find its footholds. (While I sought to create jobs via Actors Workout Community Land Trust I could no longer afford the *co-pays* of my HMO Humana— $150 for a follow up sonar cardiogram plus $40 for the cardiologist. Apparently, my heart valve is now "hanging by a thread"—aeortic valve stenosis, and I must have a cardiac catherization and probable heart valve replacement shortly). For the first time in an economic recovery, the share of additional income that has gone to corporate profits is greater than the share that has gone to employee compensation-i.e. wages and benefits. Most recently at Democratic Headquarters in Phoenix, I met Teresa Heinz Kerry, wife of Presidential candidate for 2004 John Kerry. I was deeply disappointed that John Kerry-John Edwards did not win the election in 2004, because homo sapiens first experiment in freedom is too miraculous and precious to lose!

This is the letter to the editors of the *New York Times*, the *Los Angeles Times*, the *Washington Post*, *USA Today*, and the *Wall Street Journal* I sent about Teresa and Vice President nominee John Edwards' wife, Elizabeth:

Teresa and Elizabeth Will Be USA—Now Reps to World's Women

Male representatives of the press are vicious to infer Teresa Heinz Kerry and Elizabeth Edwards are politically ambitious. They don't have to remember "it's not about them." American women evolve! Teresa and Elizabeth are benchmarks. In highly competitive fields each is a top professional—Teresa in philanthropy-management and Elizabeth in law. Teresa and Elizabeth would stand alone without politics if necessary!

Yet each is an enthusiastic supporter of her husband. Like Eleanor Roosevelt, Teresa and Elizabeth have done it all~been close friends and partners to outstanding men, borne bright, handsome-beautiful children, plus created enviable careers of service. Unlike Eleanor, each sustains a joyful, romantic relationship with her mate.

In addition each has endured the tragic loss of a brilliant intimate family member, Teresa her first husband, Senator John Heinz, in a plane crash; Elizabeth, her over-achieving high school age son Wade in an automobile accident. Teresa overcame her loss to lovingly marry again—Democratic Presidental candidate Senator John Kerry. Elizabeth—just as her daughter Kate neared attendance at Princeton—to start a second family in six-year-old Emma Claire and four-year-old Jack.

In a time when females outnumber males in the USA electorate, and when world diplomacy craves positive American role models, Teresa Heinz Kerry and Elizabeth Edwards will inspire women everywhere to achieve in their work goals, to gain equal rights with equal responsibilities and live full roles as wives, mothers and grandmothers!

So my spirit *moves.*
Every morning now at 4 a.m. before beginning to write *Moving*, Nite does his roll-over trick for me (which is reinforced when he receives 2 yummies and his wet food)! Then I take my vitamins, get a mug of coffee and sit for an hour. Nite reposes, "limp as a cat," on the back of my living room bucket chair. He has one leg draped over far enough to touch my shoulder.

Because my daughter-in-law Joanne had compassion for Nite, he escaped the prison of a Humane Society cage where he survived via only food and water for 2 and a half months. A bit of American flag visible over the pool reminds me of how blessed we Americans are to have freedom of speech, press, religion, and the right to pursue happiness (America is a *dream* which we must fulfill every day). I stare at a large framed Monet print, gifted me by Joanne (reminiscent of my visits to the Corcoran Gallery, the National Gallery in Washington, D. C., the Metropolitan Museum and the Museum of Modern Art in New York City).

The Monet evokes the smell of creosote bushes and salt air, the sound of crashing surf, the feel of wet sand squishing between my toes, the sight of pelicans swooping down to the beach. Sighting through my window the American flag flying over the pool I connect to the silence of *all that is.* Even before seeing Mel Gibson's masterpiece *The Passion*, I began my prayers by repeating the Lord's Prayer, the Twenty-third Psalm, the Beatitudes, I COR 13 and several other verses from Matthew 5. The Lord's Prayer is in Matthew 6:9~13.

"Our Father which are in heaven."

I see images of the Hubble telescope and reflect.

"We are made of elements forged in the stars and scattered through space. We are recycled stardust with the gift of consciousness," (John Noble Wilford, ibid)

"Hallowed be thy name..."

Creator, Perfection, Kingdom, Power, Wonder, Glory, Beauty, Miracle, Truth, Life, Love!

"...Give us this day our daily bread..."

Each day I ask God what *I* should *think* and what *I* should *do.*

From Paul who was once Saul I ponder (I Cor 13:4~10): *"Love is patient and kind; love is not jealous and boastful; it is not arrogant or rude. Love does not insist on its own way; it is not irritable or resentful; it does not rejoice at wrong, but rejoices in the right. Love bears all things, hopes all things, endures all things. Love never ends."*

A wonderful verse from Paul to the Corinthians...: *"When I was a child I spoke like a child, I thought like a child, I reasoned like a child. But when I became* [an adult] *I gave up childish ways."* (I Cor 13:11) brings to mind stories I've *heard* about *me* when I was a very little child(*"there was a little girl who had a little curl right in the middle of her forehead. When she was good she was very, very good. But when she was bad she was horrid!"* So intoned my Aunt Lois, Grandma Daisy's maiden sister, as she rocked me on the rocking chair). I've always credited the nursery rhyme with my decision to become an actress, but I've come to an even greater realization today. When I was a small child my mother put me in the back yard in Lincoln, Nebraska with a basket of clothespins. For hour after hour (according to mother) I didn't leave or talk or protest about being left alone while my busy mother did her never-ending work. But, now that I've become an adult I'm *not doing and saying nothing*! I've given up childish ways!

Moving to write this memoir (which must reveal *my* many sins—separation from God when I have *not* lived the above verses) I am motivated to...

"Let your light so shine before men that they can glorify your Father in Heaven"(Matthew 5:16)

So in humility and awe I *"Ask and it will be given you; seek and you will find; knock and it will be opened to you"*! (Matthew 7:7)

I was baptized a second time by emersion Sunday, April 25, 2004, by the pacesetting minister of Gary and Joanne's spirited Mountain Valley Church in Scottsdale, Arizona (church goers numbering 1500 don't yet have a sanctuary and must go to a large office space but they joyously go every Sunday to worship!). I was asked to write a testimony about *why* I wanted to be immersed. Below is what I wrote:

> I remember my baptism by sprinkling as a high point of my fourteen years. The beautiful music of the Presbyterian church(it was my boyfriend's church; he was President of my junior high school and I was vice president) eerily plays in my mind. I have never heard that particular music in a church since then.......
>
> At the end of a rich and colorful life I now spend each morning circa 4AM asking "Give me this day my daily bread."
>
> It was at such a moment that I received the clear message that I should be immersed because that's what Jesus did and *what Jesus lived and taught*(whether one is a believer or not) *is the only way homo sapiens will survive!* To have innocently endured what He did and to ask God from the cross "Forgive them for they know not what they do" *is God*! Homo sapiens must "turn the other cheek," *look for God in All* the way He did! In the Information Age I am enjoined to communicate this as only an artist can.

In the information age I am enjoined to communicate this as only an artist can.

"We are put on earth a little space that we may learn to bear the beams of love." (William Blake).
"I'm ready (moving) *here,*
The pieces of me,
I'm ready to leave a legacy,
The people of my lives come together in me,
And I'm ready to face eternity..."
(from the overture to Mary Daisy's play with music *Ordinary Jenny White*, produced in Los Angeles Equity Waiver and at the Performing Arts Center, Tempe, Arizona)

Epilogue

On October 3, 2004, I went into congestive heart failure from a congenital defective heart valve, but I did not die like hundreds of thousands did December 26,2004 when the earth *moved* under the ocean creating the tsunami!

As I entered the ER I kept saying "I can't be mad at my heart! It's beat so many beats per minute for 75 years!" A couple of days later I learned from the cardiologist who performed a cardiac catherization, "I don't know how you are still here~ you should have died with that valve." Then the night before open heart surgery my surgeon, Michael Caskey, M.D., stopped by and among the things he said to me was, "I want to be certain you understand you could die tomorrow [October 6] when the surgery is performed."

You've seen on all the many medical shows, a camera angle from the patient's point of view, as the patient is being wheeled from a room to OR, flanked by medical personnel and a couple of anxious family members. The view of ceiling tiles and florescent lights pass by relentlessly as you approach a destiny unknown. You lie helpless—totally in the hands of experts doing their jobs (hopefully excellently well!) and in the loving hands of God.

I was released from the hospital on my eighth day (I went out to dinner October 3 and was gone eight days!) I came home to no help except family and friends, especially my son Gary and his wife Joanne, who lovingly did all they could to help me recreate my life.

I believe one of the reasons I did not die in 2004 is *Moving*, which will be published at the end of summer- 2005..

It is now June 12.

I have *moved* to my 8ᵗʰ month post open heart valve-replacement surgery! I learned, after the surgery and the heart valve tissue examination, my defect was *congenital!*

I *moved* for more than 75 years with a defective heart!

I've been *moving* on my bike 10 miles a week since my 6ᵗʰ week post surgery.

I *move* swimming again.

I've *moved* to begin a new book and script-doctor a screenplay for a colleague.

I've *moved* minds at American Express and Gila River Casinos to sponsor a July/August Training of Native Americans as Actors, for children, youth and adults, with a performance of *Native American Experience Alive* at the end; and minds at the world famous Heard Museum to contribute an $8000 grant in kind for auditorium space. As the project's Director-Teacher I am *moving to engage* contract labor, create collateral material, etc…

Still *moving* at or below the poverty level I believe I am one of the richest people alive!

Pretty soon I will be gone.

But like the tiniest grain of sand in the Grand Canyon at sunrise, little pieces of me will hang around to *move* things.

In ***MOVING*** the reader will *move* to and about or
on, through and around:

ACTING Early
ACTING Professional
ACTORS STUDIO(HOLLYWOOD)
AMERICAN FILM INSTITUTE(HOLLYWOOD~REPERTORY)
ACTORS(USA RENOWNED)
Richard Dreyfuss, Academy Award winning actor
Mildred Dunnock, star of Broadway's "Death Of A Salesman"with Lee
J. Cobb
John Garfield, star of ANTA's "Peer Gynt"
Sir John Gielgud, British star and quintessential Shakespearean actor
Lee Grant, Actress/Director
Valerie Harper, star in "Mary Tyler Moore" series
Dianne Kay, Nancy in"Eight Is Enough"series
Nick Nolte,Oscar nominated Actor
Sarah Rice, ingénue in Broadway "Sweeney Todd" with Angela Lansbury
James Stewart, Academy award winning actor
Richard Thomas, star actor "The Waltons"
Stars on CBS live TV's"Studio One" (John Forsythe, Beatrice Straight,
Leslie Nielson)
Shelley Winters, Academy Award winning actress
ACTORS(ACTORS WORKOUT, INC.~AW)
Ray Anderson, #1 Interpreter Teddy Roosevelt in USA
Richard Blake, Emmy Winner~Lincoln, AW Actor Heritage Square
Centennial
Lauren Eiler, Attorney/Judge AW Actor honored at Heritage Square

Centennial

Mark DeMichele, Actors Equity Association (AEA) Actor, 1-man~14 character show

Margie Ghigo, Actress/Singer, Nat'l Board AFTRA

Buck Hart, Former Headmaster Orme School, AW Actor

Randy Kemp, Native American fine artist(USA museums & galleries), Actor/Floutist

Dan Mason, L.A. DramaLogue "Best Actor"

Tarah Paige, #1 Gymnast AZ., #1 Dancer USA(MGM Grand, Las Vegas),AW Dancer/Actor

Fred Sugerman, union Actor/Dancer, AW Co-Incorporator

Sule Greg Wilson, African American Drummer, AW talent, vet~Smithsonian Museum & Yale

AIRPLANES

First Mail Route to Omaha, Nebraska

Small Jet in Air Race to Mexico

British Airways to London, U.K.

Single Engine Plane over Lake Powell, Arizona

ANIMALS, SCORPIANS & SNAKES

Halloween

Jackrabbit Lane animals

Nite

Scorpians

Snakes

ATTORNEYS

Bob Ciancola, one time Tax Attorney Salt River Project~AW Treasurer

Lauren Eiler, Attorney/Judge AW Actor honored at Heritage Square Centennial

Neal Roberts, top Phoenix attorney suspect in Bolles murder who received immunity

Antje Roberts

Blair & Ginger Roberts

Debbie Roberts

Lois Roberts

Kimberly Roberts

**Nathaniel Taylor Roberts

**Vernetta Sweet Roberts

AUNT(Gladys Reynolds)

AUNT IN LAW(Agnes Reynolds)
BALLOONS
Bob Sparks
"Maxie" Anderson
BANKERS
Philip Carpenter, VP Wells Fargo Bank~Phoenix,~AW Treasurer
Philip Hungerford, X-President S.C. Bank, President Bala Cynwyd Jr. High School
BICYCLES
BIRTHS
Mine, Born in the Great Depression
Brother Thomas Rhodes Oliver
Children:
James Robert Mizell
Richard William Mizell
Melanie Anne Mizell
Gary Michael Mizell
Grandchildren:
Gina Marie Mizell
Daniel Joseph Mizell
BODIES
BROTHERS
Robert Merion Oliver, Jr.-("Bob")
Richard Kent Oliver, ("Dick")
Thomas Rhodes Oliver, ("Tom")
Ronald William Oliver, ("Ron")
BUSES
CAMPING
CARS
CASTING DIRECTORS
Lyn Stalmaster, casting director "Coming Home"
Tony Shepherd, great grandson L. B. Mayer, casting director Aaron Spelling
CHILDREN
James Robert Mizell, ("Jamie")
Richard William Mizell, ("Ricky")
Melanie Anne Mizell, ("Mellie")
Gary Michael Mizell, ("Gar")

CHRISTMAS
CITIES
Athens, Greece
Lima, Peru
London, U.K.
Los Angeles, California
Milan, Italy
New York City, N.Y.
Phoenix, Arizona
Philadelphia, Pennsylvania
Washington, D.C.
COACH(ACTORS)
Pre AW
Drama Logue top listed(actors trade~Los Angeles)
Screen Actors Guild Conservatory Workshops Leader
Actors Workout, Inc.(AW)
CONDUCTORS
Leonard Bernstein, New York Symphony
Koussevitsky, Tanglewood, Massachusetts
Zubin Meta, Los Angeles Symphony in La Scala, Italy
Toscanini, New York Symphony at Carnegie Hall, New York City
COUSIN(Thomas Reynolds, DDS, "Tom")
DANCE & CHOREOGRAPHERS
Kelly Brown, American Ballet Theatre star, owner Phoenix School of Ballet
Lisa Chow, Artistic Director, Desert Dance Theatre, metro- Phoenix
Judy Chruma, Local Casting"The Nutcracker" at ASU Gammage, AW choreographer
Frances Smith Cohen, Artistic Director, Dance Theatre West at the Phoenix Herberger
Agnes DeMille, Choreographer, "Brigadoon" on Broadway
Martha Graham, creator of modern dance & Merce Cunningham, choreographer
Leigh Cassidy King, Founder~Owner, Dance Centre, Phoenix, Arizona
DAUGHTER-IN-LAW
Joanne Marie Mizell
Lynn Cassidy(X-Mizell)
DEATH

Mine
Family members
Beth(mother)
Bob(brother)
Ricky(son)
Robert(father)
Ron(brother)
Verne(uncle)
Woody(husband)
My Near Death Escapes
DIRECTING Early
DIRECTING Pre AW
DIRECTING AW
DIRECTORS(USA RENOWNED)
Joseph Anthony, Actors Studio-Director, Director "Rainmaker" Broadway & film
James Edmondson, Oregon Shakespeare Festival leading actor/director
Sir Peter Hall, Director National Theatre of Great Britain
Delbert Mann, Academy Award winning director "Marty"
Sanford Meisner, Group Theatre Director/topAmerican "method" coach
Cedrick Messina, British Director of BBC's Shakespeare series
**Joseph Papp, Founder New York Shakespeare Festival
Jose Quintero, Broadway Director "Long Day's Journey Into Night"
Worthington Miner, Director of Alfred Lunt and Lynn Fontaine, director "Studio One"
Robert Wise, Academy Award winning director "Sound of Music"
DISEASE
Alcoholim
Cancer
American Cancer Society Volunteer
Don Barclay, Disney actor artist, clown painter, caricaturist Pink Pony Inn
Kax Herberger, Chair ACS event
Heart
Poliomyelitis
Spinal Meningitis
Schizophrenia
DIVORCE
EDITORS

Howard Beach, This Week Magazine
Moyca Manoil, Arizona Living Magazine
EVENTS
Assassinations
Don Bolles, Arizona Republic investigative reporter car bomb murdered
**Martin Luthur King, Civil Rights Leader
**Kennedy, John, President of the United States
**Kennedy, Robert, Attorney General USA
USA:
The Great Depression
Wars:
Iraq War
9-11
Pearl Harbor
Vietnam
WWII
World:
Spaceship Earth
Earthquake~Whittier, California
FATHER(Robert Merion Oliver, "Bob")
FINE ARTISTS
Corcoran Gallery, Washington, D.C.(up close and personal to great Impressionists)
Page E FINE ARTISTS(continued)
**Ted DeGrazia
Randy Kemp, Native American fine artist(USA museums & galleries), Actor/Floutist
Betty Banks Herbert Koch, show in USA Capitol Rotunda, NYC friend, AW rear screen
Paintings
**Leonardo da Vinci, "The Last Supper" in Milan, Italy
**Van Gogh(effect of NYC Metropolitan Museum show}
FIRST
Charlie Chaplin film
Live Show
Broadway Show
Perfect Theatre Experience
Performance

GIRLS IN AMERICA
GRANDCHILDREN
Gina Marie Mizell, "Gina"
Daniel Joseph Mizell, "Dan"
GRANDNEPHEW(Brett Zenor)
GRANDPARENTS
Fred & Elizabeth Oliver
William & Daisy Reynolds
GREAT AUNT(Lois Reynolds)
HOMES
Highfields(Harwinton, Connecticut)
Evangeline(Greenwich Village, NYC)
First Married Apartment(Jackson Heights, Long Island, N.Y.)
Jack Rabbit Lane(Scottsdale, Arizona)
Mountain Meadow Ranch(Christopher Creek, Mongollon Rim, Arizona)
Mummy Mountain Studio(Scottsdale, Arizona)
HOTELS & RESORTS
Arizona Biltmore(Phoenix, Arizona)
Camelback Inn(Scottsdale, Arizona)
Holiday Inn Sunspree Resort(Scottsdale, Arizona)
Waldorf Astoria(New York City, New York)
Wrigley Mansion(Phoenix, Arizona)
HUSBAND(Woodfin Grady Mizell, Jr.)
HELEN KELLER
MENTORS
Mildred Dunnock, star of Broadway's "Death Of A Salesman"with Lee J. Cobb
Fred Eldean, former CEO John Page Land Company who created the original land deals
for Carefree, Fountain Hills, & Laughlin, Arizona
Jack Stewart, founder of "In All the World Only One"Camelback Inn
MOTHER(Beth Claudine Reynolds Oliver,"Betty")
NEPHEWS
Ryan Mooney Oliver, ("Ryan")
Brett Oliver, ("Brett")
Page F NIECES
Cheryl Oliver Zenor, ("Cheryl")
Wendy Beth Oliver Garcia, ("Wendy Beth")

NIGHTMARES & DREAMS
OCEANS
Atlantic
Pacific
POLITICS
Sam Campana, Mayor of Scottsdale, Arizona
Barry Goldwater, Presidential Candidate, Arizona Senator
Phil Gordon, Mayor of Phoenix, Arizona
Teresa Heinz Kerry(2004 Presidential candidate John Kerry's wife)
John McCain, USA Senator from Arizona
Harry Mitchell, Mayor of Tempe, Arizona
Ronald Reagan, Governor of California
Nancy Clark Reynolds, Special Asst to Governor Ronald Reagan,Washington lobbyist
PRODUCERS
Theron Bamberger, Producer Bucks County Playhouse, #1 "stock" company in America
Grey Frederickson, producer of Godfather feature films
PROFESSIONAL JOBS(in addition to Acting/Writing/Directing/Coaching/Producing)
Arizona Association of Industries, Public Relations
Cooperage 10K(Albuquerque) Publicist
Los Angeles Actors Theatre~Los Angeles Theatre Center, Sales
Maricopa Mental Health Association Executive Director
Northbank 10K(Phoenix) Publicist
Orme School Fine Arts Festival, Theatre Workshop Director 10 years
Palo Alto Preschools(AZ., CA.) Publicist
RIVERS
Amazon(Peru)
Colorado(Arizona)
SCHOOLS
Bala Cynwyd Junior High School(Bala Cynwyd, Pennsylvania)
Lower Merion Senior High School(Ardmore, Pennsylvania)
Goucher College(Baltimore & towson, Maryland)
Alice Falvey ("Bubbles," roommate colleague at Camp Cloudmarch in Maine)
Judy Mohraz, PhD, X-President Goucher College, current CEO Piper Trust

Aida Schoenfeld("Curly," cultural inspiration)

American Academy of Dramatic Art(Carnegie Hall, New York, New York)

Arizona State University(Tempe, Arizona)

SISTER IN LAW(Jane Mooney Oliver)

SPIRITUALITY

SPORTS

"Maxie" Anderson,1st to fly the Atlantic Ocean in a balloon

Al Campanis, VP Los Angeles Dodgers

Bill Denney, Major League Baseball Player/Sports Broadcaster/AW President

Kathy Miller,winner Victoria Sporting Club award for valour in sport

Dr.Art Mollen, founder of the Phoenix 10K

Jesse Owens, Olympic gold medalist

Bobby Riggs, tennis star

Frank Shorter, Olympic gold medalist

Georgie White, pioneer Colorado River rapids trips

SWIMMING

STATES

Arizona

California

Connecticut

Nebraska

Ohio

Pennsylvania

SURVIVAL JOBS

Goucher College Waitress

NYC Wall Street Hat Check Girl

Macy's Christmas Toy Dept. Sales

Valley(San Fernando, CA.)Cab Driver

House Cleaner(metro-Phoenix)

Office Cleaner(Phoenix)

THEATRES

Actors Workout, Inc.

Actors Workout Community Land Trust(AWCLT)

Board Members

Itchy Feet Run(pre AW)

Venues

Theatre For The New Millennium(TFTNM)
Kamal Amin,X- Architect/Frank Lloyd Wright at Taliesin, Arizona, design for
TFTNM
Herman Chanen, Builder Terminal 4 Sky Harbor Airport
Dan Harkins, CEO Harkins Theatres(chain of film theatres in metro Phoenix)
John McCain
Keith Ritchie, Producer-Director NBC Phoenix KPNX, AW VP
Theatre of Dionysus~Parthanon, Athens, Greece
Importance of
Los Angeles Actors Theatre(LAAT)~Los Angeles Theatre Center(LATC)
New York Shakespeare Festival
**Joe Papp
TRAINS & SUBWAYS
UNCLE(Verne Reynolds, "Verne")
VESSELS(ON WATER)
Canoe on Amazon River, Peru
Ferry Boats~Staten Island, Catalina Island
House Boat on Lake Powell, Arizona~Utah
Inner Tubes on Verde River near Phoenix, Arizona
Ocean liner in ice NYC Harbor
Pontoon Barge through Grand Canyon
Speed Boat on Lake Powell, Arizona~Utah
VOLUNTEER(in addition to American Cancer Society above)
Church School Teacher & Supervisor
St. Joseph's Hospital Pediatrics
Teacher-Parents Org, Kiva Elementary School(Mrs. Raymond Rubicam)
WAYS OF MOVING
WRITERS(USA ACCREDITED)
James Billington, Librarian of Congress, Russian authority
Jim Byrnes, Writer, TV's"Gunsmoke"
Zane Grey(father of the American western via his son Loren Grey, PhD)
Archibald MacLeish, Poet Laurate and Librarian of Congress.
Mario Puzo, Author of "The Godfather"
Jeb Rosebrook, Writer, "Miracle on 34th Street," "Junior Bonner," TV's"The Waltons."
William Whitehead, "Best Playwright In Texas" at Alley Theatre, Houston

WRITERS(PHOENIX)
Don Bolles, Arizona Republic investigative reporter car bomb murdered, p2, 3
Machu Pichu, Peru
Kyle Lawson, Entertainment Editor, The Arizona Republic(Phoenix)
Rae Anne Marsh, dba Grammar & Glitz
Max McQueen, Entertainment Editor, The Tribune Papers(metro-Phoenix) Terry Greene Sterling
WRITER(MARY DAISY)
Pre AW
"Arizona 1776"
Father Divine, Philadelphia African American who claimed to be God
Grand Canyon
PEOPLE magazine
Havasu Canyon(west end of Grand Canyon)
"Ordinary Jenny White"(Los Angeles, Phoenix)
Jean Campbell(wife of Joseph Campbell~"The Power of Myth"re OJW)
"Counterpoint Peru"
"Reaching"(Los Angeles, Phoenix)
"Tulla"(Los Angeles)
"Zane"(Los Angeles)
Actors Workout, Inc.(AW)
"Pipe Dreams"(Phoenix)
Wayne Roth-Nelson, PhD, Environmental Scientist~University of London
"Water"
"Moving"

Printed in the United States
34101LVS00003B/57